JOURNAL FOR THE STUDY OF THE OLD TESTAMENT SUPPLEMENT SERIES
177

Sheffield Academic Press

Text-Linguistics and Biblical Hebrew

David Allan Dawson

Journal for the Study of the Old Testament
Supplement Series 177

Copyright © 1994 Sheffield Academic Press

Published by
Sheffield Academic Press Ltd
Mansion House
19 Kingfield Road
Sheffield S11 9AS
England

Typeset by Sheffield Academic Press
and
Printed on acid-free paper in Great Britain
by Bookcraft
Midsomer Norton, Somerset

British Library Cataloguing in Publication Data

A catalogue record for this book is available
from the British Library

ISBN 1-85075-490-X

CONTENTS

The bulk of this work originated in my doctoral dissertation (under Professor John Gibson at Edinburgh University, Scotland, 1993), having developed out of a marriage between my delight in text-linguistics and my love of Classical Hebrew. It quickly became apparent that if others had discovered the same loves, few of them had offered anything in print, fewer still had written for Hebrew scholars, and an exceptionally limited number had written books which could be employed by the hebraist without substantial training in modern linguistics.

My original goal was to produce a text-linguistic commentary on a particular text. Ruth, Jonah and the Joseph stories all came to mind, yet no sooner had I started on this project, than Dr Robert Longacre published his *Joseph: A Story of Divine Providence: A Text-Theoretical and Text-Linguistic analysis of Genesis 37 and 39–48* (Eisenbrauns, 1989). I had worked under Dr Longacre during linguistic training for work with Wycliffe Bible Translators several years before, and his work had always been the root of my own. I was immensely pleased to see this material come to publication. Dr Longacre's method is difficult to grasp, however, and difficult to put to practical use, for its starting point is well beyond the average hebraist's linguistic facility. As I worked with this book, and several others, I decided that I would try to put together a book which would form a bridge between the rarified works of the ultra-trained linguists and the minimally trained (in linguistics, that is) Hebrew scholars.

Thus, this book is intended for those with an interest, but little background, in modern text-linguistics. This is not to say that I have avoided issues which generally require more finely tuned training, but rather that I have sought, by use of explanations and examples, to grant to the average scholar access to all the topics covered in this volume.

I am aware that this book cannot hope to solve confusions of terminology and theory. But its principal focus is on *methodology*, and issues of terminology and theory are part of methodology. I hope to contribute to clearer thinking about these things, as I have a strong interest in clarity and 'elegance' (a term which will recur with some regularity in this volume, and which will, in due course, be defined). Much has been left out; but this is intended as a starting point. The starting point seems to have been omitted from this discipline, and there is little communication between those whose training in linguistics exceeds the norm and those whose knowledge of the Hebrew Bible is beyond compare. I have sought merely to establish a little more solidity in the link between them.

As is always the case in such works, many deserve recognition for their role in the process of getting it 'from there to here'. A great deal of help on this work has come from Professor John C.L. Gibson, whose scholarly integrity and the simple human concern which characterizes his daily life are standards which I hope to achieve in my own life. And no amount of words could express my gratitude to my parents and best friends, Frank and Ruth Dawson, for their encouragement, love and support through the years.

ABBREVIATIONS

AB	Anchor Bible
AnBib	Analecta biblica
BibSac	Bibliotheca Sacra
BKAT	Biblischer Kommentar: Altes Testament
FOTL	The Forms of the Old Testament Literature
JQR	*Jewish Quarterly Review*
JQRMS	*Jewish Quarterly Review* Monograph Series
JSOT	*Journal for the Study of the Old Testament*
JSOTSup	*Journal for the Study of the Old Testament* Supplement Series
Or	*Orientalia*
OTL	Old Testament Library
SANT	Studien zum Alten und Neuen Testament
TynBul	*Tyndale Bulletin*
VT	*Vetus Testamentun*
WBC	Word Biblical Commentary
ZAH	*Zeitschrift für Althebraistik*
ZAW	*Zeitschrift für die alttestamentliche Wissenschaft*

Chapter 1

INTRODUCTION AND EXAMINATION
OF SEVERAL RECENT PUBLICATIONS

1.1 *Introduction to the Content and Goals of this Volume*

In this work, I will examine several currently available works on Classical Hebrew,[1] explain a particular theory of linguistics and its derived approach to the data, examine a series of texts, and draw conclusions from all the above. The lynch-pin holding all this together is the question of *the role(s) of different types of clauses in different types of texts.*[2]

My goal is to measure some of the current work on this question against two basic criteria: (1) integrity of description, and (2) effectiveness of communication. In a very real sense, the author of a study offers him- or herself (or rather, the work) as a bridge between the topic studied and the reader; if the connection between the author/work and either the topic or the reader is inadequate in some way, then the author's purpose will not be accomplished in a satisfactory way. So, if a researcher approaches data with a faulty theoretical base, or faulty methodological procedures, then that end of

---

1. I use this term to refer to Hebrew of the biblical period (extending to roughly 200 BCE); it is more or less synonymous with the term Biblical Hebrew, but allows for the inclusion of non-biblical materials in the corpus; although these are not relevant for the present study, I adopt the term on principle: we are dealing with a language *per se*, not simply a set of features of some strictly limited corpus of data.

2. Jones, in 'A Synopsis of Tagmemics', commenting on Longacre's contribution of this type of enquiry, has written, 'Longacre has studied the effect of discourse types on units both large and small in texts. "In effect once a discourse type is chosen, many decisions as to structure of very small parts of it are already made [1972, p. 133]"' [p. 94]; this, in brief, is the justification for my interest in this approach: I seek to describe the motivating factors at the macro-syntactic level for the employment of micro-syntactic features.

the bridge is insecure; likewise, if one's communication of truly valid insights about the data is imprecise, or impenetrable (perhaps owing to use of unfamiliar and poorly defined vocabulary), then the other end of the bridge is insecure. Both must be solid if the work is to advance the study of the language. With these two concerns in mind, I will survey five contemporary works, and will then turn my attention to samples from the data.

Before much can be said about the data, however, my own approach to it—theory, methodology and working hypotheses—will require elucidation. In Chapter 3, therefore, I will present definitions, relate concepts and justify procedures, which will come into play in my examination of the data. This will be followed by examination of six extended sections of text from the Hebrew Bible,[3] culminating in an integrated reading of the book of Ruth, where I will examine the text in light of hypotheses developed out of the previous examinations of data. The final chapter will summarize the material contained in the previous five, and will look forward toward further application of this kind of research. The layout is as follows:

Chapter 1   Introduction and objectives, and examination of the first three works (Niccacci, *Syntax*, Eskhult, *Studies*, and Andersen, *Sentence*)

Chapter 2   Examination of Khan, *Studies*, and Longacre *Joseph*

Chapter 3   Presentation of theoretical and methodological approach to the data

Chapter 4   Presentation of worked material from Judges 2, Leviticus 14, and 6–7, and the 'Tabernacle texts' (sections from Exodus 25–40)

Chapter 5   Presentation of Judg. 10.6–12.7 (with particular interest in Reported Speech sections), and the whole text of Ruth, integrating the hypotheses examined

Chapter 6   Summary, practical applications, and review of objectives

Chapter 1 introduces the present research project, and will provide a summary of some of the major recent contributions in the field of Hebrew text-linguistics; a brief introduction to the principal theoretical questions involved in this study will be followed by an in-depth

---

3.   Judg. 2; Lev. 14.1-32; Lev. 6.1 [Heb.]–7.38; sections of Exod. 25-40 (these four data-samples are dealt with in Chapter 4]; Judg. 10.6–12.7; and the whole of the book of Ruth (these are found in Chapter 5).

analysis of one of the currently most influential works in this field,[4] and of two other significant works.[5]

The principal theoretical elements that I will explain in this chapter are these:

- the necessity of theoretical and methodological integrity and clarity;
- the primacy of the data;
- language universals, and their significance for Hebrew studies; text-level structures as describable features of language;
- bag-of-tricks languages, and, with such languages, the necessity of studying all possible features that perform the same function, in order to describe accurately the function of any one of these features;
- 'text', providing a basic definition for this term as I use it, and 'discourse', and why I avoid using it;
- text-type, and its influence on the distribution of clause-types;
- and, finally the interrelationship between micro-syntactic and macro-syntactic levels of language.

This theoretical section is followed by reviews of works by Niccacci, Eskhult and Andersen.

The following quotations from David Crystal's *Dictionary of Linguistics and Phonetics* will illustrate some of the difficulties we will face in Hebrew text-linguistics:

> One sign of immaturity [in a science] is the endless flow of terminology. The critical reader begins to wonder if some strange naming taboo attaches itself to the terms that a linguist uses, whereby, when he dies they must be buried with him.[6]

> DISCOURSE A term used in linguistics to refer to a continuous stretch of (especially spoken) language larger than a sentence—but, within this

4. A. Niccacci, *Syntax of the Verb in Biblical Hebrew Prose* (trans. W.G.E. Watson; JSOTSup, 86; Sheffield: JSOT Press, 1990).

5. M. Eskhult, *Studies in Verbal Aspect and Narrative Technique in Biblical Hebrew Prose* (Acta Universitatis Upsaliensis: Studia Semitica Upsaliensia, 12; Uppsala: Uppsala University, 1990), and F.I. Andersen, *The Sentence in Biblical Hebrew* (The Hague: Mouton, 1974).

6. D. Bolinger, *Aspects of Language* (with D.A. Sears; Harcourt Brace Jovanovich, 3rd edn, 1981), p. 554; quoted by D. Crystal, *Dictionary* (The Language Library; Oxford: Basil Blackwell, 1985), p.v.

broad notion, several different applications may be found. At its most general, a discourse is a behavioural unit which has a pre-theoretical status in linguistics: it is a set of utterances which constitute any recognizable speech event (no reference being made to its linguistic structuring, if any), e.g. a conversation, a joke, a sermon, an interview. A classification of discourse functions, with particular reference to type of subject-matter, the situation, and the behaviour of the speaker, is often carried out in socio-linguistic studies (of primitive societies, in particular), e.g. distinguishing dialogues v. monologues, or (more specifically) oratory, ritual, insults, narrative, and so on. In recent years, several linguists have attempted to discover linguistic regularities in discourses (discourse analysis or DA), using grammatical, phonological and semantic criteria (e.g. cohesion, anaphora, inter-sentence connectivity). It is now plain that there exist important linguistic dependencies between sentences, but it is less clear how far these dependencies are sufficiently systematic to enable linguistic units higher than the sentence to be established.[7] The methodology and theoretical orientation of discourse analysis (with its emphasis on well-formedness and rules governing the sequence of permissible units, in both spoken and written texts) are often contrasted with those of conversation analysis. Some linguists adopt a broader, psycholinguistic perspective in studying discourse, which they view as a dynamic process of expression and conmprehension governing the performance of people during linguistic interaction. Some adopt a sociolinguistic perspective, in which the purpose or function of the discourse is emphasised. These emphases distance the subject from 'text linguistics', when this is seen as the formal account of the linguistic principles governing the structure of texts. But there is considerable overlap between the domains of discourse analysis and text linguistics (for example, the notion of cohesion is prominent in both), and any attempt at a principled distinction would be premature.[8]

We may read these quotations with some amusement, for the first draws into focus a problem that affects the term 'discourse' in particular, with acerbic clarity, as can be seen by the definition[s] that Crystal offers. When we get into the realm of linguistics—and in particular, text-linguistics—the humour of these statements begins to

---

7. These 'linguistic dependencies' are the focus of 'text-linguistic' analyses; that these are 'sufficiently systematic to enable linguistic units higher than the sentence to be established' is indeed a matter for some debate, yet is also one of the presuppositions that undergirds the text-linguistic undertaking as a whole—and it is one that is being amply substantiated by data from the widest possible array of the world's languages, both living and dead.

8. Crystal, *Dictionary*, p. 96.

darken, for linguistics generates new terminology at a mind-boggling rate.

There are at least three things to which a reader should find access—in addition to the results of the work undertaken—in a research publication: *the author's presuppositions, theoretical perspective* and *methodology*. This is because the only means a reader has of assessing the trustworthiness and applicability of a researcher's conclusions is by evaluating them through that researcher's approach to the data. The problem, however, is that many researchers either have not learned the technique of self-analysis with regard to these concerns, or consider them of too little importance to be included in published results.

Presuppositions must be uncovered, examined, and put to the most difficult challenges throughout a researcher's work with the data, for these, if left unchallenged, can govern one's work to the point that it produces nothing of value. They must either (1) be recognized as false, and rejected, (2) be acknowledged as unproven, hypothetical, and therefore remaining suspect, or (3) be proved to be in concordance with the data, at which point they cease to be presuppositions, and become part of the researcher's theoretical base.

That theoretical base (which is, in effect, a summary of, and a set of generalizations from, data already processed) in turn gives the researcher meaningful ways of interacting with the data; that is to say, the theoretical base suggests a methodology. This methodology—or the procedures one will implement in analysing the data—will in its turn assist in organizing the data in a way that leads to solid scientific conclusions (even where these conclusions be that the processing of data according to one's methodology has led to no solid conclusions).

These conclusions are then compared with the theory's projections. Where the two are in accord, the theory is strengthened; where they are not, both must be re-examined in order that fault be found in either the methodology or the theoretical base. It must then be determined whether the inadequate approach should be altered to make room for the new results, or whether it should be jettisoned altogether in favour of another, more workable one. Any less rigorous approach to these concerns is the less objective and the less trustworthy.

In the long run, *all but the data must be considered suspect.*[9] This is true particularly when dealing with a restricted corpus of language material, since there are insufficient data to substantiate hypotheses fully. Only where the data appear to be in contradiction with all other possible explanations can it be permitted that the data be called into question. It is rare, however, that scholars go to these lengths, and many settle for 'improving' the text as a path of lesser resistance. With regard to this tendency, Niccacci writes,

> It is, in any case, a duty to presume that even the various kinds of 'glosses' or inserts also follow the rules of grammar and syntax. I think it injudicious to adopt the principle which unfortunately so many scholars follow that so-called 'difficulties' or 'mistakes' of grammar and syntax are indications of later reworking. In effect this would mean that the writers of such glosses either did not know the language or at the least were inept. I wish to reiterate here a caution against the danger of making syntax as arbitrary as literary criticism... I prefer to follow this method closely rather than 'correct' the texts using 'rules' even if difficult cases remain which require further study...[10]

I present here, in this chapter and in the following, several relatively recent works, which have to do with the assessment of syntactic features in prose. I will sketch my own theoretical and methodological bases more fully in Chapter 3; for the moment, however, the following will serve to introduce these features sufficiently to provide the reader with a starting point for understanding my assessment of these works.

9.   I acknowledge that our corpus may contain errors of transmission, and that this places the analyst in a different situation from one working in a living language, where the data can be reconfirmed when doubt exists about their accuracy. This possibility is not open to those working on Classical Hebrew, for example. However, cautious textual criticism and emendation is not what is at stake in the above statement—rather, it is that too many people engaged in analysis of this language come to it with inflexible theories and/or ideologies, which they are unwilling to re-examine in light of the data. Radical restructuring of the text is, for some, only a starting point in their protection of theory or ideology: difficulties in the text lead to rewriting the text. I will overstate this point at several stages in this volume. I recognize that the current trend in biblical scholarship is away from radical rewriting of the text, and in the direction of the position I hold. Yet much of what is available to the researcher and student, originating as it does from a different perspective, affirms this more invasive approach to the data. I emphasize the issue in this work to provoke the reader to conscious examination of his or her own approach to the data.

10.   Niccacci, *Syntax*, p. 13.

It will be clear from the comments above, and to follow, that I consider it of prime importance to import as few changes into the data as possible, and to regard the data as the anchoring point of the research process. Nonetheless, there is a rather small amount of data available to us in this language (by contemporary linguistic standards), and we are somewhat at a disadvantage. Modern descriptive linguistics,[11] however, has discovered that, despite the great number of different languages in the world (over 5000 at latest count, not including languages of the antiquities), and despite the enormous diversity exhibited among these languages, there is a remarkable degree of consistency in language features; that is to say, the world's languages demonstrate a limited number of possible variants.

To take a rather mundane example, one might expect, given the three main constituents[12] of a transitive clause (Subject, Object, and Verb), that we should be able to find the following combinations: S-V-O, S-O-V, V-S-O, V-O-S, O-S-V and O-V-S. In fact, only the first three combinations occur with any frequency as the *standard* word order for transitive clauses. The latter three are extremely uncommon, the last being virtually unheard of.[13] Thus when we look at a new language, we can start from a certain confidence that O-S-V is *not* a strong option for the normative word order of a transitive clause, and that any occurrences of the O-S-V clause-type should be examined closely, since they are highly unusual. This particular example is not of a great significance for the present topic, but a more relevant one is at hand.

One of the 'discoveries'—rather I should say 'new emphases'—of contemporary linguistics has been the analysis of large structures in texts. Thus, just as one can describe the constituent structure of a transitive clause as S-V-O (where each constituent in this formula represents a set of possible 'fillers' in the formula, for example, the

11. Please note that I make no attempt at precision in the use of the term 'descriptive'; it has been used in the past as a label for certain brands of 'structural' linguistic theories, which is not my intent here. Here, I merely mean linguistics which has as its principal concern the empirical analysis and description of the features of the data.

12. 'CONSTITUENT (CONSTITUENCY) A basic term in grammatical analysis for a linguistic unit which is a component of a larger construction' (Crystal, *Dictionary*, p. 68); I will return to this topic in Chapter 3.

13. On this topic, see, for example, Khan, *Studies*, p. 225, and his notes.

'V' represents a collection of verbs—but not just any verb: these must be transitive verbs, and so on), so one can also describe a story as a sequence of constituent units, each constituent having its proper place, and each section filled with its proper sort of 'filler'. This has allowed scholars to observe that certain features occur regularly in the world's languages at these 'larger' levels; for example, it is common, if not universal, for languages to mark the most significant event or events in a story, so that this material stands out from the rest of the story. Likewise, distinctions are normally made between background information and foreground information (regardless of the basic text-type in question), and so on.

'Language universals', as these general tendencies of human language have been dubbed,[14] give language workers the 'basic starting point' kind of information that a traveller would hope to find in a good guide-book—not the specificities like 'If you have time to kill, and wish to see a humorous spectacle, watch the changing of the guard in front of the Parliament building on Syntagma Sq. Every hour on the hour two sets of enormously tall *evzones* (guards) slowly wind up like toy soldiers, kick their heels about, and fall backwards into symmetrical little guard houses on either side of the Tomb of the Unknown Warrior...',[15] but rather general facts like 'Pharmacies: Indicated by a Byzantine-style red cross. Open Sat.–Sun. on a rotating

---

14. 'In their broadest sense, then, LANGUAGE UNIVERSALS are equivalent to the general design features of human language... FORMAL UNIVERSALS are the necessary conditions which have to be imposed on the construction of grammars in order for them to be able to operate. They include such notions as the number of components, types of rules, ordering conventions (e.g. cycles), types of transformations, and so on. SUBSTANTIVE UNIVERSALS, on the other hand, are the primitive elements in a grammar, required for the analysis of linguistic data, e.g. NP, VP, [+ grave], [+ abstract]... Some of these categories may actually be found in every language, but it is not crucial to the notion of substantive universal that they should be. All that is required is that they be constructs which need to be defined by linguistic theory *to enable cross-language generalisations to be made*, i.e. they are not terms established for the analysis of just one language, but are capable of general application... ABSOLUTE UNIVERSALS are *properties which all languages share; there are no exceptions.* RELATIVE UNIVERSALS are *general tendencies in language; there may be principled exceptions*' (Crystal, *Dictionary*, p. 321, emphasis added).

15. L. Shang-Huei Chao (ed.), *Let's Go: The Budget Guide to Greece & Turkey 1992* (London: Pan Books 1992), p. 87.

basis; signs are posted in the windows of each to indicate the nearest open pharmacy. You can also find out by phoning 166.'[16] Now, the material we are dealing with, of course, does not usually generate the kind of urgency exhibited in my analogy, but the researcher will find that a list of 'most likely language features' derived from language studies around the world will be of some considerable help in trying to answer questions about Classical Hebrew. Longacre writes,

> The linguistic specialist who takes out even a minimum of his time to read the writings of his colleagues who work in other fields of specialization, is often pleasantly surprised to find that the exercise is relevant and helpful. For one thing, languages around the world involve not only particulars but universals. The universals are partially masked by the particulars. Consequently, one often finds in comparing two languages (typically of two different language areas), a feature which is somewhat latent and covert in language B is marked and overt in language A. The student of language A, having learned of the presence of this feature in language B, returns to his own speciality with his attention now directed to a feature which had not formerly received sufficient attention from him.[17]

Another language universal is that a language will employ one of two basic techniques for marking peak situations, and other such 'text-level' features. Some languages will have one—and only one—marker for a specific function. Others chose from a variety of possibilities (Longacre calls languages of this latter type 'bag-of-tricks' languages, for obvious reasons), and the choice of which item is very often a 'stylistic'[18] one.[19]

16. Chao, *Greece*, p. 76.

17. Longacre, *Theory and Application in Processing Texts in non-Indoeuropean Languages* (Papiere zur Textlinguistik, Bd. 42; Hamburg: Helmut Buske Verlag, 1984), p.v.

18. I won't attempt to define this term closely—I tend to use it to describe the situation where a language user is faced with more than one option to perform a function, but where the differences between the options are not great; in such a case, the language user makes his choice on the basis of any number of factors, many of which are not solely related to semantics, etc. (such as energy level of the speaker), which are often too subtle to be understood well by the non-native user, for example.

19. In English, for example, we can connect two paragraphs by the words 'thus', 'therefore', 'and so', etc. without any great change in meaning or macro-syntactic significance—though the choice may still be rather rigidly controlled by other factors, such as the socio-linguistic setting.

A language with only one way to mark a peak event, (to cite an arbitrary example) in no way exhibits an impaired stylistic realm, it must be said; those nuances which indicate the 'style' of a text are simply apportioned to other facets of the language.

The role of language universals in the present study is all the greater, in that the limited scope of our data is rendered, by language universal sign-posts, not as significant a hindrance as we might otherwise have been forced to conclude; for, just as comparison of Hebrew with Ugaritic and Arabic can help us elucidate lexical and other difficulties, these language universals can indicate to us certain features that may occur in our texts, or they may indicate to us possible solutions for difficult syntactic problems. One may approach the language with a sense that one does not need to carry out an analysis with no clues whatsoever, as if performing an autopsy on an extra-terrestrial. Rather, the language lies before us (to mix metaphors) as a countryside already vaguely familiar. In the same way that we would suspect, based on our knowledge of general geography, that abundant vegetation in the cleft between two hills may indicate a water-source, we can construct initial hypotheses about our data, based on language universals, where otherwise we might not notice enough of the signs in our language to make any such observations.

Languages all over the world—and from every age from which we have language data—have, to a great extent, had to perform the same kinds of tasks (this is confirmed by the very *existence* of language universals as well as by the evidence they present to us). This is to be expected: all humans have the same size neurological language centres, and social interchange tends to demand certain general things[20] of the speaker, which individual languages must accomodate. Psycho- and neuro-linguists will affirm a certain consistency of psychological and neurological language patterning, which does not vary greatly from culture to culture, and so on.[21]

At the structural level, then, all language systems tend to have a

20. Can the reader imagine a language with *no* facility at all for discussing 'time', 'movement', 'food' or 'relatives'?

21. The question of whether we can apply such up-to-date research results to languages from millennia past is one that we cannot ever fully answer; studies in early language data (as early as we have it, that is) confirm, however, that 'language' as a human tool has not altered so significantly in the time elapsed that today's knowledge could not elucidate yesterday's data.

concept of syllable structure, of intonation patterns, of hypothesis–conclusion sentence structure, and so on; this should not evoke a sceptical response from the reader. It may, however, be less evident that languages have a strong tendency to structure larger units as well—that is, systems exist within all languages so far studied, which serve to indicate to a reader or hearer[22] that a speech has ended, or that a new scene in the story has begun, or that the key point in an exhortation has been made. These structures are sometimes subtle,[23] and will often occur in overlapping fashion to give a cumulative effect, but they exist nonetheless, and can be catalogued and codified in the same way that 'hypothetical sentence' structures (English 'if X, then Y') can be catalogued and codified.

'Universal syntactic structures', that is, those found in the vast majority of languages usually include, from smallest building block to largest unit: MORPHEME–WORD–PHRASE–CLAUSE–SENTENCE–PARAGRAPH–TEXT.[24] We are accustomed to analysing phrase-, clause-, and to some extent sentence-structure, but paragraph- and text-structure are relatively new to us.

I have avoided using the term 'discourse' here. My term 'text' is very nearly equivalent to the former, as it is used in Longacre's brand of 'Tagmemic' linguistics,[25] that is, a text (or 'discourse') is a unit of speech, whose constituents are paragraphs, and other, shorter, units; texts exhibit consistent tendencies in internal development, which features can be described linguistically. This definition, though inadequate, will suffice for the time being. It can be seen from the dictionary entry quoted at the beginning of this chapter that the term 'discourse' has a variety of uses; in the following material, I will identify each author's own use of the term, and will be specific with regard to the meaning I intend, if my own use of the term might lead to confusion. In the long run, however, I try to stay away from 'discourse' as a technical term—too many people have used it in too

22. In this work, reference, by one of these two terms, to the transmission of language material, will not exclude the other—for my purposes, the same language processes are going on whether the communication is oral or written.

23. For example, falling intonation may indicate the end of a speech.

24. The definition of those terms requiring it will be given, either where first encountered, or in Chapter 3.

25. A working introduction to this theory will be presented in Chapter 3.

many applications for it to be free enough of unwanted connotations to serve my purposes.[26]

In addition to the universal tendencies mentioned above, all languages need to be able to relate sequences of historical events; likewise, all need to be able to give lists of instructions; all need to be able to predict, exhort, describe—*and all languages need to be able to distinguish these text-types one from another.* The theoretical system presented in the following chapters is a most helpful tool for looking at this facet of language; it provides a framework for analysing and codifying the features seen at the 'text' level of language.

Words are usually the building blocks of phrases, phrases the building blocks of clauses, and so on. Texts rely on the content of their constituents in order to convey their own content; it is to be expected, then, that text-type distinctions depend heavily on the type of information encoded in clauses, and so forth, by verbal aspects, time-frames and the like, to expound the text-type being worked with. Micro-syntax and macro-syntax work hand in hand: proposing that a certain feature has macro-syntactic significance—as I will not infrequently do in the following pages—in no way deprives it of its micro-syntactic value and significance.

In addition, there are a limited number of grammatical and syntactic options in the verb system, and, therefore, these options will sometimes be called upon to perform more than one function (e.g. a clause-type that serves as the foreground form[27] in one text-type may be the furthest from the foreground in a different text-type). Nevertheless, it is important—if not essential—that the researcher acknowledge these text-type distinctions and their related verb usages in order to make sense of the data; without such distinctions, no patterns will surface to aid the researcher to understand the features being examined.

---

26. This, too, is a fairly standard language trait: development of new applications for a term is often followed by abandonment of it in other circles—cf. the same process with the word 'gay', whose more general definition as 'light-hearted' has been more or less completely abandoned by much of the English-speaking populace, owing to its more recently developed application as a term describing a sexual orientation.

27. 'Foreground' and 'background' will be defined in Chapter 3.

The essential theoretical elements that inform my methodology are:

1. that identifiable structures exist at the paragraph- and text-levels, and that these can be described;
2. that 'text-type' is one of the strongest motivating factors at macro-syntactic levels in the deployment of micro-syntactic constructions;
3. that the positing of macro-syntactic roles for certain constructions in no way lessens their micro-syntactic identities, but that both layers work hand in hand to convey a wide variety of necessary information.

These basic elements—like the dry bones in the valley—will be knit together with sinews and flesh in Chapter 3. The basic features I have described above will be sufficient for the reader to make sense of the comments that follow, on the five works to be examined. They will serve to create a reasonable context within which we can operate until such a time as a further definition of theory and methodology becomes more appropriate.

The works I will be examining in detail in this chapter and the next are:

Andersen, F.I., *The Sentence in Biblical Hebrew* (The Hague: Mouton, 1974)

Eskhult, M., *Studies in Verbal Aspect and Narrative Technique in Biblical Hebrew Prose* (Uppsala: Uppsala University Press, 1990)

Longacre, R.E., *Joseph: A Story of Divine Providence: A Text-Theoretical and Text-Linguistic Analysis of Genesis 37 and 39–48* (Winona Lake, IN: Eisenbrauns, 1989)

Khan, G., *Studies in Semitic Syntax* (Oxford: Oxford University Press, 1988)

Niccacci, A., *The Syntax of the Verb in Classical Hebrew Prose* (trans. W.G.E. Watson; JSOTSup 86; Sheffield: JSOT Press, 1990)

Each of these books contributes to a greater understanding of the text-level features of Classical Hebrew, and I will be evaluating them on the basis of the significance of that contribution (in particular, with reference to the specific concerns of this study).[28] It is only fair to acknowledge that these books may not have intended to contribute to

---

28. Which, as I mentioned above, are (1) the interrelationship between clause-types and text-types in Classical Hebrew, and (2) the question of integrity of theory and methodology in enquiries of this sort.

an enquiry of exactly this sort, and I acknowledge at the outset that, in some ways, I will not be 'giving them a fair reading'. Yet, these provide an excellent working collection for assessing the kinds of presuppositions, theoretical bases, and the like, which one finds in contemporary literature that has a bearing on the description of the text-level features of this language.

I will examine these books in two stages: the first group includes Niccacci, Eskhult and Andersen, all of whom approach their topic with macro-syntactic considerations in mind; the first two (Niccacci and Eskhult) are concerned broadly with description of the verb in Hebrew; Andersen, on the other hand, focuses on particular syntactic features and presents a fuller description of their variants and functions.

The second stage will consist of an examination Khan's *Studies*, and of Longacre's *Joseph*.[29] Khan and Longacre have more in common than their particular theoretical background (which is shared by Andersen), in that they each offer something unique in their work. In Khan's case it is clarity of presentation, matched by solidity of theoretical grounding; in Longacre's, it is his astute insight into the macro-system of language as a whole, and of Classical Hebrew in particular. As we shall see, these works also have their weak points, which are likewise instructive.

My purpose in looking at these books will be to sample the variety of theories and methodologies current in the academic world of the hebraist, with regard to analyzing larger bodies of Hebrew text.

Excursus on B.K. Waltke and M. O'Connor, An Introduction to Biblical Hebrew Syntax (Winona Lake, IN: Eisenbrauns, 1990)

Most works produced at present tend to steer rather wide of the kind of work I am engaged in in this study; those which do address the issue often do so with a wariness of the intellectual 'investment and returns' involved. Those which do attempt this work are often marred by an inadequate grounding in empirical theory, or never break out of the world of 'linguists communicating with linguists'.[30]

---

29. Longacre's approach to language has informed my own to a great degree, and his principles, for the most part, are my own. This work is dealt with in Chapter 2.

30. As I will reiterate below, in my examination of the various works in this and the next chapters.

One book that adopts the first approach is Waltke and O'Connor's *Introduction*. I have a mixed response to this impressive 'syntax'. On the one hand, it is a remarkable work, and welcome; yet it is also seriously disappointing on several levels: in the first place, the authors spend a vast amount of time on *semantic evaluation of forms* (which is grammar, not syntax), and, in all honesty, very little time on *syntax itself*. Although they do occasionally discuss word order and the like, in clauses containing various forms of the verb, they spend far more time on discussing the *meaning* rather than the *function* of those forms.[31] I have yet to find, for example, a discussion of what elements may be found, and in what order and with what significance, in a participial, or an infinitive, phrase. All this underlines a certain confusion about what constitutes grammar, and what constitutes syntax—by far, most of what purports to be syntactic description is little more than grammar where the nuance of the *form* in question is fine-tuned by a look at the context. This is not to say that I denigrate Waltke and O'Connor's volume—it is a treasury of information; my complaint on this score is solely that they don't end up doing as much syntax as one is led to expect.

In the second place, Waltke and O'Connor blow hot and cold on 'discourse analysis or text linguistics',[32] opting for 'the more traditional path' of old-style phrase and clause analysis (and which they do not do very systematically at the *syntactic* level). They write,

> We have resisted the strong claims of discourse grammarians in part for the theoretical and practical reasons mentioned earlier: *most syntax can be and has been described on the basis of the phrase, clause, and sentence.*[33] Further, it is evident that the grammatical analysis of Hebrew discourse is in its infancy. As an infant, it offers little help for the many problems of grammar which have not been well understood. Most translators, we think it fair to say, fly by the seat of their pants in interpreting the Hebrew conjugations. Hebrew grammarians have only recently come to appreciate morphemes as diverse as the 'object marker' *'t* and the enclitic *mem*. No modern grammar, further, has begun to gather together the wealth of individual studies that have been carried out in a more traditional frame-work; thus it is not surprising that some students know little about the

31. E.g. 'A *non-perfective of instruction* expresses the speaker's will in a context of legislation or teaching', Waltke and O'Connor, *Introduction*, p. 510.
32. Waltke and O'Connor, *Introduction*, pp. 53-54—the entirety of the section.
33. Emphasis added.

case functions and some commentators make egregious errors in their interpretations of prepositions. For our purposes, therefore, we are content to stay with more traditional bases than those of discourse grammar.[34]

And yet they also write,

> If we seek to systematize our understanding of textual organization, we need to introduce the notion of different levels and types of organization. Not every verse, for example, works in the same way in itself and in relation to the verses around it. We may recognize a class of major textual markers or macrosyntactic signs, by which we mean conjunctions and other expressions that bind together the sentences constituting a larger span of text.

Here follows a quote from W. Schneider, *Grammatik des biblischen Hebräisch*,[35] pointing out that certain 'signs' have macrosyntactic significance. Waltke and O'Connor follow this with a very lucid summary, then a disclaimer:

> Like the Masoretic accent system, this method of analyzing textual organization requires independent study (cf. 3.3.4).
> A simpler approach may be offered...[36]

In fact, their 'simpler approach' is not simpler, but muddier, and the simpler approach is the one they have forsaken.[37]

They detail in their book what has been written about Hebrew; at times this appears to exclude the idea of actually describing the language itself. For example, it is nearly universally accepted, nowadays, that 'narrative' is a category with particular features in Biblical Hebrew; Waltke and O'Connor accept it as such, without ever examining what that acceptance implies for language in general, nor for their description of Biblical Hebrew, as the subject of their work.[38] They have taken it on board because it is a matter of general

---

34. Waltke and O'Connor, *Introduction*, p. 55.

35. (Munich: Claudius, 1974), p. 261.

36. Waltke and O'Connor, *Introduction*, p. 634.

37. Waltke and O'Connor, *Introduction*, pp. 634ff. I do not intend this as negatively as it might sound; the fact remains that text-linguistics has already made significant contributions to the organization and simplification of Hebrew grammar and syntax. These Waltke and O'Connor eschew in favor of a method that focuses on particulars rather than patterns, to the complication and detriment of their language description.

38. See, for example, Waltke and O'Connor, *Introduction*, p. 647.

acceptance. And yet, although there is likewise a consensus of opinion that acknowledges ויהי to be an intriguing and significant feature of the language, the index directs the reader to only three locations—of these, two are tangential mentions in the context of a brief reference to someone else's work, and the third is to tell the reader that one should translate the clause ויהי היום into English as '*One day*'; it is accompanied by one example. This glossing over of such a fascinating, and textually significant, feature of the language is not helpful; they choose to do so, I believe (given their own statements in their introductory sections), because if they were to engage in a fuller treatment of the issues involved, it would take them out of their realm, and into areas they have chosen, for personal, rather than academic, reasons, to avoid.

It would be irresponsible of me to give a purely negative review of this book;[39] but to be honest there is something in the underlying principle of the work to which I take serious exception: this is a *textus receptus* approach to describing the language; it has chosen to include only what has been accepted previously, and to break no new ground—nor even to summarize current developments in a way that encourages the reader to look forward to progress and development. It is not likely that another work of a similar nature and scope will receive, for a long time to come, the support and prominence that this has received; therefore, this book will be one of the standards for this generation, and possibly more, of Hebrew students;[40] it has had an opportunity to bring the fascinating array of advances in description of the language to the broadest possible readership, in a way that could have moved the study of this language forward exponentially, yet it has chosen a safer, simpler (for the authors, but not for the student) approach. In my opinion, had the authors taken the task more 'holistically',[41] and had done the four, or seven, or ten, more years'

---

39. The introductory overviews are exceptional, for example, despite the restrictions of space which must curtail most of these discussions; and, for the most part, it is not what they cover that engenders disagreement, but, rather, what they have omitted.

40. Re-editing of some of the older standard grammars and syntaxes, with a view to bringing in modern linguistic insights, is presently underway, and promises to combine the best of both worlds—how much more, then, should we be able to find this in a work like Waltke and O'Connor!

41. I recognize that this excursus may sound rather shrill, yet I believe these

work, which would have enabled them really to write a 'syntax' based on the work available, the book would have been shorter—not because less would be said, but rather because more would have been said, with greater clarity, elegance and simplicity.

2. *Niccacci, The Syntax of the Verb in Classical Hebrew Prose*

Niccacci's *Syntax* is an attempt to describe the variety of uses of the Hebrew verb from a text-linguistic perspective. In several ways it is a strong beginning, but also exhibits several flaws.

The greatest strength of this book is that it eschews older styles of Hebrew grammatical/syntactic description,[42] in favour of an approach drawn from modern linguistics. Niccacci points out the weak points of these more 'traditional' grammars on occasion, in hopes of converting the reader to this new 'text linguistic' approach to language analysis, and in justification of his own approach:

> While it is true that Hebrew had only a limited number of verb forms at its disposal, it still seemed odd that, for example, WAYYIQTOL could be translated by virtually all the finite tenses of modern languages, as would appear from classical grammars. Nor is it easy to accept the view that QATAL, which was supposed to be the form for beginning narrative in Hebrew, could have been replaced so often in that position by the WAYYIQTOL by customary misuse. It was obvious to me that the lengthy catalogues of special cases and exceptional uses listed in the grammars only show how difficult the problem is.
>
> In turn, translators select the equivalent tenses of modern languages somewhat at random, applying their own interpretation and sensitivity.[43]

and,

> It is clear, then, that text linguistic analysis enables us to formulate a set of rules concerning the use of WAYYIQTOL and so considerably lessen the frustrating impression gained from leafing through traditional grammars: that almost any tense of modern languages can be used to translate it.[44]

complaints are inherent weaknesses in the work, and yet are often overlooked owing to the otherwise justifiably impressive nature of the volume.

42. Derived originally from grammars of Latin, hence references to 'genitive constructions', etc., which are out of place for a language with no case system.

43. Niccacci, *Syntax*, p. 9.

44. Niccacci, *Syntax*, p. 177.

His general statements with regard to language principles are often excellent. Consider the following:

> From the aspect of text linguistics every construction which breaks the narrative chain belongs to the background.[45]

> As in pure narrative the chain of WAYYIQTOLs is not interrupted without a reason.[46]

> It is clear, then, that the tense of an individual form and construction and therefore the most suitable tense for translation into modern languages is not tied to that actual form or construction but to its function in the text.[47]

In addition, this book contains some remarkably succinct statements about the syntax or functions of particular features. For example,

> In respect of linguistic attitude, WAYYIQTOL is the tense for narrative (s. 81); in respect of emphasis it denotes the foreground (s. 86); in respect of linguistic aspect it denotes degree zero (s. 88).[48]

Essentially, Niccacci's starting point, and conclusion as well, is that there are two basic features which, when examined together, provide the key to understanding the syntax of the Hebrew verb (in prose, as his title indicates). The first consists of a three-fold set of mutually exclusive categories:

> *Linguistic attitude*: Narrative/Commentary (or Discourse)
> *Emphasis/Highlighting*: Foreground/Background
> *Linguistic Perspective*: Retrieved Information/Degree Zero/Anticipated Information

The second feature is word order within the clause (he will usually refer to this as 'position in the sentence', but for the most part, he is dealing with clause-level syntax rather than sentence-level syntax—or higher).[49] These two sets of criteria are his analytical parameters.

After laying out his basic theoretical ideas in chs. 1, 2 and 3, Niccacci looks at the two 'tenses' WAYYIQTOL and QATAL in ch. 4.[50] Here, Niccacci looks at the distribution of these two

---

45. Niccacci, *Syntax*, p. 71.
46. Niccacci, *Syntax*, p. 107.
47. Niccacci, *Syntax*, pp. 164-65.
48. Niccacci, *Syntax*, p. 175.
49. See Niccacci, *Syntax*, pp. 20ff., 23, 173, *et passim*.
50. I take exception to the use in this book of the term 'tense'—though I acknowledge that some of the problem may have been engendered by the difficulties

conjugations, in narrative, and in 'discourse'.[51]

Perhaps Niccacci's strongest moment is in ch. 5, where he looks at Hebrew Narrative, and where he truly begins to engage in text-linguistic analysis, yet this is also one of his more dangerous points as well, for he is not entirely thorough, and draws conclusions that do not accurately describe the data.

He attempts a similar 'text-type-distribution' analysis in ch. 6, with reference to 'discourse', but I find his conclusions unsatisfactory, owing to his definition of this category.

Chapter 7 deals with 'Tense Shift', in which he looks at the motivation for moving away from the standard tense for the text-type being examined; this again is a strong point, in particular where he refers to narrative material; however, I take exception to some of his findings—once again with reference to 'discourse', but here with reference to other conclusions as well.

Chapter 8 layout the details of what he terms the 'two element syntactic construction'. In my opinion, however, this whole concept is based on some of his weakest prior conclusions, and therefore does not exhibit a great deal of internal strength and consistency.

Chapter 9 is Niccacci's summary of findings. He is definitely at his best when summarizing, and, where his findings are solid, his summary statements are brilliant. Where he is on less solid ground it is often difficult to make sense of his statements, particularly in comparison to alternative explanations of the data.

Niccacci's most striking contribution to the study of Hebrew syntax

of translation. 'Tense', according to Crystal, is 'a category used in the grammatical description of verbs (along with aspect and mood), referring primarily to the way the grammar marks the time at which the action denoted by the verb took place' (*Dictionary*, p. 306, a fairly standard contemporary understanding of the term). It is more or less universally agreed that Classical Hebrew does not have 'tense'-based conjugations. Niccacci himself points out on several occasions that Classical Hebrew does not exhibit tense-like features (see, for example, the above-quoted material from pp. 9 and 177), and yet he chooses this term to describe the Hebrew 'conjugations'— which term seems to me better suited to his needs; failing that, he could always choose the option of such phrases like 'QATAL-forms'. This inconsistency in adherence to the principles of modern linguistic description (which prefers labels that describe the form, rather than the function, when the form is the distinguishing feature) is only one of several minor difficulties that can be found in this work.

51. I will reserve my comments on Niccacci's category of 'discourse' until further on.

is, in my opinion, his assessment of the foreground/background opposition, as being indicated by shifts from one verb-form or syntactic construction to another. And he is very much on the right track with his distinction between 'narrative' and 'discourse', but his handling of 'discourse' is considerably muddied by his definition of this category. And again, his handling of the three-way distinction between 'recovered information', 'degree zero' and 'anticipated information' is going in the right direction, but is weakened by certain inadequacies related to other linguistic questions.

The major 'flaws' that I find in Niccacci's work are as follows:

1. He has lumped all conversational material (reported speech) into one category called 'discourse'—regardless of differences of text-type—and expects this category to show internal consistency and predictability, in spite of the fact that he does not provide parameters for distinguishing, say, between exhortations and reported history.
2. Although he opts for a text-linguistic analysis of the verb system of Classical Hebrew, he almost never gets beyond the clause level.
3. He is not rigorously thorough in his application of linguistic principles, and permits himself both short-cuts and inconsistencies.

The first 'flaw' is at the theoretical level; the second two are methodological.

With reference to my first objection: we require that our language give us many clues as to the type of material we are hearing or reading, and these clues must be more or less instantly recognizable. So, for example, we need to be able to differentiate the following phrases, in order to know what sort of social interaction is involved and expected:

> He went to the store, and he bought bread.
> Let him go to the store, and let him buy bread.

The clause types used in the two sentences immediately indicate to us the text-type we are dealing with in each case (the first is historical narration, the second is exhortation). However, if both the above sentences occurred in Reported Speech, nothing in Niccacci's description would distinguish the first from the second.[52] This is inadequate.

Niccacci recognizes the principle that each type of speech (narrative, exhortation, exposition/explanation, etc.) must use a different verb-form or construction as its main-line form. One can hardly expect the main form for story-telling to be an imperative; and, in the same way, exhortation does not rely on historical past as its main verb form; yet each occurs with regularity in 'conversational' material/reported speech—Niccacci's 'discourse' category is incapable of accounting for this.[53]

Were he to have described these syntactic structures in terms of their text-type, his analysis of 'discourse' would have greater simplicity and clarity. As it is, his analysis is over-complicated and sometimes more than a bit confusing. He concedes, however, that this category requires further work:

> The forms of discourse [conversation] still require study, though, in particular the indirect volitional forms.[54]

With reference to the second so-called 'flaw': Niccacci only once presents a longish section of Hebrew text for analysis, and this is with reference to narrative material embedded within 'discourse';[55] his analysis of this section of text is intended to discover whether or not embedded narrative (his 'discourse narrative') follows the same pattern as narrative which is not related in Reported Speech. And yet, although he insists that units exist beyond the sentence level, and hints that these units also have identifiable structures,[56] *he never looks at a complete text in an attempt to isolate such structures* before trying to identify similarity or dissimilarity to a normative pattern. This prevents him from seeing that a *variety* of features may, for example, serve to introduce a narrative unit, which discovery would in turn inform and streamline some of his other language descriptions.

The third difficulty with Niccacci is a certain tendency toward

52. See his Table 2, Niccacci, *Syntax*, pp. 168-69.
53. No fewer than fourteen possible syntactic constructions—more than half those he lists—are given as possible foreground 'discourse' clause-types, with no real indication of under what conditions they perform this function.
54. Niccacci, *Syntax*, p. 13.
55. Judg. 11.12-28, Niccacci, *Syntax*, pp. 102ff.
56. See Niccacci, *Syntax*, ch. 5.

overstatement of 'rules' of syntax, some of which are occasioned by
the theoretical and procedural difficulties mentioned above—and, as a
result, he occasionally contradicts himself. For example, Niccacci says
of the 'report QATAL' that it 'never heads a sentence' as well as that
it 'is a form with first position in the clause'.[57] These two statements
cannot be reconciled with each other, and do not describe the data.
And again, he writes, 'a very important fact concerning the use of
QATAL in discourse is that it always comes first in the sentence; this
never occurs in narrative'.[58] This statement is in fact wrong on both
counts: clear exceptions to both facets of this rule occur in Ruth, for
example.[59]

I do not often find myself in agreement with Niccacci's rules,
particularly with regard to distribution of specific syntactic constructions. Non-linguistic readers of Niccacci's work may be tempted to
think that the difficulties in understanding this work stem from their
own lack of sophistication in this discipline; Niccacci, however, must
share the responsibility for the difficulties encountered, since his work
exhibits a certain internal inconsistency.

I hasten to add, however, that Niccacci is not so much 'wrong' in
his conclusions, as he is 'only partly right'—theoretical factors that he
has overlooked provide contextual clues that clarify the distribution of
these syntactic elements, and permit a more restrained and 'more
elegant' formulation of 'rules.' Niccacci is working toward the
description of the system that governs the deployment the verb in
different clause-types in Classical Hebrew; and he is correct, both in
supposing that it is there to be discovered, and in seeking many of the
clues to it at the macro-syntactic levels. The difficulties encountered

57. Niccacci, *Syntax*, p. 43.
58. Niccacci, *Syntax*, p. 41.
59. Cf. Ruth 3.17.2 [the three indices in this form of reference identify
Chapter.Verse.Clause; this last refers to the clause within specific verse—in this
case, the second clause of Ruth 3.17] שש־השערים האלה נתן לי כי..., contrary to his
first assertion, and Ruth 4.7.2-3 ונתן לרעהו // חעלו איש שלף...(I will use this
convention [//], from time to time, where it is useful to see the text in continuous
sequence, but where it is nonetheless advantageous to bear in mind the clause
divisions of the text), contrary to his second assertion—this latter I would not call
`Narrative' and therefore the second assertion might be valid according to *my* criteria,
but it is not true according to Niccacci's, for he would not distinguish this material as
being of a separate text-type (see chapters 3, 4 and 5 in this volume, for the theory
and examples relating to this issue).

here arise out of a partially insufficient theoretical base and a few procedural short-cuts, with the result that the conclusions he comes to are less elegant than they could be, and do not fully match the data.

There are several other comments I wish to make with regard to Niccacci's analysis. First, he recognizes and focuses on macro-syntactic markers (for example, הנה and עתה); this is a strong move forward—here again, however, he will benefit from isolating distribution of these elements according to text-type.

Second, he examines forms of היה as a possible macro-syntactic markers, and makes some cogent observations. This is a significant improvement over Waltke and O'Connor (and others), and the traditional grammarians, who limit themselves to only the briefest allusions to this feature's (and others') macro-syntactic significance.

On the other hand, while he acknowledges that semantics must play a role even in macro-syntactic description,[60] he restricts his semantic analysis to grammatical forms. He overlooks the fact that, for example, היה never represents a 'full' event, by virtue of its inherent, 'stative', meaning, and thus can never be a foregrounded narrative verb. His explanation of the distribution of this verb is fairly convoluted, and could have been simplified with recognition of the stative nature of היה.[61]

One of the difficulties Niccacci runs into here is due to his apparently not having examined larger units for structural similarities. This sort of investigation would have shown that 'interruptions' to the

---

60. 'We have already stated that semantics is of importance, even if only secondary, in determining the function of a verb form or grammatical construction' (Niccacci, *Syntax*, p. 165).

61. I am aware that a case can be made for a dual semantic nature of היה, with the 'be' and the 'become' meanings treated independently—this *may* have significance for the proposed macro-syntactic functions of the word, with the 'be' occurrences having a stronger macro-syntactic effect in narrative, for example, than the 'become' occurrences. I do not see the need for this, at this point, as neither of them appear ever to be main-line verbs in the Narrative History data I have examined (definitions, and further discussion of the issue, will follow). In addition, I am sceptical of this distinction at another level: is this not simply a matter of difficulties in translation? What evidence do we have that this was a significant distinction for *native users* of the language? Until I have seen empirical evidence that the 'be' sense and the 'become' sense of this verb have distinctive distributions in the text itself, I see no need to treat them separately. 'Do not explain with two things what can be explained with one', to paraphrase the 14th c. epistemology of William of Ockham.

main narrative are marked as more or less significant on the basis of (1) how far removed the interruption is from the normal semantic, temporal, and aspectual (etc.) qualities of the main-line of the text,[62] and (2) how many non-main-line clause-types occur in tandem. This second factor is significant for evaluation of היה forms—if Niccacci were to have worked from the assumption that Classical Hebrew is a 'bag-of-tricks' language, the idea that ויהי clauses are among the possible options in the bag of tricks available for a specific task, and he would not have to claim a distinction between ויהי as a 'full form of the verb' and ויהי as a macro-syntactic marker, since ויהי as a 'full form' could still function as a macro-syntactic marker. Comparison of several large units of text would lead as well to the realization that narrative units can be broken down into smaller units without endangering the integrity of the whole, and he would not need to insist that ויהי is always a marker of continuity. (In my reading of the data, ויהי seems almost without exception to function as a paragraph-break marker, and as such is often a marker of *discontinuity*.)[63]

Third, had Niccacci analysed the structure of larger narrative units more carefully, and had he acknowledged the integrity of other text-types, he would not need to posit a difference between narrative embedded in discourse and 'narrative proper'.[64]

When analyzing the Judges 11 text as an example of narrative within 'discourse', Niccacci makes several surprising statements:

> I use the term 'narrative discourse' for this type of narrative in which the events are not reported in a detached way, as in a historian's account, but from the speaker's point of view. Naturally, verbal forms in the first and second person predominate.[65]

The claim that 'verbal forms in the first and second person predominate' is odd, particularly in light of the fact that, in the

---

62. We will return to rework this concept more deeply in Chapter Three.

63. Perhaps some of the difficulty here is related to the term 'continuity' and its cognates; I perceive an element of continuity in the function of ויהי, due to its wc + Prefix form—it is certainly more indicative of 'continuity' than the same clause would be if it contained a Suffix form of היה—yet I also want to highlight that ויהי appears to have a consistent role of the 'hinge' between paragraphs, etc. In this sense, which I consider dominant, it is an indicator of 'discontinuity'.

64. Niccacci, *Syntax*, p. 102.

65. Niccacci, *Syntax*, p. 102.

example Niccacci himself gives, in the narrative in question,[66] *all narrative clauses are in third person*; two cohortative clauses do occur, which record the messages sent to the two kings—these are not narrative, but exhortation: 'Let us pass through your land' (in vv. 17 and 19).

In addition to this, Niccacci claims that 'narrative discourse' and 'discourse proper' obey different rules, and that

> The text of Judges 11 just examined shows that QATAL is the verb form for beginning 'narrative discourse'... Now here a basic fact must be emphasized. No 'narrative discourse' begins with a WAYYIQTOL; the WAYYIQTOL is always the continuation form of an initial construction typical of discourse (cf. s. 24)... This fact reveals the fundamental difference between the WAYYIQTOL of narrative—which is either initial or the continuation of another initial WAYYIQTOL—and the WAYYIQTOL of discourse which is never initial but always the continuation of a non-narrative initial construction, different, that is, from WAYYIQTOL.[67]

Niccacci is at ease with the idea that a narrative unit can (or perhaps, 'must') be preceded by an 'antecedent construction' section—that is, a section that provides background information such as location, time reference, and so on.[68] Why is it, then, that he discounts this explanation of the opening temporal clause of the Judges narrative on the grounds that it occurs in recorded speech? This explanation actually fits the data, and eliminates the need for multiplex descriptions of this verb-form and text-type.[69] In my opinion, Niccacci considerably overworks the 'linguistic perspective (retrieved information/degree zero/anticipated information)' factor. This is in compensation for the too-broadly defined 'discourse' category; for, where he has failed to distinguish the integrity of individual text-types and the consistency with which clause types function within them, he has been forced to attempt another explanation for the bewildering remainder of material left unexplained by his other two categories (linguistic attitude: narrative/discourse; and prominence: foreground/background)—both of which categories are quite solid, apart from the ineffectively broad 'discourse' category.

---

66. Judg. 11.16-22, 27 clauses in all, by my count.

67. Niccacci, *Syntax*, pp.106-107.

68. Cf. Niccacci, *Syntax*, pp. 36-37 and p. 48.

69. I will address this problem again in Chapter 5, after we have examined some data, for I will propose another explanation for this phenomenon.

This 'linguistic perspective' category likewise has promise, but does not rise to the occasion, since it does not explain all the occurrences it purports to explain; this factor does not appear to play a major role in verb and clause usage in Classical Hebrew, and Niccacci does not seem to be on the right track in assuming it as a motivating factor for a wide array of features; other motivating factors can be demonstrated to have a far greater influence over the choice of clause type, resulting in a much clearer presentation of the micro- and macro-syntax of this language.

My last objection to Niccacci's description is again one questioning the degree of influence of a certain factor, in this case word order, within the clause. Here, I am largely in favour of Niccacci's conclusion: that the emphasis of the clause is determined by what has first position in it (excluding conjunctions such as -ו and כי); however, I feel he takes this too far. Permit me to quote at length:

> At this point we can state our opinion concerning the traditional definition which runs as follows: a clause is verbal when the predicate is a finite verb and nominal when the predicate is a noun. For this definition to be valid it should also be specified that in Hebrew a finite verbal form is predicate when it comes first in the clause. When, instead, it is preceded by an element of any kind (other than WAW) the verbal form is not the predicate and therefore the clause is nominal (CNC)...
>
> By definition, the 'subject' is the topic spoken about (usually a person or animate being) and the 'predicate' is what is said about the subject... Now the subject is a noun or noun equivalent ('noun-phrase') while the predicate is a verb ('verb-phrase'). According to modern linguists the 'noun-phrase' has first position in the sentence. It should be noted, however, that this statement does not suit Hebrew, for two reasons. First, in Hebrew the first position in the sentence is filled by the predicate, not by the subject. Second, when a Hebrew sentence begins with a noun or an adverb the predicate is not identical with the verb but in actual fact with that noun or adverb. Accordingly, what is normally the 'subject' becomes the 'predicate' and vice versa.
>
> This transformation is not exclusive to Hebrew as it occurs in other languages, ancient and modern. It is effected by nominalisation of the verbal form. To this type belong the first two constructions in Hebrew, listed above:
>
> 1) x-participle with article
> 2) x-'asher + QATAL

Typically, in Hebrew there is a way to effect the change from 'subject' to 'predicate' without nominalisation of the verb. Instead, the noun is simply placed at the head of the sentence. To this type belong the other two constructions discussed above:

3)   x-QATAL
4)   x-YIQTOL[70]

This opposition of subject and predicate seems overstated. In truth, *all* the information in a 'sentence' (by which he here means 'clause')— and not just the predicate—is vital to the meaning of the sentence, and though one element may have greater importance, this is only on a sliding scale; to label one element 'subject' and another 'predicate' in this fashion is to put into black and white that which should be described in terms of greys. Rather, is this not a case, not of the transformation of subject to predicate and vice versa, but more simply of the *de-emphasizing of the predicate and the emphasizing of the subject*, without the categories themselves being reversed? Niccacci's approach oversimpifies the phenomenon, while creating a new range of concepts and definitions for terms which served adequately in their old guise. I feel that nothing is gained in calling a noun which precedes the verb 'the predicate', rather than 'sentence-' or 'clause-initial'. Such a redefinition is extraneous—one accomplishes the same thing by giving the label 'subject-initial' clause, or some other similar (and more empirically descriptive) label; this 'transformation' of subject and predicate is not necessary, and complicates description of the language.

He is also not accurate in his assessment of 'modern linguists'; it is incorrect to say that they believe the noun phrase to be 'first in the sentence'. Perhaps this is true of those who do not engage in linguistics as a description of data (though I cannot imagine what other sort of linguistics would exhibit any integrity); it is certainly not true of linguists whose goal is to describe 'what is there'. The syntax of Classical Hebrew must be described in such a way that all syntactic options are accounted for; this is easiest if one specifies as accurately as possible what sorts of clauses (for example) have what sort of construction—for Classical Hebrew, for example, one might say that main-line narrative transitive clauses are normally V-S-O, while

70. Niccacci, *Syntax*, pp. 28-29.

background narrative transitive clauses are S-V-O and, rarely, O-S-V.[71]

Niccacci suggests that this transformation from subject to predicate and vice versa is found in modern languages, and cites the French 'c'est moi qui...' as an example.[72] This in fact is simply a stative identificational clause (identical to the likes of 'c'est un homme', 'il est professeur', 'he's my friend', and so on) which follows its standard rule for stative identificational clauses in French:

S + stative-Verb [= être] + Noun Phr. or equiv.

In this case the predicated Noun Phrase is a personal pronoun, which is modified by a relative clause (which is left incomplete in our example, but which will follow its own rules of constituent structure). There is no need to propose a shift of predicate to subject and vice versa: properly written rules forestall the need to redefine basic terms.

I do not share Niccacci's confidence in the finality of his results, as evidenced by his statement, 'scrutiny of a wider selection of texts might contribute further refinements but I do not envisage major modifications'.[73] I believe he is well on the right track, yet I *do* envisage modifications, some of which will indeed be major.[74]

71. This is, of course, a vastly oversimplified 'rule', taking no account of sentences with conjunctions, temporal phrases, adverbs, etc., each of which can be described accurately, without requiring a redefinition of terms, and without becoming too cumbersome—but this illustrates well enough the benefits of describing a feature by its own features: 'S-V-O' is a much more 'accurate' description than 'nominal clause' as opposed to 'verbal clause'. These other labels may have some value in other facets of language description, but at the level at which Niccacci, Eskhult, myself, and others, are working, it is far clearer to employ the former option.

72. Niccacci, *Syntax*, p. 29 n. 18.

73. Niccacci, *Syntax*, p. 10.

74. Lest this sound condescending, I must acknowledge my debt to Niccacci for several insights and characteristics, not the least of which, in addition to several observations on clause function in Classical Hebrew, is his example and encouragement in challenging outmoded ways of thinking.

3. *Eskhult: Studies in Verbal Aspect and Narrative*
Technique in Biblical Hebrew

Eskhult's book has a narrow focus—he looks principally at a single clause-type—but he attempts a great deal within these narrow confines. He writes,

> The aim of this study is to shed light on the system of aspectual contrasts in Biblical Hebrew, and more particularly how aspectual contrasts are used as a device in narrative technique.[75]

His basic approach is solid: he looks to the world of theoretical linguistics for direction in resolving the opacities of Hebrew syntax. Although his is essentially a micro-syntactic enquiry, with a shy courtship of macro-syntax (he does not really step outside of micro-syntax even to examine macro-syntactic function), he asserts the easily overlooked fact that 'there are factors on the clause, sentence and episode level that bear on the verbal aspect'[76] and, further, that

> it is decisive for the interpretation of classical Hebrew prose, that one is clear about which clauses carry on a narrative, and which depict a background state of affairs. In narrative discourse the skeleton is made up of sequential *wayyiqtol*-clauses, while the *subj–qtl* clause almost exclusively furnishes some background information.[77]

These are insightful observations, solidly rooted in good theory, and they lead him to posit the *(w^e)subj–qtl* clause as a feature that separates sections of main-line narrative clauses, providing a structuring mechanism for narrative texts.[78]

Eskhult is hoping to contribute to solutions in the realm of Hebrew macro-syntax; his approach is to perform a 'cross-over' attempt,

---

75. Eskhult, *Studies*, p. 9.
76. Eskhult, *Studies*, p. 121.
77. Eskhult, *Studies*, p. 43.
78. He suggests that this feature is particularly suited to a largely illiterate society, with its emphasis on the oral, rather than the written, use of narrative (Eskhult, *Studies*, p. 43); but this is somewhat irrelevant, since literate societies, with their written narrative, have the same tendency to use clause-types to endcode episode margins, etc., as do illiterate ones (see the example from Mary Shelley's *Frankenstein*, below). This foreshadows a theoretical weakness which will be betrayed more clearly by other difficulties; his theoretical base is too far removed from 'real language'.

whereby he looks to micro-syntax for help in determining the function and distribution of macro-syntactic features. He forcuses strongly on the aspectual (and thus micro-syntactic and semantic) nature of the verbal clauses under consideration.

The first of three major difficulties that I perceive in this work, however, is that Eskhult attempts much in too little space, and leaves the sceptical reader largely unconvinced.[79] There is no doubt that micro-syntax and macro-syntax interpenetrate, and he is right in assuming that the aspectual nature of these clauses is the means by which they perform their macro-syntactic functions, but the connections that Eskhult proposes are not so apparent that his substantiation of these claims is sufficient. Eskhult has left it unclear as to whether he sees himself doing clause-level analysis, or 'discourse'-level analysis;[80] and though this type of study is welcome, it does not really belong in either category, and his proposal requires a more lucidly presented, and much more thoroughly substantiated, work than this if it is to be accepted by his readers.

In addition, the extensive micro-syntactic description of the aspectual features of a few clause-types (the scope of this work extends to cover only $(w^e)subj–qatal$ clauses, with only the very briefest examination of other clause-types), with occasional reference to possible functions at higher levels, does not really constitute a macro-syntactic analysis, nor—owing to lack of thoroughly reasoned explanations for connecting micro-syntax so closely to macro-syntax—does it convince the reader to do the work more thoroughly him- or herself.

This emphasis on micro-syntax is not prerequisite to a description of macro-syntactic functions, for once one accepts that the difference in meaning conveyed by the various clause-types enables the hearer/reader to register its macro-syntactic signals, the aspectual nature of specific clause-types ceases to be central to macro-syntactic analysis. That is to say, a syntactic study needs to identify and describe the structures and functions of elements at whatever syntactic level one is working at; it does not require us to do all other levels of analysis at the same time.

79. This need not be the case; a more in-depth examination of such a broad topic has been successfully undertaken: compare the thoroughness of M. O'Connor's *Hebrew Verse Structure* (Winona Lake, IN: Eisenbrauns, 1980).

80. Eskhult uses the term 'discourse' to refer to large units of text.

This may seem at first blush either obvious or irrelevant—or simply wrong; yet macro-syntactic descriptions will benefit from the clarity gained by omitting secondarily related material. The macro-syntactic *function* of a particular clause-type may, for example, be more simply apprehended if we stay within the syntactic level where the feature is to be found, as opposed to stopping frequently to assess its aspectual connotations. We expect a book on Hebrew syntax to forego in-depth analysis of grammatical constructions, except where they substantiate a point under examination; likewise we would find a lexicon 'obsessive' which makes constant reference, on even the most minor points, to the phonological system of the language. In each of these cases, we accustomed to the fact that features that can be analyzed in their own right can become (more or less) *unquestioned* building blocks at levels further up the hierarchy; if we don't take at least *some* things as tentative starting points, we will never get off the ground.

The $(w^e)subj–qatal$ clause does warrant approach from both the macro-syntactic and the micro-syntactic directions; however, Eskhult attempts to cover too much ground in too few pages (objection no. 1), and he (like many others) is working from a theoretical base that does not direct him to focus on text-type as a conditioning factor in deployment of clause-types (objection no. 2); in addition, he does not attempt to examine this clause-type as one of several possibilities for this particular macro-syntactic function (objection no. 3)—for these reasons he describes successfully neither the aspectual relationships, nor the macro-syntactic distribution and functions, of this clause-type.

And yet, it must be said that, like Niccacci, he makes some very astute and helpful observations. Some of his summary comments are direct and incisive—the model of elegance—for example,

> Generally speaking, a clause expressing a completed action with reference to the present is static, since it refers some state to a preceding situation. Therefore, it seems natural that such a clause is construed as a descriptive, not a narrative-sequential, clause.[81]

---

81. Eskhult, *Studies*, p. 39; it should be noted, however, that such nuances of time reference are decidedly difficult to pin down. This is a constant thorn in the flesh of this study: starting from the point of aspectual contrasts (which tend to be too evasive of secure identification and codification to serve well in this role), enforces on this study a constant weakness.

With regard to my second objection, Eskhult, like Niccacci, fails to take into account that different text-types will use verbs and clauses differently; their attempts to generalize on the distribution of clause-types in Reported Speech material, in particular, are confused and unsuccessful—lacking entirely the elegance visible in their more solidly grounded observations. Weeding out *mutually exclusive occurrences*, predictable on the basis of differing text-types, would enable each of them to describe much more clearly the harmony and symmetry of the Hebrew verb system.

Eskhult writes,

> from a *discourse perspective* the contrast between 'state' and 'motion' is also a contrast between 'background' and 'foreground', which means that aspectual contrasts are liable to be used by a narrator in order to facilitate the apprehension of the structure of a story on the part of his audience. This is, however, fully pertinent to narrative portions only; in dialogue this contrast is less apparent.[82]

82. Eskhult, *Studies*, p. 121; Eskhult's summary of the role of aspectual contrasts is very much on the mark, yet as I hope to illustrate beyond doubt below, factoring in the role of *text-type* in the deployment of clause-types will improve the description even further. It is a feature of the general state of affairs in Classical Hebrew text-linguistics that Reported Speech is evaluated as a single, unified text-type—it is rare that hebraists interested in text-linguistics look at Narrative texts in Reported Speech, and compare them with Predictive, with Exhortation, with Instructions, and with Expository texts in Reported Speech, to identify features peculiar to each, and traits common to all. Another recent contribution to the discussion falls afoul of the same insufficiency: A. den Exter Blokland's 'Clause-Analysis in Biblical Hebrew Narrative—An Explanation and a Manual for Compilation' (*Trinity Journal* 11 [1990], pp. 73–102) is a bit of a rarity, in that its goal is to present a *methodology* to the reader, so that one can retreat to the study and 'do it' after him (this methodology is computer-based, however, and requires materials prepared by J.H. Sailhammer of Trinity Evangelical Divinity School, Deerfield, Illinois, which restricts its practicability). This study makes the same mistake of lumping all 'discourse' material into a single category; in the context of pointing the reader in the direction of language universals, den Exter Blokland writes, 'Linguistic reseach of the past thirty odd years has shown that texts themselves show patterns in their composition that arise from the nature of the medium language [I suspect his point would have been more clearly made had he enclosed in quotation marks the word 'language'] rather than from text-genre combined with the author's literary freedom alone. A case in point is the fact that in many languages the distribution of tenses differs according to whether the text-type is discourse or narrative. There are rules of language that determine in what tense a sentence will be cast, depending on whether the sentence forms part of a discourse or a narrative text-segment, whether it is background or

The difficulties alluded to in this reference to 'dialogue' settle calmly into place with a proper appreciation of the influence text-types exert on linguistic material. This subject will occupy our attention at considerable length in Chapter 3.

Thirdly, Eskhult no more than cursorily evaluates the range of possible features that could replace his chosen clause-type as an 'Episode Marginal Circumstantial'.[83] This is inadequate. Saturation with a range of features is the proven tendency for marking the macro-structure of a vast number of the world's languages (in particular, those that fit into the *bag-of-tricks* category).[84] Therefore, any macro-syntactic markers in Classical Hebrew (since it is a bag-of-tricks language) need to be examined in company with other options that can perform the same function. Eskhult attempts to discern the macro-syntactic contribution of the $(w^e)subj$–$qatal$ clause on the basis of its aspectual identity, without doing a thorough survey of its distribution as one of a collection of forms that can perform the same function, and therefore he presents a rather limited perspective on the matter.

In Mary Shelley's *Frankenstein*, to take a random example, we find the following clause distribution:

foreground, whether the statement is general or specific' (p. 73). Here again, the only substantial weakness in this statement is the definition of 'discourse' as a text-type parallel to 'narrative'. The dismantling of this presupposition is one of the main goals of the present volume.

83. Eskhult, *Studies*, p. 9, *et freq.*

84. There is no compendium of 'text-level features of the world's languages', and therefore these statements which refer to 'a vast number of the world's languages' may seem to beg the question. It would be irresponsible of me, however, to leave these claims totally unsupported, though I can direct the reader to no more than a token substantiation. In Mandarin (Chinese), for example, peak events are marked by a single particle—this is *not* a bag-of-tricks language; in colloquial American English (I have noticed this feature in Britain as well, though it seems less socially acceptable there), a story-teller may shift from simple past to (historical) present tense, to highlight the peak episode of a story; verb saturation, staccato clause structure, and other such features may also mark the peak episode, but *none of these is required* as is the particle in Mandarin. These languages in which one particle has one function, which none other can replace, are documented from around the world, in linguistic journals and monographs. Beyond this very short summary, I must refer the interested reader first to Longacre's *Grammar Discovery Procedures* and *Grammar of Discourse*, then to the language-specific literature listed in his bibliography, and those of others.

—a long string of 'simple past' clauses;
—a string of 11 clauses built on the verb 'to be';
—a long series of clauses with 'past perfect' forms, and the occasional 'modal clause' ('that I should...') and 'stative clause';
—then, another long string of 'simple past' clauses.

This is the distribution of clauses found at the end of Chapter 2 and the beginning of Chapter 3.[85]

The readers know that they have come to a significant break in the action of the story; they do not tend to register consciously the fact that these 'to be' clauses provide stative description, or that the past-perfect clauses are requiring them to examine prior events. It is possible (if not probable) that the same unconscious relationship to the syntax (macro-syntax) of this material is true of the author as well. An analysis of the aspectual values of these clauses is illuminating, but it is not required in order to understand the macro-syntactic significance of these features. It is clear, in addition, that a study of only the stative clauses, in this example, will not lead us to a very well-rounded understanding of the macro-syntax of this text—nor, for that matter, will it tell us all that much about the stative clauses, since we do not gain an understanding of how they work with other clause-types to perform their own macro-syntactic functions.

I hold to a basic assumption that informs and controls my own approach: when assessing the use of a specific linguistic feature, it is important to seek first its strongest motivating or conditioning factor; this will provide the observer with the clearest and most uncomplicated data from which to describe the particular feature. It is possible that Eskhult and Niccacci would affirm this as well, but their theoretical starting point directs neither of them to all the possible motivating factors.

A goal of any linguistic description is 'elegance'—that is, a linguist seeks to describe data accurately and fully, yet as economically as possible. An accurate and readable analysis of three pages in length is considered more elegant than an equally accurate, and equally readable, analysis of thirty pages in length. This goal of an elegant description reflects an underlying presupposition: that the human brain requires organization in order to encode thoughts into language—we are not capable of synthesizing vast quantities of only marginally related data

85. The chapter break occurs after the 11 *to be* clauses; cf. pp. 41-42 in the Oxford University Press's 'World Classics' edition (1980).

without some sort of organization being applied to it—and, therefore, that each language can be reduced to its principles of organizing raw data. Both Niccacci and Eskhult are shy of the mark with regard to this elegance, in that they have overlooked factors that would have streamlined their results.

Eskhult's work does contribute to our knowledge of the Hebrew verb; it does not, however, greatly advance our understanding of Hebrew macro-syntax. Analyses such as this, which focus on the inherent meaning of a form,[86] are essential for an understanding of the Hebrew verb. However, the inherent meaning of a form should in theory be described only in conjunction with the contextual meaning and function. The inherent sense of the verbless clause, for example, is exactly that which makes it the most appropriate form to use for Expository texts,[87] and the inherent sense of *wayyiqtol* forms make them the most appropriate for narrative material.[88] When a verbless clause is used in an expository text, it should raise no eyebrows; it imports little or no added nuance to the text. However, if a verbless clause occurs in a narrative text, *this* should incite comment, since it is very different from the standard form, and thus is used to contribute something to the text, by virtue of its being 'unexpected'.

When a writer seeks to explain certain syntactic features, but does so only from the perspective of the inherent meaning of that feature or form, regardless of its function in the text, we do not get a true picture of things; it is untrue that a syntactic feature always imposes its inherent meaning upon a text (for the reasons stated immediately above), and therefore an analysis from such a perspective is misleading in that we are told that these nuances are present in all occurrences of the feature or form being examined.

4. *Andersen: The Sentence in Biblical Hebrew*

What has been said in the introduction to my analysis of Khan— regarding the narrowness of his topic, and the thoroughness with which he describes it—can also be said of Andersen, although I must open my remarks on this landmark in Biblical Hebrew studies with the

---

86. As opposed to its function in its context.
87. See Chapters 3, 4 and 5, for a fuller discussion of this text-type.
88. Or it might be the evolved function which has given rise to the significance of a particular form, though this is less likely... yet another 'chicken-or-egg' situation.

comment that the average hebraist will find this one of the most unreadable books available to the Hebrew scholar.[89] For example, where the author begins to explain 'deep' grammar versus 'surface' grammar, the text reads as follows:

Consider the phrases in English:

a man,	whose name is/was Job
the king,	whose name is David
Esau,	whose name is Edom
you,	whose name is Yahweh

These all have the structure:[90]

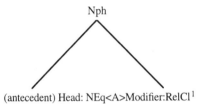

(antecedent) Head: NEq<A>Modifier:RelCl[1]

This is a 'Tagmemic' encoding of a description like the following: 'this type of Noun Phrase is composed of an antecedent (that is, a definite or an indefinite article, or the like), which is optional, followed by the 'Head' of the phrase (that is, the core unit), which can

---

89. One of the benefits of the 'Tagmemic' school of linguistics—which has given us both this book, and Khan's, and Longacre's various works, among others—is that it is empirically rooted. It has provided a systematic theory which has opened the door to a great deal of understanding of language; its theoretical underpinnings are sufficiently economical, yet all-encompassing, to permit all facets of a language to be assessed in relation to all other facets of that language (from extra-linguistic signals, such as gestures, to the structures of the largest bodies of text, and again to the most minute details of pronunciation). The drawback is that such a wealth of interrelating information requires to be put into print, and is often summarized in very dense jargon; linguists familiar with this theoretical system tend to try to include as much of this related material as possible in any given analysis, and (always trying to produce the most 'elegant' solution possible—where 'elegance' sometimes seems to refer to least number of pages rather than merely clarity and economy of logic) they tend to try to present it in a minimum of space. This leads to a vast amount of material being presented in a short-hand form resembling mathematical calculus—it is not coincidence that Andersen's and Longacre's works are alike in this.

90. Andersen, *Sentence*, p. 29.

be composed of a Noun or its equivalent (a pronoun, personal name, etc.); this is followed by a modifier, which is composed in this instance of a Relative Clause, and which is tied together with the Head section by grammatical agreement'.[91] While this approach provides the benefit of an enormous amount of linguistic analysis in a nutshell, it is all but impenetrable to one who has not mastered the theory with its idiosyncratic short-hand.

This is a significant drawback, yet Andersen's book has nontheless had widespread effect on Hebrew studies; it is cited in nearly every text dealing with the syntax of Biblical Hebrew since its publication. It is an example of the highest calibre of scholarship and of scholastic integrity, informed by language universals, and thus enabled to describe in penetrating detail a particular level of the Hebrew language. However, its transmission to the average interested hebraist has not, altogether, been a success.

Andersen engages in both 'from the bottom up' description and 'from the top down' description—that is to say, he describes the Biblical Hebrew sentence (1) in terms of what units make it up, (2) in terms of what other options might replace it in the various slots which it can fill. In addition, he describes it in terms of what effect it has on its wider context or contexts.

One of the great strengths of this book is that it does recognize the strong influence of text-type on other levels of the language, for example the author frequently deals with 'precative discourse'[92] and 'predictive discourse' in separate sections, since to mix them together would not allow certain patterns of usage to appear. In addition, the reader will find practical justification for this kind of research in statements like the following:

> The connections secured by the hierarchical grammar of Hebrew discourse are shown on p. 138. The example is instructive, because the results are different in translation when these structural signals to the higher levels of discourse structure are not heeded. RSV, to look at only one attempt, takes considerable liberties with the conjunctions, thus throwing the paragraphs into quite different arrangements, breaking some

---

91. Chapter 3 will deal at length with the principles and particulars of Tagmemic linguistic theory, but this volume will not require the reader to 'learn' any of its idiosyncratic calculus.

92. Andersen uses the term 'discourse' to refer to a longer, structured, section of text.

close linkages, and creating others where there should be a break. It omits the conjunction at the beginning of 8.18, making a break where there is sequence. It misses completely the trio of clauses governed by *pen*, which as we have seen, are unified by chiasmus. Instead, it adds a gratuitous *beware lest* to verse 17, severing its sequential connection with verse 14b.[93]

Andersen writes,

> Without explicit and methodologically rigorous definitions of basic units and relationships the classification of a linguistic datum remains whimsical, and the same clause will often be described differently by different writers, with no discussion of the reason for doing so.[94]

In his opening pages he provides a detailed introduction to his topic (the sentence), giving definitions arising out of concerns raised by modern linguistics. So, rather than saying that a sentence is 'a complete thought expressed in words' (which definition is found wanting on several counts by modern standards), he sets out what exactly can and cannot be termed a sentence for purposes of linguistic assessment.[95] This section is not vastly easier to understand than the remainder of the book, but amply repays careful study. Working through this material gives the reader great insight into the kind of analysis of data, and the kind of language description, that one must cultivate in order to do justice to the task we undertake.

The main impediment in this book is that it is exceptionally difficult to *read*. One is constantly faced with the difficult task of trying to decipher tagmemic calculus; and there are minor weaknesses where a particular remark is not clarified for the uninitiated, for example, 'such a participial phrase (incomplete clause) generally functions as a NOUN EQUIVALENT (NEq); the participle is verbal within the phrase, nominal outside it'.[96] The reader is left to divine the sense of this summary, and while the meaning is not impenetrable, it is difficult to determine that one's interpretation is exactly what the author had intended.

This book does not require further attention in this particular work, as the shortcomings of the work are immediately apparent, and the

---

93. Andersen, *Sentence*, p. 137.

94. Andersen, *Sentence*, p. 18.

95. Waltke and O'Connor, *Introduction*, pp. 77ff., borrow heavily from Andersen in their discussion of the same topic.

96. Andersen, *Sentence*, p. 24.

assets of the work have long been recognized. In addition, the principal relevance for the present study is its incorporation of the 'higher levels' of the linguistic hierarchy, and its theoretical foundations, and to these latter we will return for a more penetrating discussion in Chapter 3.

5. *Conclusions*

In this chapter I have introduced the general plan of this book: its concern that contemporary works on Hebrew text-linguistic studies fail to complete the task of communicating solid results in a form that is accessible to the readership, and the intention to provide an evaluation of some of those works, an introduction to text-linguistic theory from the 'Tagmemic' perspective, and a presentation of some worked examples as an illustration of a methodology derived from that theoretical base.

In addition, I have presented an analysis of several recent Hebrew language studies. Earlier in this chapter I used the metaphor of a bridge—the two sides of a chasm representing (a) the material to be conveyed, and (b) the readership, the bridge itself representing the author and the work—to illustrate the two elements of the communication process I would be evaluating in each of our authors. I have found each of them wanting to some degree with regard to one or the other of these two elements.

This, I want to emphasize here, does *not* mean I reject these works, nor that I do not appreciate their worth; I have found each of them helpful, and many others as well, whose weaknesses and failings have been far more significant. The choice of these authors' works was not because they are particularly glaring examples of these 'weaknesses', but rather because they are so close to a proper balance. Permit me an illustration from a different realm altogether—a sporting competition, one in which the performance is measured aesthetically: In a 10-metre diving competition, for example, two divers might do an identical dive with exactly the same execution, both making the same error (say, a large splash instead of a small one, on entering the water); the only difference between them is that one of the divers is more graceful in the air than is the other. In theory, the more graceful dive should receive the higher award. In fact, this is often *not* the case, and the *less* graceful one often receives the higher award. The reason for this is that the error—the large splash—is the more obvious in the dive which is the closer to 'perfection'. That is, the more perfect the 'ensemble', the more striking are the exceptions to that perfection. And that is the case here: the books examined in this chapter and the next are among the best text-linguistic studies available to the hebraist. Their inadequacies are the more obvious because they are seen against the background of their significant contributions to Hebrew studies.

Niccacci's book has been welcomed as an excellent study on Hebrew macro-syntax. Its major failing is its difficulty in handling 'discourse' material; the category is too broadly defined, the patterns within it do not emerge, and false conclusions are drawn. Eskhult shares the same weakness, but the final result is slightly different. Where Niccacci concludes that 'discourse' is a category with rules different from those of narrative, and much more nebulous ones, Eskhult concludes that it is the inherent 'aspect' of a form, rather than a shift to 'discourse' text-type, which governs the contribution a particular form makes to the 'whole' in which it is found. Both authors miss out principal conditioning factors, and focus on secondary ones.

Andersen, on the other hand, does not exhibit theoretical weaknesses, but rather 'fails' to communicate his results clearly. His impressive work is all too readily shelved without thorough study because it demands so much of the reader. Linguists with a rich background in theory often forget that the average reader will not understand their jargon, and will therefore not benefit from the exceptional terseness that is frequently the goal of linguists. A treatise on putting on a pair of socks, or unstopping a blocked drain, could be written in such a scientific way as to be utterly incomprehensible to the untrained reader—and, at least in the case of the blocked drain, the untrained person would be the worse off. If research is intended to make a contribution to the non-specialist's world, it must be communicated in a way that makes it accessible. Andersen certainly cannot be singled out as the worst offender in this, but it is a mark against this book that it does not communicate readily to those who would benefit most from its insights.

In the following chapter I will present analyses of two more works, one of which is a model of good scholarship and good communication, but which only lightly touches on our topic, and the other, which is also a model of good scholarship, but which is less than completely successful in communicating to Hebrew scholars.

Chapter 2

EXAMINATION OF KHAN'S 'STUDIES' AND LONGACRE'S 'JOSEPH'

1. *Introduction*

I move on now to two other recent works: Khan's and Longacre's; I have mentioned above my reasons for examining them together.[1] Khan's work will not occupy our attention for any great length, since his topic does not feature highly in the data that I myself examine; Longacre's will require the bulk of this chapter.

2. *Khan: Studies in Semitic Syntax*

This study adopts a 'comparative Semitic' approach, examining data from Arabic, Biblical Hebrew, Biblical Aramaic, Syriac, Akkadian and Amharic. The breadth of data consulted is compensated for by the narrowness of topic: Khan treats only the subjects of 'extrapositional sentences (Ex)' and 'pronominal agreement constructions with resumptive pronouns (PAR)', which he defines as follows:

> By the term 'extraposition' I understand the syntactic construction in which a noun or nominal phrase stands isolated at the front of a clause without any formal connection to the predication. The initial 'extraposed' nominal is not adjoined to any relational particle such as a preposition or an object marker and in those languages which have a case inflection it is generally in the nominative. The grammatical relation of nominal in the predication is usually indicated vicariously by means of a co-referential resumptive pronoun...

---

1. In brief, I consider these two be the best examples available to the hebraist of works with a positive view of text-linguistic research—Khan, for his clarity of communication, and integrity of methodology, and Longacre, for the rich potential of his theory and methodology, and the astute insights he offers into the text-level structures of Classical Hebrew.

'Pronominal agreement' is a construction where a noun or nominal phrase whose grammatical relation is indicated by its case inflection or by an adjoining relational particle is accompanied in the same clause by a co-referential pronoun agreeing with it in number, gender, person, and grammatical relation.

Unlike extraposed nominals, nominals which are accompanied by such 'agreement pronouns' are not restricted to initial position but may occur anywhere in the clause—the front, the interior, or the end...

Pronominal agreement constructions in which the 'agreed with' nominal occurs at the front of the clause are closely allied to extraposition.[2]

This book is well-organized, and likewise very well-written. The introductory chapter opens with some general statements on language functions, then moves on to definitions of terms, choice of languages (and sources from which data were taken), a brief yet thorough examination of previous literature on these two constructions, and a section on contemporary linguistic theory. Khan then outlines his own presuppositions and methodology,[3] with definitions given for more specific technical terms. The term 'discourse' is once again in prominence, and in this case it is defined obliquely as a 'certain stretch of text';[4] and although Khan does not clarify this further, it is to be understood as a rather vague category of a large body of text—his term 'span of discourse' seems more akin to Longacre's 'discourse'.[5]

One of the points made in Khan's section on methodology is that, with each separate language, he divides his treatment of these constructions into two sections: the first deals with the internal structure of the constructions, and the second deals with their functions within their wider context. Each of the languages mentioned above is examined in this manner, in chs. 1 through 5. This is one of the greatest strengths of this book: Khan separates the 'observable' from the 'interpreted'.

The book concludes with a chapter on Comparative Semitic Syntax, which examines the principles and merits of this discipline. Khan writes,

---

2. Khan, *Studies*, pp. xxvi-xxvii; Khan's n. 2 adds here, 'Indeed in some cases the two constructions are indistinguishable, cf. 108, 160'.
3. Khan, *Studies*, pp. xxxiii ff.
4. Khan, *Studies*, p. xxxiii.
5. Or my 'text'; see below, this chapter, and the following.

> Comparative Semitic syntax is not only of interest to the general language typologist but is also of direct relevance for the Semitist in so far as it helps to clarify the understanding of features in the individual Semitic languages.[6]

Khan's work is restrained, and, although he does not claim to be describing the macro-syntax of any of the languages he works on, he describes very well the text-level functions of these features. Had he chosen to work 'from the top down',[7] he would have had to consider many more syntactic features than he has done, describing each as an option available for use at the higher levels; however, working 'from the bottom up'[8] allows him to describe only these particular features; he need only describe the function of his chosen constructions, noting their effect on—and their function in—higher-level units. One might say that Niccacci, for example, is engaged in this same 'from the bottom up' sort of work; he, however, has set a much broader scope, attempting to describe the macro-syntax of the language by describing its micro-syntax, while Khan, on the other hand, describes a specific, limited, and closely related pair of features in terms of both its structure (micro-syntactic components) and its function (which includes its macro-syntactic significance).

Khan moves very well from micro-syntax to macro-syntax. The organization and lucid style of this work contribute a sense of 'flow' from the level of internal structure to that of contributions to macro-structure. Khan looks first at the bits and pieces making up his two contructions, and then looks at how these two constructions become 'bits and pieces' which help to make up other, larger, constructions.[9] One is instructed first in how a certain drawer is made, and then how that drawer forms an integral part of the desk.

---

6.   Khan, *Studies*, p. 233; I believe that the same is true of what I have been calling 'language universals', for the more we understand the working of the human mind with regard to its use of language, the better we will understand the vagaries of Classical Hebrew.

7.   That is, were he to start with a text or a text-type (both of which I am doing), and describe the variety of macrosyntactic features found therein, then moving from this level to the level below it (to paragraph), and to the one below that (to sentence), and so on.

8.   Starting, in this case, at the clause-level, and moving from there to sentence, and paragraph, and beyond.

9.   This is one of the basic concepts of 'Tagmemic' linguistic theory; it will be unpacked in Chapter 3.

This is a model presentation of research; it demonstrates clearly the elegance of description that is the ideal of a descriptive linguist. The clarity of this book, and the thoroughness of its treatment of this topic, particularly with the comparative methodology, are its principal strengths. If one must cite a draw-back, it would be that the topic is narrow, and provides little general insight into the system as a whole, in any of the languages examined; however, by contrast with Niccacci, for example, Khan does not attempt this goal. Would that this were but a chapter in a much larger work detailing a wider range of syntactic and macro-syntactic features.

Ex and PAR are constructions that can be considered 'exceptional' clause-types in the same sense that a Hebrew noun phrase that includes an attributive adjective or participle can be considered exceptional; both are developments away from the simplest and most common constructions of their type. Since these constructions occur but rarely in the data that I examine, there is little overlap between Khan's work and my own.[10]

Khan notes that Ex and PAR 'perform the same functions and are in most cases interchangeable', and that 'one of the most widespread functions of Ex and PAR clauses is to mark the boundaries of spans of discourse. They coincide with either the *onset* or the *closure* of a span.'[11] My own findings agree with these conclusions: exceptional clauses (of which Ex and PAR clauses are examples*) always mark in some way an interruption of the continuity of the material being presented*. The effect that these particular constructions produce does not appear to be linked to the text-type in which they are used; this may be traceable to the fact that they are exceptions more to micro-syntactic than to macro-syntactic (and, therefore, text-type-based) standards.

Khan's Table of Contents is perhaps the best summary of his approach to this material;[12] his excellent organization allows the reader to see at a glance the way he works through the functions of these two constructions in Biblical Hebrew, and his awareness of other macro-syntactic structures:[13]

---

10. Therefore my principal interest in this book, here, is with reference to its methodology and its presentation.

11. Eskhult, *Studies*, p. 78.

12. In particular, Khan, *Studies*, pp. xv-xvi.

13. Cf. pp. 86ff. (sections II.1.3 under 'Biblical Hebrew'); I find his interest in

Khan adjoins an appendix dealing with the special case of the use of these constructions in 'legal precepts', and writes,

> Extraposition occurs particularly frequently in the structure of legal formulae in the Old Testament. This is also the case with regard to post-Biblical law corpora which were composed in Hebrew, e.g. the Qumran text *serek hayyahad* (The Rule of the Community) and the halakic works of the Tannaim. It is convenient, therefore, to devote a separate section to extrapositional structures which are characteristic of this genre of text, bringing together for the sake of completeness both Biblical and post-Biblical law formulae.[14]

Khan has done well to separate out this particular context for special attention owing to the frequency of occurrence in these texts. However, I am not convinced that this actually forms an alien usage of this construction; rather it seems to me simply another context in which the construction performs the function of 'change of topic'—a function he has noted and described on pp. 79ff. Owing to the relatively 'topic-intensive' nature of legal material,[15] the topics of legal regulation change from one to the next fairly rapidly; that Ex and PAR—possible topic-changing mechanisms—are found in greater frequency in legal material than in other text-types is not enormously surprising.

Khan's work is a model of good scholarship and excellent presentation. I can find no flaws in it that impede its usefulness. We can hope that such successful research and communication becomes more and more common in our literature.

3. *Longacre: Joseph: A Story of Divine Providence: A Text-Theoretical and Text-Linguistic Analysis of Genesis 37 and 39–48*

This book represents the most significant advancement in Hebrew textlinguistics seen to date; it contains much of near-revolutionary value to the student of Classical Hebrew syntax. Several of Longacre's

---

comparing the features on which he chooses to focus, with those which can perform the same function, to be a great strength of his approach. We will look at this methodological principle in greater detail in the rest of this volume, in particular in Chapter 3.

14. Khan, *Studies*, p. 98.

15. In the sense that it tends to incorporate a lot of information into as little space as possible.

contributions are of the sort that are immediately accessible to the readership, and which prepare the way for a much clearer (more 'elegant') description of the language. Others are more esoteric, but equally important.

On the other hand, this volume suffers from some of the same difficulties as does Andersen's *Sentence*, in that it contains *so much* information that it becomes difficult to sort through. Where Andersen's difficulty, however, was that of relying too heavily (for the average reader) on linguistic jargon, Longacre's is more a matter of leapfrogging over too many steps in the theoretical logic, thus leaving behind all but the most astute reader, and fellow linguists (although even fellow linguists may not follow, if they are not familiar with the tagmemic approach to language).[16]

3.1 *General Background to the Book*

At the outset of this examination of *Joseph*, it will not be out of place to mention one of the reasons why this work is particularly valuable—a reason that is not related to the study of Hebrew in particular. Much of the development of the tagmemic school of linguistics has taken place 'in the field'. Literally. The three or four primary movers in this theoretical development have spent, between them, well over a century (a most conservative estimate) working among indigenous populations, and with previously unanalysed language material—and following this, perhaps the double of that in processing data from as wide a range of the world's languages as possible, for theoretical purposes. Tagmemics, as an approach to the data, developed—from its 'birth' in the fifties[17]—out of dissatisfaction with the fact that previously accepted theoretical models of language analysis did not deal well enough with living language data. A new model, which had an increased capacity to 'learn from' discoveries in real language data, was developed, which worked from simple basics, but which allowed for the description of finer details of language use. This capacity to

---

16. Longacre does include a 3-page appendix on tagmemic theory (pp. 311-13), from which I will quote at length in the next chapter, but this is inadequate to the task of 'educating' the readership up to a standard where the book becomes easier to follow.

17. K.L. Pike's *Language in Relation to a Unified Theory of the Structure of Human Behavior* (first published in 3 vols., 1954–1960, Summer Institute of Linguistics) is the seminal work of this approach.

'learn from' real language data has produced a theoretical model that finds the basic patterns, and the permutations thereof, within any language studied; and the results of these analyses are particularly well-suited for comparative linguistic research. The end result is that 'language universals' are constantly compared with data from specific languages in a way that advances the study of both. Longacre has long been at the forefront of this development, and is without doubt the text-linguist with the greatest exposure to the breadth of the world's language data, of anyone in print today.[18]

A sample of Longacre's collation of language data resulting in an appreciation of language universals is the following:

> The successive events of a narrative paragraph may be given as a series of what I call build-ups, each in a separate sentence, or the whole narrative action may be expressed in one long run-on sentence with but one final verb at its end, i.e. in a one-sentence paragraph. What is the rationale of this choice? Is this pure caprice?
>
> At this point the study of whole discourses is helpful. In fact, a perusal of the Wojokeso corpus of text material (Longacre 1972a, Text)[19] suggests a resolution of the problem. There is a narrative discourse which has narrative paragraphs composed of fair-to-middling-length sentences until one reaches what is really the *denouement* of the whole story. At this point, we find a long run-on structure in which all the events are lumped together in one paragraph-length sentence. Similarly, we have a procedural discourse on housebuilding, in which likewise we find sentences of fair-to-middling length until we reach the *target procedure* where the house is finished and the couple move in to spend their first night in it. Here again we find a long run-on one-sentence paragraph in which all the steps of the paragraph are in one page-length sentence. Sentence is here being used in both narrative and procedural discourse to mark the *peak* of the discourse in the surface structure, which corresponds to either denouement in narrative discourse, or to target procedure in procedural discourse.

---

18. This is not an idle claim: Longacre, after working for many years in the field on the languages of indigenous people groups of Mexico, has gone on to work with Pacific, North American and African languages (in each case, he has worked with not one, but scores, of languages from these regions), in addition to the biblical languages; the bibliography in *Joseph* lists 20 articles and books—only a fraction of his publications.

19. I.e. Longacre's *Hierarchy and Universality of Discourse Constituents in New Guinea Languages*. I. *Discussion*. II. *Texts* (Washington: Georgetown University Press, 1972).

Parallels are not lacking elsewhere. Thus, Charles Green has pointed out to me that a not dissimilar phenomenon is found in Hemingway's story, 'The short happy life of Francis Macomber'. Here, at the climax of the story where the main character of the story is shot in the back of the head (accidentally?) by his wife, we find a long run-on, rollicking sentence not unlike in kind from what we have mentioned in the Wojokeso discourses. Something similar is found in the text of the Greek New Testament. We find in the account of the feeding of the five thousand (Matthew 14:13-21) an absolutely unparalleled string of participles in sentence-initial position precisely at the denouement of the account (Matthew 14:19), where Jesus takes the loaves, multiplies them, and feeds the people.[20]

My praise of Longacre's depth of experience and knowledge may seem out of place; his credentials, however, are not likely to have preceded him very far into this discipline (as he writes primarily for linguistics publications)—though not for want of influence—Khan, for example, writes,

> My methodology has been inspired mainly by the work of Joseph Grimes, Robert Longacre, and Teun van Dijk. The value of their approach to the analysis of discourse is that it is largely empirical. This applies especially to the work of Grimes and Longacre, who have both carried out extensive field work in a large number of language communities.[21]

Most of Longacre's writing has been for linguists—in particular, field linguists—thus it is not surprising that few hebraists are aware of his work; thus, the idea that this book needs to be given considerable attention will not be immediately evident to the average biblical scholar.[22]

---

20. Longacre, *Discourse*, pp. 30-31.

21. Khan, *Studies*, p. xxxiv; In a note on this section, Khan writes, 'Andersen's study of the sentence in Biblical Hebrew was in fact based mainly on the methodology which was developed by Longacre'; he states later, in the text, 'I have, however, rejected the more abstract methods of discourse analysis, many of which are still embroiled in theoretical preliminaries and show little concern for the direct analysis of texts' (*Studies,* p. xxxiv, reflecting in his own approach the priorities of the Tagmemic school of linguistics).

22. In fact, only one of the entries under his name in the bibliography of *Joseph* was published in the literature hebraists are most likely to consult—hence my 'touting' of his background and achievements: although his is not a name on the lips of most biblical scholars (they will not have seen much of his published material), he is one who has earned the right to speak with authority on the subject at hand.

3.2 *Contents of Longacre's Joseph*

Joseph is organized into four parts: Part One introduces the text-unit (Gen. 37 and 39–48) and gives the broader interpretative and text-linguistic features of the story; Part Two looks at the unit in terms of textlinguistic observations (observations more specific to the language features, such as 'off-the-line' material, ויהי and its text-level functions, etc., than his comments in Part One) and sociolinguistic observations (relating primarily to questions of mitigation and deference in Hortatory portions of Reported Speech); Part Three focuses on Participant Reference, and Dialogue; and Part Four is a presentation of the entire text examined in this study, presented in a typographical arrangement intended to highlight the text-linguistic features noted in the preceding analysis (particularly those commented on in Part Two). This is followed by a short appendix on tagmemic linguistic theory.

3.2.1 *'Part One'*

The broader movement of this book is discernible from the Table of Contents, once the intricacies of the individual chapters are understood. Longacre starts by setting the broader context—the whole of the historical material, from Genesis 1 through to the end of 2 Kings—and presenting part of his methodology (Introduction), then he moves to the narrower context of the תלדות of Jacob.[23] Here he looks at the articulation of episodes in the Joseph story, examining devices that signal the boundaries of the major sections (ch. 1). In ch. 2 he looks at 'macro-structures'—by which he means 'an overall meaning and plan'.[24] In ch. 1, then, he presents the surface structure organization of the story, and in ch. 2 he looks at the underlying flow of *issues, meaning and plan*.

---

23. His understanding of the way the Joseph story fits into its nearer context leads him to leap over the Judah and Tamar section (Gen. 38)—an approach that will not appeal to all; in addition the explanatory material concerning his decision is pared to a minimum, where it would have contributed to the reader's understanding of the material that follows to know how Longacre has come to the conclusions he does.

24. Longacre, *Joseph*, p. 43; I use this term to refer to the constituent structure of the largest units of language, referring to 'episodes' of a story, etc.—but *in the sense of the surface structure itself* (paragraphs, etc.), rather than the 'notional' or 'deep' (cognitive) level. To refer to what Longacre terms 'macrostructure', I would probably borrow his alternative expression: 'overall meaning and plan'. His term is derived from van Dijk's work (see his 'References' section, p. 316).

3.2.2 *'Part Two'*

In Part Two, Longacre presents a more meticulous analysis of the surface structure of the language, and here we begin to see the revolutionary ideas he has to offer. His summary of the assumptions and conclusions of this section is unusual, as it approaches the grammar of this language in a manner significantly different from that seen in the majority of current Hebrew language studies:

> Typically, within a grammar of a given language all the uses of each tense/aspect or mode of a language are listed and described *en bloc* in the same section of the grammar... Part 2 of this volume is, among other things, a challenge to this time-honored way of describing the functions of the verb forms of a verb system within a language. Rather, I posit here that *(a)* every language has a system of discourse types (e.g., narrative, predictive, hortatory, procedural, expository, and others); *(b)* each discourse type has its own characteristic constellation of verb forms that figure in that type; *(c)* the uses of [a] given tense/aspect/mood form are most surely and concretely described in relation to a given discourse type. These assumptions inform chapters 3, 4, and 5 of this volume, where they are illustrated in regard to narrative, predictive, expository, and hortatory discourse.
>
> The constellation of verb forms that figure in a given discourse type are structured so that one or more privileged forms constitute the mainline or backbone of each type, while other forms can be shown to encode progressive degrees of departure from the mainline. This is developed empirically in chapter 3 in regard to narrative discourse and the verb forms that characterize it. Here the *waw*-consecutive imperfect is seen to be mainline in that it is punctiliar, and sequential in function; the perfect is found to be (as a whole) a non-punctiliar and non-sequential kind of past tense in narrative; the imperfect and the participles are, respectively, implicitly and explicitly durative in the framework of the story; *hāyâ* clauses and verbless clauses represent stative elements toward the bottom of the scheme; and negated clauses rank lowest.
>
> In regard to these various matters, Biblical Hebrew can be shown more and more to be a rather run-of-the-mill example of a language with a special narrative or 'consecutive' tense—a statement that can be easily documented in regard to the narrative structures of a variety of African languages (cf. Longacre, in press). Some of the latter have consecutive forms that necessarily depend on a special initial form that must precede them; other such languages simply have a special consecutive form that need not have a special initial form to initiate the chain in narrative. Biblical Hebrew belongs to the latter type of language, but traditionally has been described as if it belongs to the former type. Thus the legend has

grown up that a *waw*-consecutive perfect must similarly follow an imperfect (or some other tense/aspect/mood form).[25]

Longacre's ch. 3 discusses the different kinds of clauses one can find in Narrative History,[26] dividing them into 'on-the-line' and 'off-the-line' options. Longacre writes,

> Discourse grammarians are coming to recognize more and more that in the telling of a story, one particular tense is favored as the carrier of the backbone or storyline of the story while other tenses serve to present the background, supportive, and depictive material in the story.[27]

> I have assumed, then, that the storyline or the backbone of a discourse in Biblical Hebrew is conveyed by the use of clauses that begin with a *waw*-consecutive verb—in the balance of this book simply called the *preterite*.[28]

Included here is a reference to היה, which is worth quoting in toto:

> It is immediately necessary, however, to qualify the above hypothesis in one important particular. The verb *hāyâ*, 'be', even in its form *wayhî*, 'and it happened', does not function on the storyline of a narrative. In this respect, the behavior of Hebrew is similar to that of a great many contemporary languages around the world. For example, English uses its past tense to encode the storyline of a story, but the verb *be* (and some other stative verbs)—even when in the past tense (for example, forms such as *was*, *were*—is typically descriptive and depictive and does not figure on the backbone of a story. This is simply a peculiarity of the verb *be*, in many languages past and present.[29]

Longacre adds to these insights discussions of permutations of the mainline clause-type, then looks at off-the-line material, giving a description of the potential offline clause-types for Narrative History.

---

25. Longacre, *Joseph*, pp. 59-60; it is strongly tempting to go on—the material that follows this is equally significant—but I will discuss these elements in my Chapter 3.

26. Longacre's term is simply 'narrative'—I will use my own terms for text-types throughout this examination of *Joseph*; they will be explained more fully in Chapter 3.

27. Longacre, *Joseph*, p. 64; this comment develops from an allusion to GKC's recognition 'that the so-called waw-consecutive is a special narrative tense' [*in loc.*].

28. Longacre, *Joseph*, p. 65; Longacre chooses the term 'preterite' in order to disassociate this conjugation from the 'prefixal' conjugation, on the basis that the two are apparently historically unrelated.

29. Longacre, *Joseph*, p. 66.

In sub-section 3. of ch. 3, we come upon 'a verbal rank scheme' for Narrative History;[30] this is one of the most immediately accessible— and revolutionary—contributions of the book. Longacre here presents, on half a page, a summary of the way clause-types function in Narrative History, in the form of a 'cline'[31] (see below).

In the next two chapters, Longacre posits verb rank clines for Predictive and Hortatory text-types, and describes verb ranking for Expository, as well, though he 'declines' to posit a cline for the last, citing the need for more analysis of Expository material in the Hebrew Bible as the reason for his hesitation.[32]

NARRATIVE DISCOURSE VERB-RANK CLINE[33]

Band 1: Storyline	1. Preterite
Band 2: Backgrounded Actions	2.1 Perfect 2.2 Noun + Perfect (with noun in focus)
Band 3: Backgrounded Activities	3.1 *hinnēh* + participle 3.2 Participle 3.3 Noun + participle
Band 4: Setting	4.1 Preterite of *hāyâ*, 'be' 4.2 Perfect of *hāyâ*, 'be' 4.3 Nominal clause (verbless) 4.4 Existential clause with yes
Band 5:	5. Negation of verb clause: irrealis (any band) —'momentous negation'[34] promotes 5. to 2.1/2.2.

30. Longacre, by contrast with Niccacci, writes, 'I do not find per se that the grand dichotomy verb clause versus noun clause is useful. Rather I absorb it into a rank scheme that can be thought of as the *verbal spectrum for narrative*...In this scheme I assume a cline, a structural slope from clauses that are relatively dynamic to clauses that are relatively static...' (*Joseph*, p. 81; cf. Niccacci, pp. 23ff.).

31. This he defines as 'a scheme symbolising degrees of departure from the storyline' (Longacre, *Joseph*, p. 82 n. 6).

32. Longacre, *Joseph*, p. 107, for Predictive; p. 121, for Hortatory; and pp. 111-12, for Expository. I will not include these charts here, as they will be reproduced in the following chapter.

33. Longacre, *Joseph*, p. 81.

34. 'Momentous negation' describes the situation where the absence of a certain event carries the narrative line forward (Longacre gives the example of the failure of the dove to return to the ark in the Flood Story, *Joseph*, p. 85).

We now have the mixed pleasure of seeing this model become even more complex, in that we can look not only at 'discourse' identities, but also at paragraph identities. Longacre has isolated certain language universals concerning the nature and functions of paragraphs,[35] based on their structures and functions, and he describes nine types of paragraphs (sequence, simple, reason, result, comment, amplification, paraphrase, coordinate, and antithetical),[36] each of which may be encoded differently according to the text-type in which they occur— that is a narrative history reason paragraph will not be encoded in exactly the same manner as an expository reason paragraph.[37]

Longacre's definitions of paragraph, and especially of sentence, are distinctive enough to warrant mention at this point. Paragraphs are identified as such by their *internal structure*: 'any group of sentences that go together by virtue of cohesion and/or coherence can be shown to have the structure of an (embedded) paragraph of a recognizable type'.[38] 'Sentences' are 'the basic building blocks of the paragraph'; and 'a sentence in Hebrew is considered to be basically a unit with a main clause (and a main verb), to which may be attached such subordinate clauses as adverbial clauses and relative clauses'.[39]

In the remainder of Part 2, Longacre offers examples of the paragraph types he has found in the Joseph story. This goes at a stunning pace, and those not already familiar with Longacre's approach to paragraph analysis and identification will be hard pressed to make sense of it.[40] In the long run, the section on paragraphs yields little readily accessible material; and comprehension of this material is

---

35. Cf. his *An Apparatus for the Identification of Paragraph Types* (Notes on Linguistics, 15, Dallas: Summer Institute of Linguistics, 1980).

36. See Longacre, *Joseph*, p. 85ff.

37. This stands to reason, for we cannot expect narrative history (which focuses on the past) and expository (which is in essence atemporal) to rely on the same structures.

38. Longacre, *Joseph*, p. 62.

39. Longacre, *Joseph*, p. 84.

40. This is more evidence that the book was written with a strong bias toward communicating with *linguists*, rather than hebraists—another detail that points in this direction is that all the Hebrew is transliterated, and this is certainly not traceable to publishing difficulties as was the case with Andersen's work (see Andersen, *Sentence*, note, p. 16). But then, Longacre's goal here is to give us the benefit of his best thinking on the subject—he can hardly be expected to give a full introductory course in general- and text-linguistics at the same time.

rendered the more difficult owing to lack of thorough explanation of how paragraphs enter into the interworkings of clauses and texts, which we see so succinctly and lucidly displayed in his 'clines'.[41]

3.2.3 *Part Three*

These verb-clines are a radical innovation in the description of the Hebrew verb-system; Longacre, however, goes beyond the verbs to other elements of Biblical Hebrew. With reference to 'discourse-level' analysis, he describes the verb-system as one string in a 'double-helix'[42]—the other being composed of participant reference and speech interaction.

Part One of this book dealt with macrostructures and the larger context of the Joseph story; Part Two analysed verbs and clause-types according to discourse and paragraph distribution and functions—the first strand of the double-helix. Part Three deals with the second strand of the double-helix, and is structured as follows: ch. 6 looks at participant reference (nouns, pronouns and verb affixes), ch. 7 at variants in speech-introduction formulae, and ch. 8 at the role of dialogue in the narrative. One might say that clause-types, paragraph-types and text-types are the bones of the text, and participant reference, speech formulae and dialogue are its soft-tissue.

The reader will do well to keep a finger at pp. 141-43 while working through ch. 6, for, while the theoretical base of this section is more accessible than that of the section on paragraphs, Longacre tends to refer to it in rather abbreviated (if not jargonal) terms. In addition, everything in this chapter refers to the 'level' of participant reference; and yet (by oversight, apparently) these *levels* are never identified and defined as such—three lists are given; none of these refer, in their titles, in their contents, and in the notes following, to 'levels' of any sort; the reader eventually discerns that it is the first list that supplies us with the appropriate key, but such opacities as these are not required in an already difficult book.

The analysis is rather unremarkable except for one thing; the author writes,

41. My own focus in this work is the relationship between clause-types and text-types; I will very rarely refer to Longacre's approach to paragraph-types; though this material is valuable, entering that domain in this volume would require several scores of extra pages of theoretical material, and a similar amount of processed examples.

42. Longacre, *Joseph*, p. 140.

> One cannot read *Joseph*[43] carefully without being puzzled by the alterna-
> tion between references on level 4 (pronouns) and on level 5 (verb
> affixes) in relation to expressing the object (which is almost entirely a
> matter of the third person object since *Joseph* is a narrative told in third
> person). I propose here the view that resort to level 5 (the object suffix)
> rather than to level 4 (sign of accusative *'et* + pronoun) has to do not with
> thematicity as such but rather with dominance patterns... Succinctly, level
> 5 is used rather than level 4 to express a dominance pattern in which the
> participant(s) referred to by the object suffix is under the dominance of
> someone else.[44]

After reaffirming his belief that this does indeed accurately reflect the
data in the Joseph story, he goes on to state,

> Further research is needed to see whether this claim can be extended to
> Biblical Hebrew as a whole. Whatever the outcome of this question, it
> seems clear that this claim cannot be made in regard to certain non-narra-
> tive discourses, e.g., the poetry of the Psalms.[45]

Longacre's ch. 6 is 16 pages long; its contents are condensed from
what might have been 40 pages, were it written in 'plain English'.
This section is meant to prepare us to make use of the participant
reference interplay, along with the paragraph structures, the
'discourse-level' peaks and boundaries, and so on, of Part Four. It
seems to me an inadequate preparation for those not already schooled
in tracing participant reference and in interpreting it along with other
clues from the 'discourse-' or text-level; it is no easy task for one *with*
that background.[46]

Next, after leading the reader through some more rather 'jargon-
ish' analysis in ch. 7 (where, once again, the crucial information about
the 'calculus' employed is difficult to locate; in this instance it is
hidden at the end of paragraph 1.2. on p. 162), the author gives a
concise summary of his findings about speech-introduction formulae,
which are derived not only from the Joseph story, but from other
material in the Hebrew Bible as well. This summary indicates the

43. He refers here to the Hebrew text of the story.
44. Longacre, *Joseph*, p. 155.
45. Longacre, *Joseph*, p. 157 n. 2.
46. As I have said, the author was *not* engaged in writing an introductory
textbook on analysis procedures, but it is nevertheless helpful when a writer conveys
sufficient introductory material to allow interested readers to follow the development
of ideas.

significance, for the narration, of speech formula variants.[47] Once the jargon has been gotten through, this material could easily inspire hebraists to further examination of data.

His ch. 8 is perhaps not as revolutionary for Hebrew linguistics as is the earlier material on verb ranks, but it is in its own way significant. The chapter opens with this comment:

> It is obvious, even on cursory examination, that much of the narrative we have been examining is carried forward via sections of dialogue. A story moves along not only by virtue of what people are reported to do, but also by what they say. Saying is indeed a special kind of doing for which we reserve the special name *speech act.*[48]

Longacre has two foci here: (1) he examines each dialogue for its internal nuances, and (2) he examines this material to see how it fits into the overall structure and flow of the narrative. The significance of this is that we come to terms with speech material as *a narrative device for the advancement of the story-line*, in addition to considering it as a stylistic technique or simply as a reflection of speech patterns of daily life, which indicates *conversations are narrative units in the same way that simple narrative statements are narrative units.*

The conclusion to this chapter serves, in a way, as a conclusion to the whole book, for what follows. Part Four ('A Constituent Display of Joseph'), and an appendix on tagmemic linguistic theory, are somewhat loosely tied to the rest of the work. Longacre writes,

> In backing away a bit from the mass of detail presented in this chapter and in considering again the constituent structure of the story as a whole, I note that the narrative sequence paragraph and the simpler sort of dialogue paragraph carry in a somewhat routine way the burden of propelling the story forward. Most other paragraph types (excluding probably the narrative amplification paragraph) have other more specialized uses. Among the paragraphs that picture interaction patterns, the complex dialogue, the execution, and the stimulus-response paragraphs especially serve to underscore the more dramatic parts of the story. These paragraph types have therefore been analyzed with special attention to details of their structure; they are too important to the structure of the whole to be passed over lightly and summarily.[49]

47. Longacre, *Joseph*, pp. 183-84.
48. Longacre, *Joseph*, p. 185.
49. Longacre, *Joseph*, p. 205.

3.2.4 *Part Four*

Part Four is Longacre's presentation of a formatted text of the Joseph story, with its translation. If one has internalized the system and the calculus of Longacre's approach to the text—neither of which have been presented here for the first-time reader—there is much to be gained from studying this section. If one is not familiar with his approach, this section is at best fascinating, and at worst, thoroughly off-putting. In the main, Part Four is a graphic presentation of the text according to the analyses sampled in the preceding pages; it lays out the text in a fashion that allows the reader (if he or she has digested the nightmarish formatting code) to see, at a glance, the text in terms of its structure and sub-structures, as they have surfaced through Longacre's analysis. This is a very useful tool to have at hand, but—as is an inherent danger with all reductions from verbal explanation to graphic representation—it is difficult to make use of unless one has mastered theory in excess of what Longacre presents in this book.

3.3 *Conclusions*

Much of what Longacre has presented us with is new, or, rather, has not been seen before in publications intended for hebraists' eyes (it is not by any means 'new' in linguistic circles). What we have seen here—the concept of text-types, each with their own deployment of clause-types; the necessity of describing a form in terms of its role in specific text-types; the concept of mainline versus offline material, with the identification of the 'preterite' as the mainline form in narrative history, excepting such forms of היה—these, as well as participant reference tracking, speech formula variations, hortatory variants, and other features as well, are relatively uncharted territory for the hebraist. And, apart from a few shortcuts in explanations, and a few oversights in formatting, the presentation is not exceptionally difficult to get through, provided the reader takes the time to internalize the hoard of new concepts. There is an enormous amount of material to get to grips with, however, and it is difficult (1) to make sense of it as a whole, and (2) to know what to do with it afterward.

A part of me feels that the only response one can offer is applause: it's been a very fine performance, and I shall remember it fondly, but I couldn't hope to do any of it myself. And that, in fact, is one thing I am not happy about, for text-linguistic analysis is *not* innately difficult, and it deserves a warm recommendation to the hebraist. This study is so far beyond the level of language work done by most Hebrew scholars that its effect may be minimized as a result of the way it has been communicated. This is a book about a text, not a manual for analysis. And while Longacre writes sufficient introductory material about his approach to the text to enable the reader to gain at least cursory benefit from his book, it does not inspire the reader with confidence to continue the work him- or herself.

This point is debatable, of course; yet it is disappointing that there is nothing available to hebraists that equips them *as hebraists*—rather than forcing them out of their field—to do the kinds of research that they, as hebraists, are beginning to find intriguing. That is to say, there is no doubt that linguistics is a science, and that thoroughly trained linguists will inevitably produce more incisive works than will the marginally trained linguistic dabbler; nonetheless, however, there is ample room for linguistic research among people whose training is primarily as hebraists. It is these, in fact, who often have the deeper, intuitive, grasp of the sense of the text. Equipped with a manageable theoretical base, they will produce solid, valuable linguistic research.

It is time for an intermediate literature, neither 'quantum-linguistics' treatises which are only understood by other 'quantum' linguists, nor unscientific, non-linguistic treatises which serve only to drive the study of Hebrew further away from helpful approaches to the language—but rather *a literature intended to provide theory and methods that do not overwhelm the hebraist, a literature that is unafraid to proceed slowly enough that the reader can actually become familiar with the procedures, and return with them to the data to do his or her own testing of hypotheses.*

Khan's *Studies*, by contrast with Longacre's *Joseph*, is well explained, and does not overwhelm the reader with its contents, in part because it does not launch the reader into a new world quite so thoroughly as does Longacre's.

Because I find Longacre's approach to the text so valuable, and relatively accessible, at a *logical* level—if perhaps not entirely well communicated in *Joseph*—the remaining three chapters of this volume will present an explanation of this approach, and an application of some of its more basic principles to Hebrew text samples.

Chapter 3

AN INTRODUCTION TO THE TAGMEMIC MODEL
AND METHODOLOGY OF TEXT ANALYSIS

1. *The Purpose of this Chapter, and its Relation to the Rest of this Volume*

I have cited the topic of this study as 'the role(s) of different types of clauses in different types of texts';[1] and if the goal of the first two chapters has been to measure the success of those who have entered the field (examining their 'integrity of description' and the 'effectiveness of their communication'), then the goal of the two chapters that follow this one is to outline for the reader some of the first steps in producing an analysis that will pass both examinations. It is necessary, in that case, to set out some definitions, to tie together some concepts, and to detail the procedures to be used, in such a way that the reader is not left behind in the analyses that follow.

2. *Introduction to 'Tagmemic' Theory*

In this section, we will look at several of the essential elements of the Tagmemic school of linguistics. But why should we do this? What is to be gained by focusing on this particular approach? According to Longacre,

> Broadly conceived, tagmemics is discourse about linguistic patterns. It is not interested merely in setting up abstract strings of symbols which will get us to terminal strings in the most economical way. To tagmemicists such preoccupation misses the point. Rather we want to posit in each language a system of labeled patterns that will at least to some degree parallel the system of intuitively felt patterns used by speaker and hearer. The

---

1.   Chapter 1, section 1.1.

patterns and parts of patterns that we posit must be labeled for the simple reason that we want to discourse about them. We want to be able to show the system of patterns and to contrast one pattern with another.[2]

And Jones writes,

> Linguistic tagmemics is concerned with discovering the patterns and regularities of language, and with stating these as consistently, systematically, and elegantly as possible.[3]

> Of particular significance [in terms of contributions of the tagmemic approach to language analysis], I think, has been the focus by various tagmemicists on the discourse FUNCTIONS of various units and constructions. Longacre and his colleagues have found discourse functions for many particles and affixes that had previously been little understood or else simply glossed as 'emphasis'.[4] I (1977)[5] have suggested discourse functions for clefts, pseudo-clefts, and various other constructions in English. Larry Jones and I (1979)[6] have suggested that tense/aspect/mood, many particles, affixes, and some special constructions function in a number of languages to mark different levels of significant information in texts (e.g., to distinguish peak, pivotal events, ordinary events, significant background, and ordinary background). In discourse analysis, as well as other areas just mentioned, tagmemics offers a significant theory of linguistics.[7]

Longacre's comment about 'setting up abstract strings of symbols which will get us to terminal strings in the most economical way' is intended to contrast tagmemics with the majority of other approaches to language description. He substantiates this contrast with a comparison of two different descriptions of Turkish verbs; the first is from Gleason, and Lees ('the usual Americanist way of plotting relative

2.   Longacre, 'Tagmemics', *Word* 36.2 (1985), pp. 137-38.

3.   L.K. Jones, 'A Synopsis of Tagmemics', *Syntax and Semantics* 13 ('Current Approaches to Syntax') (1980), pp. 77-96 (86).

4.   Here we might refer to T. Muraoka, *Emphatic Words and Structures in Biblical Hebrew* (Leiden: Brill, 1985), which has examined a variety of morphemes and structures under the banner of 'emphasis', some of which certainly have macro-syntactic significance, but which receive no consideration as macro-syntactic features.

5.   L.K. Jones, *Theme in English Expository Discourse* (Lake Bluff, IL: Jupiter Press, 1977).

6.   L.B. Jones and L.K. Jones, 'Multiple Levels of Information in Discourse', in L.K. Jones (ed.), *Discourse Studies in Mesoamerican Languages* (Dallas: Summer Institute of Linguistics and University of Texas at Arlington, 1979), pp. 3-27.

7.   Jones, 'Synopsis', pp. 94ff.

orders of affixes within a verb structure');[8] the second is his own, tagmemically based, description. These two show the efficacy of the tagmemic approach in describing systems, rather than just sequences.[9]

This focus on systems, relative 'user-friendliness', and 'intuitively felt patterns' has encouraged the development in tagmemic circles of new ideas about the description of text-level features, and some of these are particularly helpful for the kind of work we are undertaking in this study.

The second reason for turning to tagmemics at this stage is that which is reflected in Longacre's comments about 'intuitively felt patterns'. We readily acknowledge that we tell stories mostly in past tense, we give predictions mostly in future, and so on. Tagmemics has provided a means of analyzing and describing that feature of language, in a simple and straightforward manner. The fact that these and other features which we will address in this study are readily verifiable at the 'common sense' level means that we will not need, on the one hand, a lengthy and heavy introduction in *all* the details of the theory used, in order to see the validity of the results, nor, on the other hand, will we be encumbered with a 'write-up' filled with jargon and convoluted explanation. Tagmemics—for our purposes—gives us simple tools to work with, and then turns us loose to get to work.

My results will not seem to be tied exclusively to any one theory, and that is intentional, for the things I describe in this study are readily accessible via a common-sense approach to the language, once the analyst has been alerted to their possible presence, and thus we do not need to bury them in theory-specific communication.[10]

Jones remarks on the practical applications of tagmemics:

> A primary task of a linguistics theory is to account for the empirical data. As an important corollary, the theory ought to have practical uses in dealing with language. There have been numerous practical applications of

---

8. Longacre, 'Tagmemics', p. 138.

9. Longacre, 'Tagmemics', pp. 138ff.

10. Of course, my write-up will bear the imprint of my own theoretical base, but this, it is hoped, will be relatively transparent. Likewise, it is obvious that in certain applications, the tagmemic approach will result in highly tagmemic-specific analytical write-ups (theoretical questions tend to require more jargon, and more short-hand type graphic representations than others, for example); nevertheless, in the case of a rather elementary description of the language features we are here examining, uncomplicated non-technical language will suffice for the presentation of results.

tagmemic theory, and I believe that the great applicability of tagmemics is a significant strength in its favor. One application has been as a heuristic for helping students to understand the nature of language. But this is not all. There have been numerous successful applications of the theory to translation, language learning, literacy, and linguistic analysis—particularly in the study of unwritten and 'exotic' languages. In addition, there have been many applications in other disciplines, including, most notably, anthropology (since tagmemics is a theory not only of language, but also of human behavior).[11]

For the analysis of unwritten languages, discovery procedures have evolved, perhaps better called ANALYTICAL TECHNIQUES. These do NOT, however, constitute a mechanical algorithm that automatically outputs an analysis. Practical goals of a theory hold pure theory-building in check, since 'fruitful theory must to some extent be limited by analytical techniques for processing or evaluating data. Tagmemics has oscillation between theory and method rather than a one-way priority...'[12]

2.1 *Foundations*

This enquiry has to do with texts, and text-level features; and in this chapter I will be working through sufficient text-linguistic theory to enable us to approach the data (in the following two chapters) in an informed manner. Yet it must be said that many in the Tagmemic School of linguistics have eschewed text-linguistics in the same way as have classical hebraists: much of the material published by tagmemic linguists stays within the traditional bounds of clause-level analysis; this fact limits, from one direction, the amount of published material that can be drawn into the discussion of Classical Hebrew text-linguistics from a tagmemic viewpoint. The second limiting factor is that a great deal of tagmemic publication takes the form of language 'write-ups'—reports on features of a specific language, or grammars of specific languages—the majority of tagmemic publications are examples of language analysis, rather than explanations of it.[13] These

---

11. One might add here that one of the more surprising applications of this theory has been in the field of music, or, more specifically, ethnomusicology, and has resulted in a variety of analytical apparatuses with a very profitable degree of flexibility—an essential feature when dealing with non-western music systems.

12. Jones here refers the reader to Pike, *Language*, p. 509; Jones, 'Synopsis', pp. 86ff.

13. For example, the list of references in Longacre's 'Discourse' (in Brend and Pike (eds.), *Tagmemics*, pp. 1-44) includes 65 articles or books on tagmemic analysis; 39 of these (60%) are reports on specific languages (Western Bukidnon

are occasioned largely by the work of Wycliffe Bible Translators and Summer Institute of Linguistics workers, whose Bible translation responsibilities require the parallel production of language descriptions. Since this group of linguists comprises the greatest number of users of this linguistic school, so this format has become the standard one for publication of new results. Those trained in this school of linguistics are accustomed to looking for new ideas in reports on Bolivian ritual poetry, to help them solve difficult problems in the Narrative History of a Philippine language, for example, and are able to sort through such reports in a way that others do not attempt.[14] It is regrettable that there is little attempt at collation of this material for more ready use by other language students.[15]

Tagmemics has nonetheless produced one of the most functional and profitable text-linguistic theories available to those who take up an interest in the issue.[16] Here, we will look at some broader concepts which undergird the material that follows; this will be divided into two sections. I will first deal with several basic *principles*, with which

Manobo, Kaiwa Guarani, Daga, Isthmus Zapotec, and so on), and many address only specific features of these languages (e.g. H. Popovich, 'Large Grammatical Units and Space-Time Setting in Maxakali'); see his pp. 41ff.

14. These factors account for the relative paucity of references in my own bibliography and notes to tagmemic works; there is little point in extending the material to include such works as Harold Popovich's (cited in the previous note), since these do not bear to any great degree on the things that we must discuss here. I have included in this bibliography those works which are the most directly relevant to this work, and while I have not avoided language-specific materials, the actual number of books and articles on tagmemics is rather smaller than one might expect.

15. Longacre's 'Discourse' is a rare example of a tagmemic article which is a collation and synopsis of language features rather than a description of language-specific features.

16. For a closer look at the origins and development of this school of language analysis, I refer the reader to V.G. Waterhouse's *The History and Development of Tagmemics* (Janua Linguarum, Series Critica 16; The Hague: Mouton, 1974), to L.K. Jones' 'Synopsis of Tagmemics', and to Longacre's 'Discourse' (in Brend and Pike [eds.], *Tagmemics*), and 'Tagmemics' *Word* 36.2 (1985), pp. 137-77. The former two are partial to Kenneth Pike's approach, while I follow more closely Longacre's; those interested in comparing the two would do to start with Longacre's 'Tagmemics', followed by *idem*, with K. Pike and E.G. Pike, *Grammatical Analysis*. The main differences are in Pike's use of a 'four-cell tagmeme', whereas Longacre employs a 'two-cell tagmeme', with the remaining material from Pike's other two cells dealt with as 'Deep-' or 'Notional Structure' (see below, this chapter).

I will not interact to any significant degree once they have been explained, but they are requisite elements of the endeavour. I will follow this with explanations of other features of the model that either are particularly important to the theoretical base (e.g. 'Syntagmeme') or will be referred to with some frequency in the analyses that follow (e.g. 'Exponence').

2.1.1 *Two Fundamentals: Empirical Analysis and 'Language as a Part of Human Behaviour'*

Before turning to these elements of the theory, however, I would like to single out two concepts that are particularly foundational. The first is 'Empirical Analysis'.

It is important to let the data define the questions asked of it, rather than a theoretical model. It has been found that the Tagmemic model is sufficiently 'alive' to the features of 'real language' that it does not need to impose structure on the language being analysed; rather, the structure that surfaces as one works with language inevitably fits within the range of possibilities anticipated by the theory. The fact that the theory concerns itself with 'deep' (cognitive) structure(s) as well as with surface structures means that there is no preconceived idea of how a deep structure 'notion' 'must' be encoded at the surface structure level. Yet this interest in deep structure also informs the linguist of the things that will need to be expressed, as a general rule, in any language. The wide-ranging research that has been conducted in real language also informs the linguist about the range of options for encoding these 'notions'. In the long run, language data is considered the unchangeable truth; it is what exists as language—even were it found to be an ungrammatical sample, for example, tagmemic theory enables the researcher to propose (if he or she so choose) explanations as to 'why' that particular ungrammatical construction was elicited. For the most part, tagmemicists process *vast* amounts of data in their analyses, in order to 'discover' the systems inherent in the language, and to secure their descriptions thereof. This is the only way to work with real language data, it is presumed, because an alleged pattern seen in four texts may no longer hold true after fifteen have been examined—if it doesn't, some other pattern will surface with the greater amount of data; if the alleged hypothesis *does* hold true, then the data substantiate the hypothesis. *The data constitute the only unquestionable 'fact' of the language.*

The second of these two concepts is 'Language as a part of human Behaviour'. No one would deny that language is a feature of human behaviour; and none would deny that language is expressed within a context. Tagmemics, however, takes these two facts strongly into consideration in its analysis. A political speech makes sense within its political and social context, for example. A series of instructions is elucidated by the details of its setting. These 'truths' are, for the most part, self-evident. Tagmemics, however, makes more consistent reference to them as explanatory contexts than other approaches tend to do. Often, it will be setting and context that help sift out patterns in difficult data. This is not to say that every bit of data must be explained exhaustively according to its context; this would be an overstatement. Features can be examined apart from their context, of course, but a full explanation will include reference to setting, appropriate sociolinguistic usage, and so on. The Gettysburg Address, for example, can be examined as a unit—to discover its internal structure, its lexical cohesion, and so on—and a great deal can be learnt of its use of language; but no one would suggest that an understanding of the context in which it was composed and first delivered brings no greater understanding to the meaning, and—yes—structure, of the text. These 'context concerns' form the centre of attention in such disciplines as psycholinguistics and sociolinguistics, yet never should they be relegated entirely to these disciplines. Just how much of this needs to enter the level of grammatical and syntactic description is a matter for debate, but the principle stands: *Language exists as a part of a wider context of human behaviour, and this context bears on the use of language features.*

2.1.2 *'Sub-Basic' Concepts*

The concepts dealt with above are likewise 'sub-basic'[17] in that they are fundamental to everything in this model; those which follow are no less fundamental, but they will not require further attention once their place in the theory is seen. We cannot really 'deal with them briefly, then forget them'—but, in fact, once we have examined them, they will not command our attention again except as undergirding for other features, and at these points I will address them only briefly.

---

17. I do not recall seeing this term elsewhere; it seems an appropriate coinage for the task it must perform, however. No significance should be deduced from it beyond a label for an evanescent category.

2.1.2.1 *Patterning*

The concept of 'Patterning' is basic to all theories of description. That a piece of data can be compared to other pieces of data, and that knowledge can be gained from doing so, presupposes that a unifying pattern can be sought and described. Longacre writes,

> Central to human behavior is PATTERNING. A noted encephalographist has written astutely about patterning. 'The first significant attribute of a pattern is that you can remember it and compare it with another pattern. This is what distinguishes it from random events or chaos. For the notion of random implies that disorder is beyond comparison; you cannot remember chaos or compare one chaos with another chaos; there is no plural of the word. Pattern is a quality of familiar things and familiar things are comparable. It is much nearer the truth to say that man abhors chaos than to say that nature abhors a vacuum... Broadly speaking one may say that the sciences derive from pattern-seeking, the arts from pattern-making, though there is a much more intimate relation between the seeking and making of patterns than this would suggest.'[18]
>
> Granted the centrality of patterning in human behavior it follows that we should require that a linguistic theory give centrality to linguistic patterns. In measuring the fit of a theory with the empirical facts of individual languages we should require that a theory lead to a description in which patterns are thrown into bold relief. Or, in terms of evaluating two grammars of the same language, one important criterion of evaluation is that we recognize as superior the grammar which sets forth the patterns of a language in the more straightforward and direct manner.[19]

So what we are about as text-linguistic grammarians is *the clear description of the patterns that occur at the 'text' level.* Some language scholars may be sceptical about such a level; the next section will address some of the elements that help identify its existence.

2.1.2.2 *Closure and Choice*

I will borrow wholesale, here, from Longacre:

> Aside from this general argument in favor of linguistic patterns, we argue that *CLOSURE* and *CHOICE*, observed in people's use of language, also point to the reality of linguistic patterning. The speaker acts as if he were using units which start and stop. He backtracks and corrects himself if

---

18. Quoted by Longacre from W. Grey Walker, *The Living Brain* (New York, 1953), p. 69.

19. Longacre, *Discovery*, pp. 13-14; this last 'criterion of evaluation' is termed 'elegance' (see below).

proper closure is not given. He hesitates at certain points as if he were confronted with a choice of item or construction. After partially or wholly articulating one item or construction he may backtrack and correct himself by choosing another item or construction. The hearer likewise demands closure of units and has opinions about choices—as is often evident by his responses. Speaker and hearer alike seem to be doing something more direct than applying a complicated series of rules to speech; rather they seem to be referring to an inventory of patterns.[20]

In other words, there are such things as linguistic units, which have beginnings and ends. Texts, for example, begin and end; this justifies our examining them as units. If patterns surface, their existence as functional units is confirmed. That a speaker may backtrack to correct something suggests that it is possible to say something in more than one way, hence the question is not only one of 'grammaticality' versus 'ungrammaticality', it is also one of appropriateness.

The concept of 'choice'—where the speaker, for example, searches among alternatives for the best way of saying something—implies that there are points where the language speaker may choose between permissible options, which in turn implies 'sub-units'. If one may hesitate over the choice of whether to employ a pronominal substitute or the full noun phrase, this indicates, on the one hand, that both options are permissible (though contextual, or perhaps 'stylistic', factors may exert considerable pressure on the choice to be made), and on the other hand, that the point of hesitation marks a *functional point of articulation*—the material preceding it does not unerringly determine what follows it. That written language is generally edited before transmission to its intended receptor in no way challenges this description of language processes; the writer, just as much as the speaker, goes through the same backtracking and choosing processes. These processes, whether written or spoken, underline the 'articulated' nature of language.[21] I will return to this concept of 'options' shortly.

20. Longacre, *Discovery*, pp. 14-15; see also his 'Tagmemics', esp. p. 137.
21. 'Articulated', that is, as in 'segmented', or 'jointed'. It is worth noting another point here, as well: In this age of printed text, it is often overlooked that such conventions as spacing between printed words, punctuation to indicate phrase, clause and sentence divisions, paragraph indentation, and such things as chapter headings, are artificial, *yet they represent linguistic realities*. These distinctions exist at the spoken level as well, yet they are often rendered into spoken language by such 'suprasegmental' features as intonation patterns, hesitations, and the like. No one would deny the functional reality of the 'word level', but this, in some languages is

2.1.2.3 *'Notional' or 'Deep' Structure versus 'Surface' Structure*
The level of 'Patterns' is found not exclusively in the outward structure of each individual language, but rather firstly in the language
centre of the human brain. There are discoverable tendencies at this
level, which begin the process of language structuring. This level is
called 'Notional Structure' by Longacre, *et al.*, and 'Deep Structure'
by others.[22] People who speak several languages sometimes find themselves unable, in trying to express a thought, to find words and structures all of which belong to the same language; they know what they
want to say, but are unable to get it out.[23] They are sure of what they
want to say (the deep structure level provides no difficulties), but the
framing of their thought in real speech doesn't come together
properly (the surface structure poses problems—in this case, the
competing surface structure rules of different languages intermingle
and become confused). Crystal gives an example that helps to clarify
this concept of 'deep structure':

> This level provides information which enables us to distinguish between
> the alternative interpretations of sentences which have the same surface
> form (i.e. they are ambiguous), e.g. *flying planes can be dangerous*,
> where *flying planes* can be related to two underlying sentences, *Planes
> which fly*... and *To fly planes*... It is also a way of relating sentences
> which have different surface forms but the same underlying meaning, as
> in the relationship between active and passive structures, e.g. *The panda
> chased the man* as opposed to *The man was chased by the panda*.[24]

not easily pinned down in definition (are the Hebrew elements -בּ, -לֹ, and the like, to
be considered words? and what about אֵת, which is sometimes independent,
sometimes a bound form? And perhaps most significantly, *why* or *why not?*)—in the
same way, text, paragraph and sentence units are difficult to pin down. It is my
contention that the major reason these are viewed more skeptically by the traditional
syntactician is that there is no inherited concept that has been handed on into the
standard grammars, etc., in the same way as were the concepts of syllable, word,
phrase and clause. Yet if we were to carry out linguistic analysis of the Ionic Greek
dialect before the period of word separation, would we have the same confidence in
word separation as we now claim to have? Language scholars have long been guilty
of a certain kind of imperialism which receives warmly that which it has been taught,
but rejects as sub-standard that which others have been taught, or have discovered.

22. My tendency is to use the two terms interchangeably, with a slight preference
for the latter. No ideological or theoretical significance need be attributed to this,
other than my own preference for more self-explanatory labels.

23. This difficulty is not limited to multi-lingual people...!

24. Crystal, *Dictionary*, p. 85.

Longacre, in a recommendation of the strengths of the tagmemic approach to language analysis, writes,

> It is precisely because tagmemics, however much as it may be become interested in deep structure, continues to be very interested in surface structures that the previous sections of this article, although referring to studies completed some time ago, are valid today. Devices for investigating and describing surface structures in the world's languages (as given above) rest on a considerable backlog of experience in languages around the world and apparently do not need much immediate modification. As the schools of grammar—noticeably stratificational, transformational-generative, and tagmemic—draw together in a common focus on meaning, it will still remain that, of these various schools, the school which is most interested in surface structure is the tagmemic school. Tagmemicists should continue to unapologetically be interested in the way in which a language of necessity must express itself and encode the deep structures that people use as the natural apparatus of human thought.
>
> Tagmemics offers more than a quick-and-convenient approach to language analysis. It opens up vistas of research—some of which are still relatively unexplored—and a program for linguistic activity for many years to come.[25]

2.1.2.4 *'Particle', 'Wave' and 'Field'*
Of these, Crystal writes,

> PARTICLE... (2) A term used in tagmemic analysis to refer to a linguistic unit seen as a discrete entity, definable in terms of features. It is contrasted with 'wave' (where the unit's contextual variability is analysed) and 'field' (where its distribution is described).[26]

Jones describes this set of concepts in terms of 'Perspective':

25. Longacre, 'Tagmemics', pp. 174-75; the directions for new 'vistas of research' that are indicated by the tagmemic school of linguistics are all the more varied and the richer for hebraists—on the one hand, because of the wealth of help it offers (through its copious processing of surface structure analysis of living language data) in suggesting solutions to difficulties of Hebrew language description, and on the other hand, through its relatively practical nature (a combination of its commitment to 'intuitively felt patterns' ['Tagmemics', p. 138] and its ability to communicate details of form and function without heavy reliance on jargon and idiosyncratic calculus).

26. Clearly, then, this is *not* the more familiar definition of the term 'particle', which is defined in Crystal as '(1) A term used in grammatical description to refer to an invariable item with grammatical function, especially one which does not readily fit into a standard classification of parts of speech'; both, Crystal, *Dictionary*, p. 222.

Tagmemic theory formally recognizes a varying observer PERSPECTIVE. At least three different, but complementary, perspectives may be used to view the same items. In a STATIC view ['particle'], items as individual, discrete things are in focus. A DYNAMIC view ['wave'] focuses on the dynamics of items overlapping, blending, and merging with each other. Finally, in a RELATIONAL perspective ['field'], focus is on the relationships between units, noting networks, fields, or matrices. Any one of the three perspectives may underlie a particular linguistic description. A description from one perspective complements, and adds to, a description from one of the other perspectives, but does not replace it. Here also tagmemics leaves room for more than one correct description or grammar.[27]

If one analyzes the clause אני יהוה, in terms of its components, we would describe it as a verbless clause with the structure 'Pronoun as Subject, plus a Proper Noun as Predicate Nominal'. We have just analysed it as a 'particle'. If we look at it from a 'wave' perspective, we would examine it in terms of all possible variants (one might decide to look at all simple S-P Verbless clauses, with no marginal phrases (temporal, attributive, appositional, etc.) added, or one might look at all Verbless clauses together;[28] this is an examination of *variants* of the clause-type. If we begin to examine how S-P Verbless clauses, or all Verbless clauses together, function in the language (for example, as boundary markers in Narrative History), then we begin to look at Verbless clauses from a 'field' perspective. These terms will rarely recur in this volume, but the concept is basic to everything forward from this point.

2.1.3 *'Basic' Concepts*
The preceding material is vital; without it, what follows will not make sense. The *terminology* presented above is less important, however, for I will not belabour it in what follows. The next set of concepts, on the other hand, will be referred to by their 'labels' with some regularity in the following material, therefore it is distinguished from that

---

27. Jones, 'Synopsis', p. 80.

28. As does Andersen, in *The Hebrew Verbless Clause in the Pentateuch* (JBL Monograph Series, 14; Nashville: Abingdon, 1970); cf. Waterhouse, *History*, who describes the concept 'wave' as the 'DYNAMIC view', in which 'structure is made up of waves, with nuclei and margins' (p. 6)—'nuclei' being the essential part of the unit, and 'margins' being the optional extras, thus accounting for the sum total of possible permutations of the unit's structure.

which I have just covered. These concepts have a more *direct* relevance to the analyses I will carry out below than do those introduced
above.

2.1.3.1 *Hierarchical Linguistic Structure*

In his Appendix on tagmemics, in *Joseph*, Longacre deals briefly with
the three 'crucial' concepts of tagmemics.[29] One of these is
'hierarchical linguistic structure'.[30] This refers to a series of levels of
language: [MORPHEME—STEM—] WORD—PHRASE—CLAUSE—
SENTENCE—PARAGRAPH—'DISCOURSE'.[31] These are surface
structure terms, which are roughly paralleled in deep structure.[32]
Apart from the last one or two, these distinctions do not usually raise
questions among hebraists, since we are still accustomed to a more
'intuitive' approach to language description, and we tend to be aware
of such things at an intuitive level. Longacre writes,

> Hierarchy is the spacing of constructions on levels from morpheme (level
> of zero internal grammatical construction) up to discourse (level of maxi-
> mal grammatical construction). With these two levels as lower and upper
> bounds of hierarchy the other levels take their place as intermediate levels
> of combination: stem, word, phrase, clause, sentence and paragraph.
> Stems are derivational units. Words are inflectional units. Phrases express
> modification or linkage. Clauses express predications. Sentences are
> propositions which may concatenate, oppose, balance, or report predica-
> tions. Paragraphs are units developing a discourse. The levels are partly
> defined by such internal characteristics as these, partly by their hierarchi-
> cal placement on the scale from morpheme to discourse.[33]

2.1.3.2 *'Slot/Class' and 'Filler/Set'*

These are more often referred to in the literature as 'slot' and 'filler'
than as 'class' and 'set' (or 'filler' set), and this is my convention
as well. This concept is one of the most central to the Tagmemic

---

29. Longacre, *Joseph*, pp. 311ff.

30. Longacre, *Joseph*, p. 311.

31. His 'discourse' equals my 'text'.

32. For a complete treatment of these two 'layers'—beyond what I have given
above—I must direct the reader to Longacre's *Grammar*, particularly pp. 322-27 and
273-74.

33. Longacre, 'Tagmemics', p. 143; those who are looking for a fuller, more scientific, definition of these levels would do well to consult Longacre's linguistic
books (e.g. *Philippine Languages*, pp. vi-xxvii, 1-3, 53, *et passim*; *Grammar*,
pp. 77-80, 269-336).

School of linguistics, and plays a central role in the shaping of other characteristics of the theory.

A man gets dressed to go to work in a bank in Edinburgh, Scotland. There are certain things he must wear, of course: shoes, socks, trousers, shirt, tie and jacket being the basics. Now, he has a choice of which shirt to wear (it must be white, however—this *is* Edinburgh, not Rome), and he can choose from among several dark suits, or combinations of trousers and jackets; he has a fairly wide variety of socks, and more than a few ties. He has a choice between three different pairs of black shoes. Yet the ensemble is more or less dictated by custom.

There is a typical 'slot–filler' relationship involved here. In each case, a required piece of clothing is supplied from a collection of suitable options: the man undoubtedly has several good shirts which are not white, yet these are not appropriate under the circumstances; he has many pairs of socks (some of which will go very well with the suit and shoes he has chosen), but it would be socially unacceptable for him to wear one of these in place of the required necktie. In the same way, grammatical (and other) relations can be described as a 'slot' into which an item is fitted; the item is chosen from among a set of acceptable 'fillers'.

The following clauses appear very similar, yet they reflect different patterns:

She is my aunt.	Subj. + Cop.Vb.(V1) + Pred.Nominal[34]
She is fun.	Subj. + Cop.Vb.(V1) + Pred.Complement
She is driving.	Subj. + Pred.(V2)

The first clause is a 'stative identificational' clause; the second, a 'stative descriptive' clause; the third, an intransitive clause. Although the word 'is' occurs in all three samples, the conjugated verb is interchangeable. This can be expressed by defining two different sets of verbs which provide the acceptable options for these two different slots—for example, 'V1' could be defined as any finite form of the verbs 'to be' and 'to become'[35] (this permits the construction of a

---

34. The '+' sign is used to indicate that a certain element is required rather than optional (in which case it would be marked with ±).

35. The acceptable way of conjugating these verbs would be dealt with elsewhere in the grammar.

clause like 'she had become my aunt'[36]), while 'V2' might be defined as any finite form of any intransitive verb,[37] granting the possibility of clauses like 'she sighed', and 'she will elope', or even 'she exists'. The slot is called Verb in both cases, but in a tagmemic approach they would be given labels that distinguish them one from another. The 'filler' set would be likewise labeled so that it matched up accurately with its corresponding 'slot'.

2.1.3.3 *'Constituent Structure' Analysis*

The sort of description of clauses that I have undertaken superficially in the above section is often called constituent structure: when one looks at the way a unit is composed, taking it apart to identify its bits and pieces, one is engaging in constituent structure analysis. Such an approach allows us to detail the patterns that surface as we compare like with like, and divide the unit into the elements which make it up.

2.1.3.4 *'Tagmeme' and 'Syntagmeme'*

All tagmemic textbooks I have come across tend to deal with this concept (*the* identifying feature of 'Tagmemic' theory) in a perfunctory way, assuming that it is a concept easily grasped. And, when one has seen countless tagmemic grammars, phonologies, scientific papers and so on, the existence of these two categories as language realities is clear beyond question—it does indeed become a concept easy to grasp.[38] Yet, the first time around is not so simple.

In short, a SYNTAGMEME is a formula, representing a language unit; this formula is made up of sub-units, which are called TAGMEMES. Each tagmeme refers to that set of options which can function in the slot represented by the tagmeme; and each option will be described by a syntagmeme (a Clause syntagmeme will be composed of tagmemes, some of which might represent Phrases, and a Phrase syntagmeme will be composed of Word-level tagmemes—and so the arrangement progresses through the grammatical hierarchy. Waterhouse describes these categories as follows:

---

36. An odd example, perhaps, but grammatically correct.
37. These 'rules' make no effort to be grammatically complete.
38. Compare the ease with which one recognizes the color 'yellow', or the sound of a violin—and the difficulties one has in trying to describe them.

[The tagmeme can be defined as] a functional slot in a grammatical construction correlated with the lexical item or class of items which could be said to fulfill that function... A TAGMEME, then, is the correlation of a functional slot on a specific level within a hierarchy with the class of items that fill the slot. Thus a class is said to fill a slot. A class may also be said to manifest a tagmeme, or a specific member of a class may be said to manifest the tagmeme. The slot is not viewed as a location in a linear sequence—although it may be that—but rather as a function in a construction type. Neither the slot nor the class that fills it is considered to be the tagmeme by itself. For this reason, the basic tagmemic notation is dual, with labels for both slot and class, and a colon inserted between them, without intervening space. The colon is to be read 'filled by'. Tagmemes may be obligatory, marked +. Optional tagmemes are marked ±. The occurrence of an optional tagmeme does not thereby constitute it obligatory; hence it is still marked ±. The marking as either obligatory or optional is part of the notation for the tagmemic unit itself; thus there is no intervening space between it and the slot label. A typical notation for a tagmeme would be + *S:n* (= 'obligatory subject slot filled by noun'), or ± *L:loc* (= 'optional location slot filled by location word').[39]

A SYNTAGMEME is a construction on a given hierarchical level whose constituent parts are tagmemes.[40]

Thus, we could say that אני יהוה is a simple realization of the Hebrew 'Naming'-type Stative Identificational Clause syntagmeme:

Verbless Cl. : { +S : PPron +P : Pnm }[41]

where the subject 'slot' of the clause can be filled with a selection from the 'filler' set 'Personal Pronoun' (Ppron—which will be defined elsewhere); the predicate 'slot' can be filled by any member of the 'filler' set 'Personal Name (Pnm—likewise defined elsewhere),

---

39. Waterhouse, *History*, pp. 10ff.

40. Waterhouse, *History*, p.11.

41. Items within brackets {...} purport to be tagmemes. I make no claims, however, to grammatical completeness. Waterhouse points out that Longacre's notation 'has used the slot label alone; this does not however, mean that the filler class is overlooked. Rather, the simpler notation is merely a convention for ease of transcription' (*in loc.*—I tend to use this simplification as well); Elson and Pickett likewise simplify the calculus for representing language features [B. Elson and V. Pickett, *An Introduction to Morphology and Syntax* (Santa Ana, CA: Summer Institute of Linguistics, 2nd edn, 1964). It is helpful to remember that it is the commonality of *theoretical* starting points which unifies the tagmemic school of language analysis and description, rather than a specific set of notational conventions.

although it is clear that this must be an 'open' set, allowing for an unlimited number of possibilities, unlike 'Ppron', which will be a 'closed' filler set.

Our Edinburgh banker will serve to illustrate these concepts further. The syntagmeme '[Male] Banker's Uniform' might be written as follows:

> B's Uniform: {+ Suit(S1) + Shirt(Sr1) + Tie(T1) + Socks(So1) +
> Shoes(Sh1) }

where 'S1', 'Sr1', 'T1', 'So1', and 'Sh1' are *tagmemes* of the [Male] Banker's Uniform *syntagmeme*. 'Suit(S1)' can also be analysed as a syntagmeme:

> Suit(S1): { + Dark Jacket + Dark Trousers }

'Suit(S1)' is a *tagmeme* when analysed as part of the Banker's Uniform; it is a *syntagmeme* when analysed in terms of what elements make it up.

This brief discussion has presented what is known as 'two-cell tagmemics', which records the 'slot' (e.g. Subject) and the 'filler' (e.g. Personal Pronoun); other versions of tagmemics exist, and are superior to this simplified model for the reduction of language rules to a shorthand 'calculus'.

The standard approach adopted by a large percentage of Summer Institute of Linguistics—Wycliffe Bible Translators personnel is that of *four-cell tagmemics*, where, in addition to the two cells representing 'slot' and 'filler', two more describe the 'role' (e.g. Subject as *Agent*) and the 'cohesion' (this can be explained best by avoiding the calculus and jargon of the system; it refers to such things as 'agreement in gender, number and case', and thus defines the *kind* of relations that exist between the different tagmemes of the syntagmeme).[42]

The reader may be permitted a sigh of relief that precise understanding of all this is not required in order to follow the remaining material; one might be the more grateful at not being required to

---

42. The definitive work for learning the mysteries of four-cell tagmemics is Pike and Pike, *Grammatical Analysis*; a briefer, and much more accessible, explanation of this apparatus is offered in Jones, 'Synopsis', section 1.3, 'Terms and Relations', pp. 80ff.—this also contains a very lucid summary of the basic concepts of syntagmeme and tagmeme.

digest the 'nine-cell' tagmeme, which was the literal 'grand-daddy' of them all.[43]

The interaction between 'tagmeme', 'syntagmeme' and 'structural hierarchy' is what interests us in particular at this point. These three elements Longacre set out as the crucial features of tagmemics for following such a work as *Joseph*; they are the core of what I am presenting as well.[44]

In our Intransitive clause sample, above ('she is driving'), the 'tagmeme' that fills the Predicate slot in the Intransitive Cl. 'syntagmeme' is an Intransitive Verb Phrase. The Subject slot is filled by a Noun Phrase or equivalent (in this case, a Personal Pronoun). The Intransitive Clause syntagmeme could be set out as below:

Intransitive Cl. = { + Subject + Predicate}

where

Subject	=	{Noun Phrase}
		{Pronoun}
		{Proper Name}
		(etc.)
Predicate	=	{Intransitive Verb Phrase}

'Noun Phrase' and 'Intransitive Verb Phrase' are themselves units that can be described as syntagmemes with 'slots' into which other 'syntagmemes' fit as 'tagmemes' within the phrase ('fillers'). Each of these tagmemes ({Noun Phrase}, {Intransitive Verb Phrase}, etc.) may perform widely differing functions in different contexts; these functions are defined by the syntagmeme for each of those contexts. So, we can say that the syntagmeme defines the function of certain tagmemes in certain specified contexts, and the tagmeme describes the constituent structure of the syntagmeme.

This is a radically simplified demonstration of how the 'syntag-memes' of one level of the hierarchy tend to look for fillers from a

43. Even the greatest of the creative masterminds behind this theory found that one unwieldy. The desire to describe as many features of a unit in as short a space as possible was the motivation for these creations; but they also must be usable and at least somewhat self-explanatory, and this one 'went the way of all flesh'. The tag-memic model is constantly evolving under pressures from new language data, and from field linguists who require manageable tools. This is one of its greatest strengths.

44. Longacre, *Joseph*, p. 311.

lower level of the hierarchy. *'Syntagmeme' can be roughly defined as a linguistic <u>unit</u>, while 'tagmeme' can be roughly defined as a <u>sub-unit within a unit</u>.*

2.1.3.5 *Exponence*

We can now begin to reconstitute[45] Longacre's incredibly dense summary of this material:

> Tagmeme and syntagmeme are correlative concepts in that (1) the functions of the various tagmemes are expounded by sets of syntagmemes (including those of zero internal structure), and (2) a syntagmeme is composed of tagmemes. I call the first relation *exponence* and the second *composition*. Thus, not only can syntagmemes of zero internal grammatical structure, such as *John* and *Bill*, occur as subject and object in a transitive clause, but compound words such as (the) *redcoat*, (the) *gentleman*, or (the) *oarsman* may occur there as well; phrases such as *the oldest man in the group*, *an imprudent young officer* or *a crippled sailor* can occur; and even a few clauses such as *That he came early* (*impressed Bill*).[46]

If 'syntagmeme' is roughly equivalent to 'unit', and 'tagmeme' is roughly equivalent to 'sub-unit within a unit', we must also say that when we begin to look at a sub-unit on its own (as opposed to within its unit/syntagmeme), then we are looking at it *as a syntagmeme in its own right*. We view it now as something with its own structure, rather than viewing as something that has horizontal relations with other tagmemes, inside another unit. In most cases this means moving down one level in the linguistic hierarchy.[47]

Longacre has written that 'the functions of the various tagmemes are expounded by sets of syntagmemes (including those of zero internal structure)'; in our earlier example of the Intransitive Clause syntagmeme, the 'functions' are 'Subject' and 'Predicate'; these are tagmemes, and are 'slots' into which certain appropriate 'fillers' can be inserted. The fillers themselves, however, are also syntagmemes

---

45. As one would 'reconstitute', say, instant coffee.

46. Longacre, *Joseph*, p. 312; his explanation in 'Tagmemics' is fuller, and more readable, but relies heavily on Turkish and Trique language data which he presents in the text, in graphic representations which are not reproducible here; in addition to this fact, any meaningful quotation from that source on our subject would extend to several pages of our text—nevertheless, these pages are the most helpful summary I have yet seen of the twin concepts of 'tagmeme' and 'syntagmeme' (pp. 138-43).

47. A point to which we will return shortly.

(e.g. 'Noun Phrase' or 'Personal Pronoun')—they are only considered 'tagmemes' when examined in terms of their function within the Intransitive Clause syntagmeme—and, as syntagmemes, can be looked at in terms of their own tagmemes. And so a syntagmeme of the Noun Phrase might look like this:[48]

Noun Phrase = { ± Det. ± Modifier (1) + Substantive ± Modifier (2) }

where

Determiner	=	{Cardinal Number}
		{'the'}
		{'a'}
		(etc.)
Modifier (1)	=	{Adjective Phrase}
		{Ordinal Number}
		(etc.)
Substantive	=	{Noun}
		{Present Participle}
		(etc.)
Modifier (2)	=	{Possessive Noun Phrase}
		{Verb Clause}
		(etc.)

With this array of syntagmemes, the following are accounted for as possible Noun Phrases:

'six yellow dogs'
'the first five hundred winners'
'a growing distrust of their frequent prevaricating'
'the last time I was there'

and so on (and all this is in order to explain the term 'exponence').[49] The section above dealing with Modifier (1)'s 'filler' options, for example, could be articulated in lay terms as 'Modifier (1) may be expounded by an Adjective Phrase, and Ordinal Number...' These exponential relations can be broken down and qualified further.

---

48. Again, I must stress that these 'syntagmemes' make no claim to complete accuracy; their purpose is to demonstrate features of this model—were they grammatically complete descriptions of the real-language clause-type, their complexity might muddy rather than clarify the points under consideration.

49. I am presuming that the concept of 'composition' as introduced above is more or less self-explanatory.

2.1.3.5.1 *Primary Exponence*

I have said above that a slot tends to be filled by a syntagmeme from the next lower level of the linguistic hierarchy; Longacre terms this 'primary' exponence.[50] A hypothetical sentence[51] tends to be composed of a pair of clauses; the clauses will likely be composed of phrases, and the phrases themselves, of words. This is sort of exponence is the most readily understood.

2.1.3.5.2 *Recursive Exponence*

Longacre writes:

> Recursive exponents of tagmemes are from the same level as the tagmemes themselves. Thus, stem can occur within stem as in *ungentlemanliness* which is a noun stem[52] the exponent of whose theme tagmeme is an adjective stem[53] *ungentlemanly*. In turn the exponent of the theme tagmeme of the latter is another adjective stem *gentlemanly*. The exponent of the theme tagmeme of the latter is a noun stem *gentleman* which has two theme tagmemes whose exponents are morphemes *gentle* and *man*. Three derivative morphemes *-ness*, *un-*, and *-ly* manifest the tagmemes nominalizer, privative, and adjectivizer.[54]

'Recursive' exponence occurs when a unit fills a slot in a syntagmeme of that same level, for example, 'a growing distrust of their frequent prevaricating', where the modifier 'of their frequent prevaricating'—itself defined by the Noun Phrase syntagmeme—occurs as a tagmeme within a Noun Phrase: a Phrase within a Phrase.

On the above two kinds of exponence, Longacre makes these comments:

> Secondary exponence (recursion) does not vitiate the witness of primary exponence to hierarchical structure in language. Recursion is identifiable as something apart from primary exponence. Thus, derivative affixes in English are a recognizable category of affixes. When we find several of these affixes occurring together in the same form,[55] then we know that we have an instance of recursive exponence on the stem level. On the phrase-level recursion is identifiable by the occurrence of prepositions or

---

50. Longacre, *Joseph*, p. 312.
51. E.g. 'If he wanted to come, he should have said so'.
52. 'Stem' is the hierarchical level of the tagmeme in question.
53. I.e. the same hierarchical level; 'theme tagmeme' is the nuclear element of a stem, and, in primary exponence, contains a morpheme.
54. Longacre, 'Tagmemics', p. 145.
55. That is, in the same linguistic unit.

noun-phrase initial items (*of, the, that*) in what is apparently phrase-medial; these relators or initial items signal onset of a phrase acting as recursive exponent of a tagmeme within another phrase. On the sentence level tell-tale distribution of such conjunctions as *and, but, or, if* and *unless* mark recursion.

While primary exponence gives strings in n-ary relations, recursive exponence creates nests of constructions which can never be successfully analyzed as simple linear strings and often are binary. Thus the English sentence quoted above [*Had they taken a sword and threatened to run him through or held a club ready to dash out his brains, he would have died saying, 'No. Never.'*] is not a simple chain of clauses: (1) *Had they taken a sword*, and (2) *had they threatened to run him through*, or (3) *had they held a club ready to dash out his brains*, (4) *he would have died saying, 'No. Never.'* A nest is a structure amenable only to some sort of immediate-constituent analysis. To analyze it as a linear string with order classes is to understructure it. The lowest layer in a nest is composed, however, of descending exponents. Ultimately, then, a nest of phrases is composed of words and a nest of sentences is composed of clauses.[56]

Recursion is more frequent on the stem, phrase, sentence, paragraph and discourse levels, and less frequent on the word and clause levels, which tend to be linear strings. Recursive or non-recursive propensities of a given level constitute a further characteristic of that level. We have already illustrated recursion for stems, phrases, and sentences. In regard to discourse it is necessary to note only that *scarcely any discourse of much length and complexity is a simple sequence of paragraphs*.[57] Rather such a discourse contains subdiscourses, subplots, and subnarratives. In brief, it has discourse level tagmemes (e.g., episodes) whose exponents are themselves discourses. Paragraphs can likewise contain subparagraphs.[58]

56. His own note on this section reads, 'Some languages contain certain syntagmemes (e.g. numeral or adjective phrases) that occur only as secondary exponents. Thus if a numeral phrase occurs only as a modifier of a noun then it is always a phrase-level recursive exponent, that is, while itself a phrase it occurs only as an exponent of a phrase-level tagmeme (Longacre, 'Tagmemics', p. 175 n. 3).

57. Italics my own; this is the principal reason for the complexity of Longacre's graphic presentation of the text of the Joseph story (*Joseph*, Part Four, pp. 209-310), and one of the principal reasons for my presenting so much tagmemic theory at this stage—our investigations below will reveal patterns that are recognizable when these tendencies of language structuring have been explained to some degree. Tagmemics is not the only school of linguistics that is capable of describing these patterns, but it is one of the best, not least because, once the principles have been understood, jargon can be left behind, and explanations be given in lay terms.

58. Longacre, 'Tagmemics', pp. 146-47.

2.1.3.5.3 *Back-Looping Exponence*

In this case, 'a higher-level unit fills a slot in a lower level'.[59] We have seen an example of this in 'the last time I was there'; 'I was there' is a Stative Descriptive Clause, which occurs as a 'Modifier' tagmeme in a Noun Phrase: a Clause within a Phrase.

Likewise a sentence can occur within a Phrase: 'his "if-we'd-done-it-my-way,-it-would-have-worked" comments'—a Sentence within a Phrase.

2.1.3.5.4 *Level-Skipping Exponence*

This is slightly more difficult to illustrate than the others, since it functions more often at the higher levels (which I have not yet described adequately enough to use as examples) than the lower ones. The principle is this: In primary exponence, a slot is normally filled by a unit from the next lower level; if this level is skipped, and the unit which fills the slot comes from an even lower level that normal level, we then have 'level-skipping' exponence, for example, 'If you can join me, we'll go together. Otherwise, I'll look for someone else'. In this case, we have two hypothetical sentences; in the first one, both the protasis and the conclusion are expounded by clauses; in the second, however, only the conclusion is expounded by a clause—the protasis ('otherwise') is expounded by a word (skipping both the clause and the phrase levels). *Elliptical units* fall under this category, and I will occasionally refer to them by that term; at this stage, however, it is to our advantage to underline that the same mechanism (that is, 'exponence') is taking place, regardless of the unit that fills the slot—whether large or small.

2.3.1.6 *Embedding*

A shorthand term for both 'recursive' exponence and 'back-looping' exponence is 'embedding'. One could say that 'a growing distrust of their frequent prevaricating' is a Noun Phrase in which the Modifier of the Noun Phrase 'a growing distrust' is *expounded recursively* by another Noun Phrase—'of their frequent prevaricating'. This specifies the exact relationship of the filler to the slot. In this volume, as is done in many others, I will sacrifice some of this precision, and will bypass explicit statement of the nature of this exponence (except where an

---

59. Longacre, *Joseph*, p. 312.

explicit statement is necessary); the result is that I will describe the above phrase as 'a Noun Phrase that contains an embedded Noun Phrase'. In this enquiry I will refer to 'a Narrative text embedded in an Expository text', 'a Predictive paragraph embedded in a Narrative History speech formula', and so on. *The concept of embedding is the most important to my later discussion of those which have been described so far*; the material preceding this has served primarily as background so that this feature may be the more readily understood.

By way of further clarification of this concept, we can draw connections between it and other concepts we have looked at. The most cogent of these is the twinned concepts of 'Slot' and 'Filler'. The mechanism of exponence (and, therefore, of embedding) is *the direct connection* between the slot and the filler.[60] By referring to the relationship between two units, of 'embedding', I am highlighting the fact that 'paragraph X' is functionally related to 'clause Y' (e.g. where a paragraph of Reported Speech fills the Direct Object slot in a Transitive Clause). The same is true of this concept's connection to the 'Tagmeme–Syntagmeme' pair of concepts—'paragraph X' is a manifestation of the 'tagmeme P', in and of itself, yet it functions with other tagmemes to create a permissible manifestation of the 'syntagmeme Q', which results in 'clause Y [the Reported Speech paragraph embedded in the Transitive Speech Formula Clause]'.

This concept of 'embedding' is a considerable help in elucidating the *grammatical* role of Reported Speech in, say, Narrative History, since it highlights the interconnectedness between Reported Speech and the framework that supports it. This is essential for the integrity of the framework, and also permits us to examine Reported Speech as individual, fully self-contained, units, which also happen to function as part of something else. The benefit of this is that we are able to ask questions of individual Reported Speech texts, and to compare them selectively (for example, to other units of the same text-type), so as to gain a greater understanding of the features of distinctive text-types. Likewise, we gain insights into the nature of Reported Speech as a grammatical/ syntactic mechanism by approaching it in this way. I will, as I have intimated above, return to this in fuller detail in Chapter 5.

60. Although the terms 'embedding' and 'embedded' could be used to described 'level-skipping exponence' (see immediately above), it serves primarily to indicate the insertion of a larger unit into a slot normally filled by a smaller one. Both situations are manifestations of the 'Slot–Filler' interrelationship.

2.2 *Specific Features of the 'Text' Level*

I will now look at the highest level of the linguistic hierarchy—
'Text'—from a variety of vantage points. That such a level exists is
indicated both by behavioural evidence (people usually know when an
oral report, or a conversation, or a joke, is finished, for example),
and by linguistic evidence (languages tend to demonstrate linguistic
patterning at the text level, for example, languages tend to mark the
'peak' event of a story).[61]

2.2.1 *The Identity of the Text*

Our first approach to the text will be to examine the varieties of texts,
or 'text-types'. I will look first at several binary parameters that will
be used to build a matrix for the identification of text-types.[62]

2.2.1.1 *The First Parameter: 'Agent Orientation'*

'Agent Orientation' (abbreviated 'AO') is a feature of texts that
highlight the *participants*. For example, a story generally highlights
the activities (or lack thereof) of a participant, or several participants;
a theoretical paper about, say, a matrix for distinguishing text-types,
does not focus on participants—if any are mentioned (for example,
the reader, or the author) it will only be obliquely, and their activities
as related in the text will have little to do with the flow of the text.

Again, if a builder is explaining the day's schedule to a team of
workers, reference will have to be made to *who* is to do what, where
a manual on how to rewire a house will prioritize the *activities per-
formed* rather than the people doing them (it makes no difference *who*
does them, as long as they are done in the manner required by safety,
by the housing code, etc.).

2.2.1.2 *The Second Parameter: 'Contingent Temporal Succession'*

Of the three parameters that will define our matrix, this may be the
most difficult to grasp. 'Contingent Temporal Succession' (abbreviated
'CTS') refers to whether or not events or doings in a text are related
to (or 'contingent upon') prior events or doings.

---

61. See below, this chapter.

62. This material is derived from Longacre's *Grammar*, pp. 3-6; the vast majority
of the terminology is his own, yet I will only reference extended quoted material; I
am too greatly in his debt for this material to reference every allusion to his publications. Having said that, I must add that his own *explanations* of these concepts,
except in the classroom, achieve minimalist standards.

Events in a story, or instructions on how to assemble a model air-plane, typically exhibit a certain temporal development: each activity develops in some way out of—or is at least sequentially related to—previous activity. This is not as true of a lecture on the nature of metamorphic rock in southern Scotland, or an ideological pamphlet about how life would be better if humanity truly put Marxist Socialism into action.

A good example of this contrast can be seen in the first chapter of the Gospel of John. In the first five verses (in particular, but this is also true of vv. 6-18), the text describes the *nature* of 'the Word', and there is only minimal reference to sequences of events—most of the clauses are stative. In v. 19, however, the treatment of events changes, and one event leads to another, and the emphasis is on *sequence* rather than *state*.

Longacre points out[63] that 'Narrative and procedural discourse have chronological linkage, while expository and hortatory discourse have logical linkage', which may be a useful confirmatory criterion in text-type identification.

2.2.1.3 *The Matrix with Two Parameters*
When we put these two parameters together, their combinations define four broad categories—NARRATIVE, PROCEDURAL, BEHAV-IOURAL and EXPOSITORY.

	+ Agent Orientation	– Agent Orientation
+ CTS	NARRATIVE	PROCEDURAL
– CTS	BEHAVIOURAL	EXPOSITORY

I will come back to this matrix shortly, to add another parameter, and will interact with its categories more fully at that time; until then, Longacre's brief summary of these classifications will suffice:

> Narrative discourse (broadly conceived) is plus in respect to both para-meters. Procedural discourse (how to do it, how it was done, how it takes place) is plus in respect to contingent succession (the steps of a procedure are ordered) but minus in respect to the agent orientation (attention is on

---

63. Longacre, 'Discourse', pp. 19-20.

what is done or made, not on who does it). Behavioral discourse (a broad category including exhortation, eulogy and political speeches of candidates) is minus in regard to contingent succession but plus in regard to agent orientation (it deals with how people did or should behave). Expository discourse is minus in respect to both parameters.

A certain care has been taken in positing these initial parameters, for if they are defined too broadly we get into difficulty in classifying some discourses. Thus, Hebrews chapter 11 is really an expository discourse on faith. On first inspection, however, there are difficulties in classifying this discourse. If, for example, we were to define the first parameter simply as chronological succession (as in Longacre 1976),[64] then Hebrews 11 would be plus in respect to this parameter since it orders its examples of believing men and women according to the chronological framework of the Old Testament. It is plain, however, that the chapter does not present the actions of any person of faith as dependent on those of a person previously mentioned. There is chronological succession, but not contingent succession. The writer is exemplifying faith and simply mentions his various examples in the order in which they are mentioned in the Old Testament. Likewise, while there is a great deal of action and many agents mentioned in the chapter, the chapter is oriented towards those agents who act as examples of faith. Furthermore, there is disparity instead of identity of reference. Actually, then, if we define our two parameters carefully enough, Hebrews 11—unlike true narratives—is minus with respect to both parameters.[65]

I am not content to leave this section without clarifying one thing further. Longacre's discussion above of Hebrews 11 with reference to Agent Orientation is unclear. He writes that, 'the chapter is oriented towards those agents who act as examples of faith'; this, I believe is slightly misleading, since he is trying to explain why the text is to be considered '–Agent Orientation'. One might more clearly say, 'the chapter is oriented towards *faith itself*, and because faith is a human response to circumstances, this requires the text to deal with agents and events. Thus, though there is to some degree a highlighting of agents and actions, this is only to achieve the goal of speaking about *faith*.'

---

64. His exact reference here is opaque; he lists three works in his bibliography that appeared in 1976—it is unlikely, however, that they did not share the same definition of these categories.

65. Longacre, *Grammar*, pp. 3-4; although his contribution to Brend and Pike, *Tagmemics* ('Discourse,' pp. 1-44), is concerned largely with the developmental history of this area of analysis, he provides here as well a good summary of these parameters and their resultant text-types (pp. 18ff.).

2.2.1.4 *The Third Parameter: 'Projection'*

Waterhouse writes, concerning the above-described four 'types of discourse':

> At workshops of the Summer Institute of Linguistics in the Philippines in 1967–68, Longacre began work on a broad front in a variety of languages. This resulted in a three-volume work (Longacre 1968–96): *Discourse, Paragraph, and Sentence Structure in Selected Philippine Languages.*[66] He found four major types of discourse: narrative, procedural, expository, and hortatory. These occurred in most languages investigated. Narrative discourse was that which told some type of story. Procedural discourse told how something was done or made. Hortatory discourse attempted to influence or change conduct or outlook. Each type of discourse was described in terms of its chronological and person orientation; its initiating, closing and nuclear tagmemes; and the types of linkage of units within it.[67]

A matrix with only two binary oppositions does not allow us to differentiate texts that are clearly different in make-up. For example, one Procedural text may record how something was made or done, but another Procedural text may *instruct* the reader for the making or the doing. 'Narrative discourse' includes prophetic, as well as historical, narratives. To represent these in the matrix we require another parameter: *Projection*.

This parameter is, I think, the easiest to grasp. If a text is 'plus Projection', it looks toward the future in some way; if it is 'minus Projection', it does not. For example, a set of instructions about how to turn lead into gold, will be 'plus projection'; a lab report about how lead *was* turned into gold, will be 'minus projection'.[68] A prophecy about the fall of an empire, and the historical report of its fall, differ in terms of 'Projection'.

2.2.1.5 *The Matrix with Three Parameters*

The addition of Projection to the matrix divides it into eight sections, and gives us a means of defining eight notional text-types:

---

66. (Summer Institute of Linguistics Publications in Linguistics and Related Fields, 21; Santa Ana, CA: Summer Institute of Linguistics, 1968).

67. Waterhouse, *History*, pp. 48-49.

68. And fictional. These parameters do not have to do with such things as truth content, injection of humour, and other such features.

	+ Agent Orientation	– Agent Orientation	
+ CTS	NARRATIVE Prediction ——————— Story	PROCEDURAL How-to-do-it ——————— How-it-was-done	+ Proj. – Proj.
– CTS	BEHAVIOURAL Exhortation Promisory Speech ——————— Eulogy	EXPOSITORY Budget Proposal Futuristic Essay ——————— Scientific Paper	+ Proj. – Proj.

These categories, though descriptive of the 'deep structure' of language, are commonly seen in the surface structures of languages as well, and therefore provide labels, and rationale, for handling them independently of one another. This is the greatest value of such a matrix: it enhances our perception of distinctions that are marked (perhaps only subtly) in real language data.

These eight categories[69] are distinctive, and, in those which are distinctive for a given language, they are marked by the surface structure of that language.[70] It would be beneficial, perhaps, to illustrate these notional categories, giving an example from each, on the same topic. For the sake of simplicity we will take 'tying one's shoes' as the subject:

In the Narrative category (+ AO, + CTS), we could have a prediction

---

69. My own 'technical labels' for these categories (by which I will refer to them in the analyses that follow) are slightly different from those given above; they are: Narrative Prediction, and Narrative History; Procedural/Instructional, and Procedural/Lab Report; Hortatory (which is the only type of Behavioural text we encounter in the texts examined in this study); and Expository (when a strict distinction between '± Projection' texts is required, I refer to the former as Expository/ 'What-it-will-be', and the latter as Expository/'What-it-was'). I will always capitalize these terms when they refer to text-types.

70. Not all of these categories are distinguished in the surface structure of each language, and in some languages the 'encoding' of one notional structure may be very similar to, or may partially or completely overlap, the 'encoding' of another.

about a child tying its shoes—'at the age of four, he will tie his shoes without help; he will reach down, take a lace in each hand, and cross them; he will then...' and so on (+ Proj.); likewise, the same thing could be looked on in the past, as history—'and at the age of four, he suddenly knew how to tie his shoes: he just reached down, took a lace in each hand...' and so forth (– Proj.).

If the topic of tying shoes is found in the Procedural category (– AO, + CTS), the agent will be mentioned only because the activity requires one; so, a set of clinical instructions will write, 'when the laces have been crossed, one lace is tucked under the crossing, and the two are pulled reasonably tight; a bow is formed next, by...' (+ Proj.); this can be contrasted with a lab report on how this action is accomplished: 'the wearer crossed the laces, and tucked one under the other; the laces were then drawn tight enough for comfort, and a bow was then formed. This was done by folding one of the laces...' (– Proj.).

In the Behavioural category (+ AO, – CTS), an exhortation by a judgmental peer might run like this: 'If you want your laces to stay tied, you've got to tie them tighter. Pull the laces harder...when you're doing the bow, hold onto it longer...and make sure before you start that your laces are even...don't cross the laces the wrong way either, when you're making the first knot...' and so on (+ Proj.); a ' – Proj.' example of this might be imagined as a reflection by a widow on the precision with which her husband used to tie his shoes: 'he always made sure his bows were the same length, and he would make sure he had pulled the laces securely tight before he began the process. He didn't mind if he had to do it twice, but it had to be right. He had a habit of patting each side of the shoe when he had finished, and he usually brushed them off with his hand just before starting to tie them...'

In the Expository category (– AO, – CTS), we are dealing with primarily descriptive material. A ' + Proj.' Expository text might read, 'When the child learns to tie a shoe properly, the bow will be neat and secure, the laces even. The foot will be comfortable in the shoe, and the laces will not be too tight'; if such a text is ' – Proj.', the time reference will not be future—it may be present or past (though the addition of further parameters could differentiate past from present): 'The shoe was beautifully tied; the laces were not too tight, and the bows were even and...'

This rather exhaustive run on the permutations of 'shoe-tying' texts should aid the reader to relate these categories to real language data.

2.2.1.6 *The Question of other Parameters*

This matrix could be complicated by the addition of other parameters; Longacre suggests the addition of 'Tension'. This is a category which permits distinction between, say, an account of history, such as the book of Judges, where similarity of events, and repetition, feature more highly than does the building of tension through a series of scenes until a climax of tension is achieved and released, such as is seen in the individual histories in Judges, or in the Gospel of John. This same parameter is decisive in the distinction between a theological essay that is merely 'exploratory' and one with a polemic thrust (e.g. one of Martin Luther's treatises against the theology of the Roman Catholic Church of his day).

Sociolinguistic factors enter the picture as well, and complicate it to a certain degree, especially with regard to Hortatory texts.[71]

In addition, I have alluded to other factors that could be included; however, for each step toward greater specificity we sacrifice simplicity and clarity. For the present work, I will limit differentiation to the three parameters given in the matrix above.

2.2.2 *The Internal Structure of Texts*

At this juncture, we shift our attention to the internal structure of these text-level units. This structure is marked by features that can be collected into two loose groups: the first includes those features which tend to extend throughout the length of the text—they are roughly similar to the 'warp' in woven cloth; the second includes those features which tend to break up those in the first category—they are comparable to the 'weft' in woven cloth. As with woven cloth, it is the working together of these features that results in a completed product.

2.2.2.1 *'Longitudinal' Features of Texts*

These are those features that extend throughout the text; they include two pairs of categories that are in opposition to one another, as well as several other features that tend to be examined in terms of the way they thread their way through the text.

71. As we have already noted with regard to Longacre's treatment of these texts in *Joseph*.

'Main-Line' versus 'Off-Line'

Many have remarked on the predominance of the wc + Prefix conjugation in storytelling/historical sections of the Hebrew Bible; it has been dubbed 'the narrative form'. It forms the backbone of the story, but is occasionally interrupted with clauses of different types. It is comparable to the English 'simple past', the French 'passé simple', the German 'Imperfekt'. All these forms characterize Narrative History in the same way that command forms characterize Hortatory texts. These are the forms that are responsible for moving the 'story'/'exhortation' forward towards its end. Longacre terms these 'on-the-line' or 'mainline'.[72] It has been found that every distinctive text-type in a language has a clause-type that it prefers; I have already mentioned command forms for Hortatory—I might also point to the tendency for English Procedural texts to employ the passive forms (particularly Procedural/ Lab Report texts, using the passive forms of past tenses), and the tendency world-wide for Expository texts to rely on stative clauses.

In addition, there occur other clause-types, which do not have the job of moving the text inexorably forward; these usually contain material that sets the scene, or in some other way departs from the main task assigned to a clause in their particular text-type. In Narrative History, a Verbless clause is an anomaly—it adds detail to the context, but does not advance the story; conversely such a clause-type is the main-line form of Expository texts[73]—where a clause with a Suffix form of (e.g.) עשׂה is inserted, then, it provides an event-setting which sets the scene for observations that relate to that context. This type of clause, too, can (rather, *must*) be analysed according to its text-type. Consider the following example:

> Mistress Madwin had a third bed brought in and hastily assembled and made up. One of the beds already there stretched nearly from wall to wall in length, and had obviously been meant for Loial from the start. There was barely room to walk between the beds. As soon as the innkeeper was gone, Rand turned to the others. Loial had pushed the still-covered chest under his bed and was trying the mattress. Hurin was setting out the saddlebags.
>
> 'Do either of you know why that captain was so suspicious of us? He was, I'm sure of it.' He shook his head. 'I almost think he thought we might steal that statue, the way he was talking.'[74]

72. Longacre, *Joseph*, pp. 64ff.
73. Or so I propose; we will return to this at several points in Chapters 4 and 5.
74. R. Jordan, *The Great Hunt* (New York: Tom Doherty Associates, 1991), p. 316.

Who is the speaker in the second paragraph—who is 'he' who shakes his head? How can we tell? At first blush, the identity of the speaker is left ambiguous; however, if one traces through the previous clauses to the *last clause in simple past* (the main-line form in English for story-telling), we find that all ambiguity is resolved. Mistress Madwin has left the room; and the other two characters are occupied with things that are recorded only as *off-line clauses* (a sequence of three passive causative clauses are followed by several descriptive clauses, two imperfect clauses, and one pluperfect clause). *Only* Rand is the subject of main-line clauses.[75]

'Foreground' versus 'Background'

The opposition between main-line and off-line is a syntactic question; the opposition 'foreground' versus 'background' is similar, but is more a 'notional' distinction—in some ways, it is a deep structure distinction that is encoded by a surface structure opposition of mainline clauses versus off-line clauses. Foreground material is that which moves the story/exhortation/instructions/etc. toward its essential goal (whether that be the highlighting and resolution of a peak event, or some other text-type-appropriate goal). Background material is that which does not significantly advance the story/etc. Both 'off-line' and 'background' material can be categorized in terms of 'distance from the main-line' or 'degree of backgrounding'; the more unlike the main-line clause-type an off-line clause-type can be shown to be (in terms of its tense–aspect–mood values, for example), the further off-line it can be said to be. This is the principle behind Longacre's clines.[76]

Payne's contribution to Longacre's *Theory and Application in Processing Texts in Non-Indoeuropean Languages*,[77] though borne of

---

75. Here we have an example of the interplay between several kinds of text-level phenomena, the one (in this case, the analysis of main-line and off-line forms) helping resolve difficulties in another (the question of participant reference, which will be discussed below, in this chapter). This is a case where either the writer was conscious of these features in writing this section, or his innate grasp of language style has led him to craft this section in such a way as to maintain tension (through ambiguity) without abandoning clarity altogether.

76. I have already commented briefly on these in our examination of *Joseph*; they will receive in-depth attention later in this chapter.

77. D. Payne, 'Activity as the Encoding of Foregrounding in Narrative: A Case Study of an Asheninca [Central Peru] Legend', in Longacre (ed.), *Theory and*

research using a somewhat different model, provides a helpful tool for assessing degree of foregrounding. The researcher assesses clauses in terms of *high* versus *low activity*, with various factors being important:

Mode —	Realis (e.g. Affirmative, Non-Future, Indicative)	Irrealis (e.g. Negative, Future, Conditional)
Aspect —	Telic (e.g. Perfective, Punctual)	Atelic (e.g. Stative or Durative)
Agent —	Agentive (e.g. Volitional, Intentional)	Non-Agentive (e.g. Involuntary, Accidental)
Object —	Transitive (e.g. Individuated Object)	Intransitive (e.g. Non-Individuated Object)[78]

The oppositions 'main-line' versus 'off-line' and 'foreground' versus 'background' are more readily apprehended when seen in their setting; and when we are working through texts, we will have ample occasion to cite examples and fine-tune these concepts.

Participant Reference

This term refers to where and how participants enter, are referred to, and exit, their texts. It is found that repetition of a person's name, for example (in a story), when the context identifies the person without him or her being named, can signal an important moment in the storyline.

This is a topic that itself warrants a volume this size; yet, analysis of this feature of texts will not figure highly in the material which follows—the scope of this study will be sufficiently limited that I will only make occasional reference to participant tracking (when, for example, it provides significant confirmation of a doubtful hypothesis).

Application in Processing Texts in Non-Indoeuropean Languages (Papiere zur Textlinguistik, 43; Hamburg: Helmut Buske Verlag, 1984).

78. Payne, 'Activity', pp. 63-64; this Transitive–Intransitive opposition is defined differently from what we are accustomed to, and the Object category is evaluated on a 'sliding scale' of sorts, so this approach would need to be examined in closer detail than the above were it to be considered for application to our data; but this much gives a good understanding of the issues involved in differentiating foreground and background; even the title of this article suggests the 'deep structure' nature of foregrounding, with its reference to 'encoding' (the process whereby deep structure language propositions, etc., are rendered according to the surface structure rules of any given language).

Topical Cohesion

Topical cohesion is a feature of texts similar to that of Participant reference; it refers to the continuity, or lack thereof, through a text of the topic(s) referred to in that text. Tracking their introduction, maintenance, relinquishment and possible reintroduction feeds information into an analysis of a text's internal structure. By and large, this approach to the text will, like the above, serve no more than a confirmatory role in the analyses that follow this chapter.

Other 'Longitudinal' Features of Texts

Other elements of a text may be examined for their clues to the overall construction of the text. An example of such an element is temporal reference—where does it occur? and in what kinds of clauses? Is all passage of time explicitly marked?—and so on. Lexical cohesion is another example: how many times do words having to do with '*X*' occur in this stretch of text? Is that consistent with the rest of this text? and so forth. A good theoretical base will suggest likely features to watch out for, and while any feature of a text can be examined to see if it has a text-level role, some leads will be more productive than others.

'Profile' Features of Texts

Features such as topical or lexical cohesion are examined in terms of their continuity through the text. Other features are not. These are 'one off' features, and the ensemble of these solitary occurrences usually tell us much about the text as a whole. We will examine these features in terms of their deep structure concepts and then in terms of how they are realized in surface structure.

Plot

It may seem odd to run across this term here; is it not a literary analyst's term? Have we wandered outside our own domain? This may in fact be true, but it merely underlines the interdependency of these various ways of approaching texts. Each is seeking to understand how the human mind creates and communicates meaning; many of the underlying truths will surface through application of widely differing procedures. This simply confirms the existence of these features as real, rather than theoretical.

One such feature is 'plot'. Literary analysts (not to mention secondary school teachers) have long considered this one of the structural givens of Narrative History. That stories tend to have a beginning, development, high point and conclusion is fairly well acknowledged. As a result of studying a wide range of languages, which have a wide range of storytelling techniques, a hypothetical underlying structure has been proposed.

Longacre proposes seven elements underlying the typical Narrative History text:

1.	Exposition	'Lay something out'
2.	Inciting Moment	'Get something going'
3.	Developing Conflict	'Keep the heat on'
4.	Climax	'Knot it all up proper'
5.	Denouement	'Loosen it'
6.	Final Suspense	'Keep untangling'
7.	Conclusion	'Wrap it up'[79]

These elements underlie and inform the surface structure of not only Narrative History texts, but also the other text-types. Perhaps some of the terms may seem a bit alien for such a text-type as Procedural/ Instructional, or Hortatory, but the concepts of beginning, sustaining, coming to the 'point', settling everything out and concluding, can be found to have their place in texts of any variety of text-type.

Constituent Structure
As with any underlying, deep-structure 'notion', realization of these concepts as surface structure features is not always straightforward, but there is enough consistency to propose a set of [roughly] corresponding features:

I	Title
II	Aperture
III	Stage
IV	(Pre-Peak) Episodes
V	Peak
VI	'Peak Prime'[80]
VII	(Post-Peak) Episodes
VIII	Closure
IX	Finis

79. Longacre, *Grammar*, pp. 20ff.

80. This term is used where the deep structure 'climax' is encoded as more than one surface structure peak; in languages that employ specific peak-marking devices (a specific particle, for example), when such a device is used to mark two different episodes, the second will be referred to by this term.

I, II and IX are identified by Longacre as 'formulaic',[81] and are surface structure features only. As is always the case in mapping relations between deep and surface structure features, one cannot always map one-to-one correlations—in this case, for example, the deep structure features '2. Inciting Moment' and '3. Developing Conflict' both realize as 'IV. (Pre-Peak) Episodes'. The deep structure features do not require us to seek exact replications in the surface structure, rather they permit us to look for a range of potential structures in the texts we examine. If we sought a specific system of surface features the underlying organization of the text might elude us.[82] Suffice it to say, we are engaged in looking at texts to discover what they show us in terms of their patterning; the awareness of deep structure features will alert us to language tendencies that may be reflected in surface structures in our texts, which might otherwise escape our notice.

Internal features or units that function to build tension or release it, to confirm a point, to identify the key exhortation, and so on, suggest an overall pattern to the text, a pattern of ebb and flow, of rise and fall, which gives a sense of a unified whole. These features suggest where we will find breaks in the text, and also that we will find functional sections bracketed by those breaks—and that these breaks and functional sections fit into an overall plan.

These deep- and surface-structure features give to the text a 'profile'. This sort of thing can be illustrated readily from familiar stories, such as 'The Boy who Cried "Wolf!"'. A boy, sent to watch the flock of sheep in the hills, became lonely, and twice raised the alarm when there was in fact no threat, to alleviate his loneliness. The villagers ceased to trust his alarm-cry, and when the sheep were indeed threatened by the wolf, the boy could raise no help. Additionally, this story had a moral, and the listeners were meant to take to heart the value of integrity and the consequences of sacrificing it. Now, I haven't rigged the data; this is a well-known story, told in a

---

81. Longacre, *Grammar*, p. 20.

82. To go into greater detail on the nature of correlations between deep and surface structure features would muddy the waters here significantly. The purpose of raising the issue is to demonstrate the fact that these surface-level features are grounded in basic human functions, that they have a real cognitive existence which is not derived from, for example, conventions of literary style—in fact, the converse is true, that conventions of literary style, etc., derive from the normal innate human tendency to organize texts along these lines.

very similar fashion in a wide variety of cultures. But it is the *sequence of episodes*—the rising and falling of tension in the story-line, and the like, which breaks it into sections—which we recall, rather than the word-for-word tale that we first heard. At a subconscious/intuitive level, we have internalized the 'profile' of this story, rather than simply its surface structure encoding. The only way we have been able to absorb this 'profile', however, is by interpreting the clues left for us in such things as the introduction of off-line material to break the flow, and the repetition of key words, phrases and structures, which create for us the patterns of the story.

2.2.3 *The Overlapping and Interleaving of Features*

In looking at texts, then, we are faced with more than a handful of different types of features, some of which form part of the continuity of the text, others of which function to segment it. These features work together; rarely is there significant disharmony in the indicators of the structure of a text (e.g. a text in which the participant reference, lexical cohesion, backgrounding versus foregrounding, and plot structure, all seemed to indicate radically different text structures). Rather, all these features tend to point the same direction toward a harmony of results. Thus, one often finds that the 'Exposition Stage' section of a story is set apart from the remainder by containing a much higher proportion of off-line material, and that boundaries, which are indicated by breaks in the main line, are also confirmed by topic shifts, introduction of new characters, and the like. Even when exploring only *one* surface-level feature (e.g. a particular clause-type, as does Eskhult),[83] therefore, it is wise to keep an eye on other features of the text, in order to see the single feature within its larger and more holistic context.[84]

---

83. Eskhult, *Studies.*

84. In my comments on Eskhult's *Studies* I have criticised his narrowness, for this very reason; likewise I have affirmed Khan's endeavour to identify features other than Ex and PAR which could perform the same function(s). Khan stands a better chance of understanding his chosen grammatical feature than Eskhult does, because he sees it in a wider context.

3. *Methodology*

With these comments[85] on the tagmemic model of text analysis, I have endeavoured to present a sufficient theoretical base so that we can test a few hypotheses raised by the model, against data from the Hebrew Bible. The intermediate step, however, is to discuss the kind of approach to the text this theoretical base will lead us to employ. There will be two sections to this: (1) a set of general principles; and (2) those general principles, given specific characteristics to fit our specific context, and to meet our specific needs.

3.1 *General Principles*
Before going into the specifics of how to approach a text for analysis using the 'Tagmemic' model, I must lay out a few basics—these form, as it were, the *Credo*:

3.1.1 *The Primacy of the Data*
Our first principle of methodology *must* be that the data are worthy of analysis. If we approach a text (or any other research data, for that matter) with the conscious or unconscious presupposition that it can only be as we expect it to be before our contact with it, then we are suggesting that the system we impose upon the text has greater value than the system which produced it (i.e. that if the two are not identical, the former is above suspicion). This is rarely the case.

Moreover, such a presupposition forgets that we go to the data to be informed about the world that produced them, and that if such an attitude had prevailed among previous researchers, the very presuppositions with which we approach the data would never have evolved.

We *must* consider the possibility that the data can correct our presuppositions, else we might as well give up 'scientific endeavour' altogether. The language had a life of its own before we came to it

---

85. In an earlier version of this study, I used the phrase 'these few comments'. It has been suggested that this might annoy the reader, as thirty pages of tagmemic theory will hardly seem like 'a few comments'. Yet, the reader will surely be aware that this has been a rather sketchy introduction to the model; a much more thorough introduction would be needed to do justice to the security with which this model allows us to describe linguistic nuances.

with our 'theory'. We must discover how it came to be the way it is,[86] and our only means to this end is to let it speak to us with its own voice.

3.1.2 *Selecting a Manageable Task*

With a healthy respect for the integrity of the data, we must then decide what we would like to ask. We must use wise restraint in this. Our selection of a topic must be informed by such concerns as (1) the size and characteristics of the database, and (2) the amount of time the researcher intends to give to the study—other factors, such as the needs of the academic community at the time of research, will enter the debate as well. There is little point in asking of Hebrew data, 'what is the text-linguistic structure of the Pentateuch?', or 'what is the function of syntax in poetic texts?', unless we are prepared for a long and exhausting project, for example.[87] The choice of which topic to pursue will determine, to a surprising extent, the *value*, as well as the accuracy, of the results.

3.1.3 *The Theoretical Starting Point*

Using the theoretical base introduced above for discovering text-types, it would be foolish to embark on a phonological enquiry like 'which syllable structures are permissible?'. This is because the model one works from will be predisposed to function better for some kinds of enquiries than for others. In addition, when one examines a language from the perspective of a certain model, one will find that the state of description, to date, of that language, will inevitably show certain gaps when compared to what *might* surface if description were carried out to its fullest on that language, using the model in question; that is, certain questions, for which this model would be a particularly helpful tool, will already have answers, and others will not. Therefore, we must allow the model we choose to help us determine the enquiry in which it will function.

---

86. Those who are more favorable to text-critical work will respond here that this is also their goal; the difference I would cite between these two goals lies in the underlying assumption of the one that the text is largely 'in a form intelligible to the original users, if not to us' (my own view), while that of the other is that the text has departed substantially from its original integrity, and that we have the knowledge and tools to restore it (it is this latter assumption of which I am skeptical).

87. The additional fact that the groundwork for such a study has not yet been adequately laid is another consideration.

3.1.4 *Working with a Hypothesis*

Once we have determined the scope, and starting point, of our topic, we are embarked on a process that will be governed largely by the question we ask.

Selecting a Working Hypothesis and a Data Sample

I have enumerated several factors above which will influence the choice of question(s) we will ask of the data. The question must also be formulated in such a way to lead us to a productive answer. '*Do verbs have a macro-syntactic significance?*' would be next to useless as working hypothesis; we need a starting point that will result in a concrete observation about the language. 'Does the distribution of verbs with היה in non-'Reported Speech' sections of Narrative History, in comparison with other clause-types, indicate possible macro-syntactic significance?' is a much more functional hypothesis.[88]

Once we have chosen a topic, a theoretical starting point, and a working hypothesis, we must also decide what will be included in our data sample. In most language studies, the database is more or less theoretically, if perhaps not functionally, unlimited—since living speakers will continually be creating further data—and therefore the researcher must select appropriate material for a study (that is, material particularly suited to the study undertaken). Thus, if one is wanting to discover the text-level features of hortatory texts, it is unhelpful to include prophetic narrative, expository and procedural texts in the database, since these will clutter the study, making seeing patterns that much more difficult. On the other hand, if one is wanting to determine the similarities and dissimilarities between expository texts and hortatory texts, it is wise to have several of both on hand to allow suspicions to be confirmed or denied. In short, choices must be made about the type of data examined, and the quantities thereof. Other factors may influence the choice as well; if—as is true in the case of Classical Hebrew—the integrity of the data may be called into

---

88. In fact, this is a kind of sub-hypothesis, since it would be correlative to other questions we must ask at the same time. Perhaps the 'umbrella' hypothesis might be: 'Do suspected clause-level macro-syntactic devices for non-Reported Speech of Narrative History converge to frame a complete picture of the constituent structure of the text?'. Were we to be strictly legalistic about this, hypotheses could not be framed as questions, but would have to take the form of 'if–then' sentences. This last scruple is perhaps helpful on occasion, but I tend to bypass it, since the question form accomplishes the task sufficiently well, and without any great ambiguity.

question on the grounds of textual variants and other, similar difficulties, it may be wise to look first at less suspect texts, so that the results achieved can be evaluated without undue complications.

These choices, like any others in the process, add an element of subjectivity to the endeavour, and this, of course, must be kept to a minimum. Restrictions on the database are going to limit the scope of the results to an equal degree, and so should be made wisely. On the other hand, however, language contains such variety that simply taking a handful of data at random rarely allows patterns to surface (unless one is, for example, studying the frequency of a particular feature in a specifically random sample of data).

Working to Disprove the Hypothesis
Now comes the difficult part: we have to disprove the hypothesis. If we *cannot* do that, only then have we substantiated it. This is a difficult discipline for a mind trained in 'the Arts'; 'pure' scientists are more familiar with this principle. And yet all of us are aware that if a theory about a feature is to become accepted as 'true', it must be able to withstand all challenges; therefore, if the researcher proposing a hypothesis throws as many of these challenges at the data as possible, he or she stands the better chance of ushering the hypothesis into the realms of accepted truth.

But this is tremendously difficult to do; once an hypothesis has led the researcher to propose a solution, it is difficult to get it out of one's head, and to ask of it if it might, in fact, be better explained another way. Yet this is the *only* way of securing the proposal.

3.1.5 *Charting*
This is, strictly speaking, not a 'general principle', in the same way the previous five sections have been, yet it nonetheless deserves attention at this point. When one examines 'texts', the very size of the units of data imposes some difficulty; therefore, how we handle our data is at least as important as in other types of research. When studying whales, one's 'field' methods will be slightly different from those used to study goldfish. Beavon writes,

> The analysis of texts depends on the use of charts. The better the chart,
> the more readily one sees the structure of the discourse.[89]

89. Beavon, 'A Partial Typology of Konzime (Bantu [Cameroon]) Discourse',

Choice of charting techniques must eventually rest with the individual using them; and, of course, the more creative the person, the wider variety of charting techniques available. The principal issues which must be resolved here are (1) the construction of a chart that actually allows patterns to surface, and (2) achieving a balance between clarity and detail. If too much detail is highlighted, clarity is obscured, and patterns may be overlooked; if too little detail is included, patterns may be overlooked.

3.1.6 *Drawing Conclusions and 'Feeding' the Theoretical Base*

This stage involves determining what, exactly, the data have brought forth during the enquiry. There are two facets to this: (1) description of the results in and of themselves; and (2) comparison of these results with those which the theoretical base led the researcher to expect at the outset. The first requires little comment, other than that it is wise—for the sake of one's reputation as a scholar, if for none other—to be circumspect in one's write-up, and that one's goal in this description is (a) to be true to the data, and (b) to communicate clearly one's findings as economically as possible—in a word, 'elegantly'.

The second, on the other hand, is less transparent. The point is this: if we start by assuming the primacy of the data, and something goes awry, then we must ask questions of (1) our theoretical base, and (2) our methodology. If, for example, we look for a strongly suspected pattern, and find none, we must ask if our charting technique, or perhaps our choice of data-sample, has been at fault. Yet, perhaps the charting technique and the data-sample were beyond reproach—then it is time to ask the same question of the theoretical base, since it suggested that such a pattern would exist.

Returning to the example we used earlier, a phonological survey of possible syllable-types: if our theory says that certain patterns are never permitted, and yet we find words in which these patterns exist, then we must ask if perhaps we have erred when dividing our words into syllables, and have included phonemes in certain syllables that actually belong in others. If this does not seem to be the case, then we must *amend our theory to permit such syllable-types.*

---

p. 250 (in Longacre [ed.], *Theory*, pp. 210-55); here 'discourse' is used in the sense of 'text'.

3.2 *Specific Methodological Plan for Chapters 4 and 5*

Having now become somewhat acquainted with some of the factors that inform one's approach to the text, the reader will now be able to see how these qualify my own approach to the data in the analyses that follow.

3.2.1 *Yet again, 'The Primacy of the Data'*[90]

I have argued that the data are the only independently existing, and in that sense the only *truly real*, element of language description. The models and procedures with which we approach the data serve merely to aid us to determine what the data really are. This means, then, that textual emendation of the book of Exodus, for example, will be a last resort during this enquiry; it means as well that questions of scribal additions to the text of Ruth will not deter us from examining the text as a unit, for we presume that scribes were the literati of their day, and if they 'contributed' to a text, they will have done so in way that did not violate the kinds of patterns we wish to examine. In short, it means that, in the pages to follow, I will be prepared to call into question theory and methodology before calling into question the data pool.

3.2.2 *Selecting a Manageable Task*

This is a slightly different matter. Given that I have chosen (a) to evaluate several other works at the outset of this volume, and (b) to introduce the tagmemic model of linguistic analysis, and the principles of its methodology (in rather a greater degree of detail than is usually

---

90. I may be accused of whipping a dead horse, here. The overstatement of this principle, however, is for polemic reasons; it is clear from even a cursory examination of the history of biblical studies, that unchallenged presuppositions have controlled the field for extended periods, resulting in what might be termed a rather insular attitude among scholars. Modern linguistics, with its greater openmindedness to new discoveries from the data, has much to offer the study of Classical Hebrew, but for the most part, hebraists are less than enthusiastic about its benefits. The perspective of 'if it ain't broke, don't fix it' appears to be in the mind of the reticent biblical shcolars here, yet the fact remains that the 'old ways' have programmed the researcher to find only what has already been found in the data, rather than anything new. It 'ain't broke', but the data have been pointing in directions that are obscured by the presuppositions of the 'old ways'; we must allow our presuppositions to be corrected by new insights from the data.

seen in such works), I am then left with less space in which to present substantiation of my 'claims', than I would like. I have chosen to compensate for this factor in two ways: (1) I have selected a narrowly circumscribed topic for examination; and (2) I have decided to address this topic with a lessened concern for thorough substantiation than would otherwise have been the case, in order that a greater number of seeming 'loose ends' from the previous chapters may be tied together for the reader.[91] And since the theoretical base I have elucidated here has focused to a fair degree on the identification of text-types, and on questions of main-line versus off-line—and since these were singled out in Longacre's work on Genesis 37, 39–48, as his most significant insight for contemporary text-linguistic description of Classical Hebrew—it is most apposite that we turn our attention to identification of Classical Hebrew text-types, and their attendant main-line and off-line clause-types.

3.2.3 *The Theoretical Starting Point*
We have looked at Longacre's matrix of 'notional' text-types, and I have cited his 'verb rank clines' of main-line and off-line forms as being particularly productive for Classical Hebrew; we have also looked at constituent structure of texts as something that may be marked by off-line features. I will therefore take as my starting point these theoretical concepts, and examine the data to see whether they are, in fact, viable for describing our language. I have also dealt bluntly with Niccacci and Eskhult, in terms of their treatment of 'discourse' (i.e. 'Reported Speech'), and have suggested that their analyses are deficient because they do not deal well with this feature of the text. Therefore, the enquiry about text-types, main-line versus off-line clause-types, and constituent structure of texts, will do well to include reference to the Reported Speech feature as well.

The sections that follow present the verb-rank clines for four text-types as a hypothetical representation of what this theoretical base leads us to suspect.

---

91. All this is based on my firm conviction that treatments of broader topics, with fuller substantiation, will appear in the not too distant future to offset the shortcomings of this particular study.

The Narrative History Cline

Although this cline has already been presented above in the discussion of Longacre's *Joseph*, I include it here for the sake of completeness.[92]

NARRATIVE DISCOURSE TEXT-TYPE VERB-RANK CLINE	
Band 1: Storyline	1. Preterite
Band 2: Backgrounded Actions	2.1 Perfect 2.2 Noun + Perfect (with noun in focus)
Band 3: Backgrounded Activities	3.1 *hinnēh* + participle 3.2 Participle 3.3 Noun + participle
Band 4: Setting	4.1 Preterite of *hāyâ*, 'be' 4.2 Perfect of *hāyâ*, 'be' 4.3 Nominal clause (verbless) 4.4 Existential clause with *yēš*
Band 5:	5. Negation of verb clause: irrealis (any band) —'momentous negation' promotes 5. to 2.1/2.2.

The Narrative Prediction Cline[93]

NARRATIVE PREDICTION TEXT-TYPE VERB-RANK CLINE	
Band 1: Line of Prediction	1. wc + Suffix
Band 2: Backgrounded Predictions	2.1 Prefix 2.2 Noun + Suffix (with noun in focus)
Band 3: Backgrounded Activities	3.1 *hinnēh* + participle 3.2 Participle 3.3 Noun + participle
Band 4: Setting	4.1 wc + Suffix of *hāyâ* 4.2 Prefix of *hāyâ* 4.3 Nominal clause (verbless) 4.4 Existential clause with *yēš*

92. Longacre, *Joseph*, p. 81; I have stated that I believe that the degree of detail in these 'clines' is difficult to accept with unreserved confidence, and these various, finely tuned, layers will not be contrasted with one another in the analyses to follow.

93. Longacre, *Joseph*, p. 107.

The Hortatory Cline[94]

HORTATORY TEXT-TYPE VERB-RANK CLINE	
Band 1:	1.1 Imperative (2nd person)
Primary Line of	1.2 Cohortative (1st person)
Exhortation	1.3 Jussive (3rd person)
Band 2:	2.1 '*l* + Jussive / Prefix
Secondary Line of	2.2 'Modal' Prefix
Exhortation	
Band 3:	3.1 wc + Suffix
Results / Consequences	3.2 '*l* / pn + Prefix
(Motivation)	3.3 Suffix (with future reference)
Band 4:	4.1 Suffix (with past reference)
Setting	4.2 Participles
(Problem)	4.3 Nominal clause (verbless)

The Expository Cline

Longacre does not posit a cline for Expository texts. Sufficient research has not yet been done to permit such a specific hypothesis, but I will hazard here a tentative cline:

EXPOSITORY TEXT-TYPE VERB-RANK CLINE	
Band 1:	1.1 Nominal clause (Verbless)
Primary Line of	1.2 Existential clauses (with '*ên* or *yēš*)
Exposition	
Band 2:	[Clauses with *hāyâ*]
Secondary Line of	
Exposition	
Band 3:	
Band 4:	[Here we would expect to find those clause-
Contest / Setting	types which have the greatest amount of
	action and transitivity][95]

3.2.4 *A Working Hypothesis and Data Sample*

The theoretical details are coming together enough now that we can formulate a working hypothesis. So far, we have affirmed (a) the

---

94. Longacre, *Joseph*, p. 121.

95. I refer the reader again to Longacre, *Joseph*, pp. 111ff.: 'Elements at the bottom of the clines for Narrative, Procedural, and Hortatory discourse have the highest ranking in Expository' [p. 111]—conversely, those clause-types which are at the top of the other clines will be at the bottom of this one. I will examine this more closely in the next two chapters, but my results even then will remain tentative.

primacy and integrity of the data, (b) the need to select a fairly restricted topic, which (c) ought to be related to the material presented in Longacre's matrix and clines, and to 'Reported Speech' versus 'non-Reported Speech'. Therefore, I have chosen to ask, as a preparation to shaping a working hypothesis, '*Can we substantiate the existence of main-line clause-types for more than just the Narrative History text-type? and do these have relevance for Reported Speech as well?*'

If we frame these in terms of a testable hypothesis, we might say the following:

> Main-line clause-types are text-type specific, and can be described as such; they will predominate in the text, and text-types can be identified by the predominant clause-type.

> The main-line clause-type for the Narrative History text-type is the wc + Prefix clause.

> The main-line for the (Narrative) Predictive[96] text-type is the wc + Suffix clause.

> The main-line clause-type for the Hortatory text-type is built on a 'command' form.

> The main-line clause-type for the Expository text-types is the Verbless clause.

> Other text-types, whose clines have not been described nor intimated by Longacre in *Joseph* will be identified first by features other than 'main-line' clause-types (as these have not yet been proposed), and then clause distribution within those texts for which we have able to posit a text-type identity, will be examined with a view toward proposing their main-line forms.

> The constituent structure of texts will be marked by divergences from the main-line form in all text-types; off-line marking of constituent structure will be confirmed by other types of marking devices, and will reflect a comprehensible underlying notional structure;

> The results of the above analyses will be expected to hold true for Reported Speech as well.

This sequence of hypotheses is simply a specific outworking of the question we have posed above, though it may look like a series of rather too loosely related studies. In addition, one may be tempted to

---

96. I will occasionally refer to this using both labels, to reaffirm the close connection between this text-type and Narrative History.

object that I have proposed to keep this enquiry rather severely circumscribed, and that this list does not seem in keeping with that goal. However, my charting techniques and so on will enable me to kill several birds with one stone; therefore I will have occasion to test more than one hypothesis with it.

In spite of claims at several earlier points that the corpus of data is small, I will, nonetheless, need to restrict further the material I examine. Given the issues with which I am concerned, and the space limitations of this particular study, I will work with no more than, say, a dozen texts, and not many of these in great depth.

It will be advantageous to employ texts with clear boundaries, for this grants a ready assurance that we are dealing with a structural unit that is natural, rather than artificial and perhaps misleading. Shorter texts will be easier to work with than long ones, but they will need to be of such a length as to show at least some internal structure—fewer than 50 clauses in a text, to pick a number somewhat at random, would mean that the text will not be likely to show us much about the language's mechanisms for marking paragraph divisions, and so on.

As I mentioned earlier in this chapter, textual concerns with the Hebrew Bible recommend to us that we avoid, where possible, texts that contain seriously suspect sections. It will be seen that our choice is not severely restricted by this caution.

Since I am taking as a starting point the more readily accepted view that the wc + Prefix forms are the main-line forms for Narrative History texts, it will be wise to examine this hypothesis first, both to confirm its veracity and to demonstrate the effectiveness of the charting techniques before moving on to texts-types whose results may be received with less confidence.

Following this, a text from another text-type will be required. Since I cannot hope to substantiate the existence and nature of every text-type in the matrix—owing primarily to the limitations of this study—some will have to be left behind. Hortatory texts are particularly familiar, and that they employ command forms is not difficult to grasp; therefore, I will take for granted, in this study, Longacre's Hortatory Verb-Rank Cline. In addition, Narrative Prophecy has received similar attention in the literature to that received by Narrative History, and its characteristics are likewise more readily accepted without extensive proof—for the sake of this preliminary study, that is—and therefore I will 'borrow' Longacre's cline for this text-type as well. Because there is considerable Procedural/ Instructional material in the Hebrew Bible, this is a logical choice for the next text-type to be examined. Several of these suit the needs of this study admirably (being well-defined units of a reasonable length, with few textual difficulties). In addition (and perhaps most importantly), we are fortunate to have a pair of texts—those concerning the building of the Tabernacle—that differ from one another solely by text-type: one is a set of instructions, the second is a report about the completed process. This pair of texts will allow me to compare these two text-types without the complication of differing subject matter.

These are the major factors involved in the choice of texts I will look at in this study; there should be little cause for complaint with regard to the decisions made (particularly in that, at the end of this study, I will not make any hard and fast claims to accuracy, but rather claim only to have pointed the way forward in this discipline).

3.2.5 *The Charting Methodology*

Because my first hypothesis centres on the question of whether the wc + Prefix clause-type can be demonstrated to be the main-line clause-type for Narrative History, my first decision regarding the analysis that follows was to display the text 'one clause per line'; I have also chosen to separate out those factors which were irrelevant to my quest. This means that syntactically subordinated material is placed in a separate column, because clause-initial particles preclude the use of the wc + Prefix form, and therefore the absence of such a form is easily predictable. For the same reason, Reported Speech material is separated from non-Reported Speech material (because the former clearly contains other text-types than Narrative History, and would clutter up the Narrative History material if included with it, to the point that no patterns in Narrative History would be discernible)— but, because Reported Speech might, nonetheless, contain some Narrative History material, I have decided that subordinated material should likewise be placed in a column separate from non-subordinated Reported Speech material, in order that similar processes of evaluation may be carried out on Reported Speech sections as on non-Reported Speech sections.[97]

---

97. And because it was found that subordinated clauses more than occasionally contained, on the one hand, clauses coordinated within that subordination, and on the other hand, clauses subordinated within that subordination, it was decided to allow

The distribution of clauses in non-subordinated non-Reported Speech material can thus be examined to see if patterns regarding this distribution can be found, drawing from the three theoretical starting points considered to be primary: (1) text-type identification according to the matrix; (2) main-line clause-type identification, in comparison with Longacre's clines; and (3) the reliability of off-line clause-types as constituent structure / macro-syntactic markers.

Because these patterns are more visible if the clause-types are immediately discernible, it was decided to use a colour-coding scheme.[98]

3.2.6 *Drawing Conclusions and Feeding the Theoretical Base*

I have talked about the primacy of the data, and that the results of the research must be allowed to inform one's approach to the data, and one's theoretical base. It might, therefore, be instructive for the reader to have a look behind the scenes, so to speak, at earlier, preliminary studies, with regard to some of the abandoned hypotheses which at one point accompanied or preceded the ones given above.

At the outset, I examined Hosea, hoping to propose something with regard to its constituent structure based on clause-type distribution.

the distinction to be marked in the charting: where subordination—or other break in the flow from one clause to the next—occurred, a space was inserted between lines; otherwise, whether within subordination, Reported Speech, or neither, no space was inserted, implying continuity.

98. In the dissertation that lies behind this study, 16 colours were originally used to mark by circling all manner of possible macro-syntactic indicators; this rather robust spectrum was found confusing by all but myself, so it was pared down to eight by coalescing such categories as *hinnēh*, *lo'*, and *yēš* (among others), into a single category, and by eliminating others from the marking scheme altogether (e.g. infinitives, which were found to have no substantial relation to the hypotheses under examination). This color-coding was perhaps the most striking feature of the original charting procedure, and enormously helpful. Owing to printing restrictions, this color-coding scheme cannot be reproduced for this volume. An alternative scheme would be to *underline* those items considered to be the principal marking device for the main-line, and *circle* any feature of interest that was not the main-line marker (e.g. the wc + Prefix forms in a Narrative History text would be underlined, and such features as *hinnēh*, Suffix forms, and Verbless clauses would be circled; this scheme is less satisfactory, however, for it fails to provide a means for identifying at a glance different text-types, marking items according to *function* rather than *form*, and the function of a form will necessarily vary according to the text-type in which it is found.

This was not successful, since I had not yet investigated the Narrative text-types, nor had I begun to suspect that 'poetic' style might not permit as simple an approach as I was hoping to adopt; I found this material difficult to work with for these reasons, and no patterns surfaced. I next looked at Jonah, then Ruth, and these Narrative History texts proved more fruitful.

I had initially presupposed that infinitives were clause-level features, and I attempted to examine them as macro-syntactically significant; this was relatively fruitless, and I dropped it from my 'theory'. In addition, it looked as though participles had a rather interesting distribution—that they were used attributively or substantively only in subordinated material, and predicatively only in non-subordinated material (i.e. that they had a non-overlapping distribution)—this, however, was *not* borne out by examinations of other data, and turned out to have been a result of faulty analysis of a few occurrences of the participle. My methodology was adjusted to prevent further mistakes.

Further, I had taken strong exception to Niccacci's claim that 'narrative discourse' was describably distinct from Narrative History found outside of Reported Speech. I challenged this in my work with the data, and was both justified, and corrected, by the data: I found that, yes, what Niccacci calls 'narrative discourse' is indeed distinctive, but that this is traceable to *factors related to the embedding of a unit of Reported Speech in the Speech Formula clause*, rather than it being a distinctive type of text in its own right. In this case, I had distrusted Niccacci's observations, while they were accurate, and yet found a different explanation which, I believe, describes the data more accurately and elegantly than his.

4. *Final Comments: On the Relationship of this Chapter to the Following Two Chapters*

It will be clear to the reader, both from the nature of this volume, and from the way the preceding sections have been written sometimes in future tense, sometimes in present, and sometimes in past tense, that the analysis that follows this section was undertaken prior to it. Yet, as data returns us to theory and methodology, which then inspires us to return to the data, this is not unfitting. The approach which we will undertake with regard to the following material has been adequately laid out in this chapter; further explanations, and reiterations, of the 'hows and whys' of this analysis will accompany the procedures themselves. The conclusions drawn from the analysis will be interspersed in the accompanying comments, and will be summarized in the final chapter. The reader should be in no doubt, however: the material that follows this chapter is not intended to be a thoroughgoing text-linguistic analysis, but serves, rather, as an illustration of the application of Tagmemic text-linguistic theory and methodologies to Classical Hebrew data.

Chapter 4

TEXT-LINGUISTIC ANALYSIS OF NARRATIVE
AND NON-NARRATIVE TEXT-TYPES, WITH DATA SAMPLES
FROM JUDGES, LEVITICUS, AND EXODUS

1. *Introduction*

Now that we have examined the theory and methodology that will
instruct our approach to the data, we can look at a few texts. I propose
first to analyze briefly a short section from Judges which will give us
a chance to test the water with that linguistic text-type which is best
known in biblical studies—Narrative History. I will then turn to some
Procedural/Instructional material, from Leviticus; also from Leviticus
is a text that will illustrate the concept of 'embedding'. The final
section in this chapter will look at material from Exodus on the
building of the Tabernacle, another Narrative History text, and its
parallel, a Procedural/Instructional text. This will give us a chance to
look at a new text-type in contrast with a nearly identical version in
the more familiar Narrative History text-type.[1]

1.   In phonological analysis (analysis of the sound system of a language), for
example, one looks for 'minimal pairs' of words to confirm that a certain pair of
sounds are contrastive at the 'emic' level (significant for the language, able to carry
distinctions of meaning, etc.), rather than contrastive at the 'etic' level (below the
level of awareness of the native speaker, etc.)—the words קָרָא, 'call', and קָרַע,
'tear', demonstrate that the contrast between א and ע is significant for Classical
Hebrew. On the other hand, the English /k/ sound may have as many as nine 'etic'
variants (distinguished by where the consonant is articulated, and how it is released);
yet it is impossible to find a 'minimal pair' where the difference in meaning between
two words can be attributed to a contrast between any of these variants (for example
an aspirated /k/ and an unaspirated /k/). Finding a minimal pair where one word had
an aspirated /k/, and another of a different meaning, whose only phonetic difference
was a lack of aspiration after the /k/, would be sure evidence of aspiration as a significant feature of the language in question. In the same way, the existence of these two
nearly identical Exodus texts is a substantial confirmation of the existence of different

I have noted the frequency with which Hebrew narrative text level patterns have been acknowledged by contemporary (as well as earlier) writers. This being the most common text-type in the Hebrew Bible, its features are more readily perceived. My treatment of Judges 2, a Narrative History text, will be brief, for two reasons: (1) it is assumed that the reader will not be surprised at the basic text-level features of Narrative History (its predominating forms, etc.), these features often having been discussed in the literature; and (2) we will be returning to another Narrative History text in the following chapter, where we will examine in much greater detail those and other text-level features.

2. *Judges 2*

The choice of Judges 2 for our examination is somewhat arbitrary, yet because it is not very complex in structure, does not present any serious textual difficulties, and does not rely heavily on reported speech as a means of carrying the story-line forward, it is a good starting point.[2]

A glance at the role of Judges 2 in the book of Judges will be helpful. Judges 2 is part of the introduction to the series of stories which follow and which focus on specific leaders. In this chapter, however, a synopsis is given, highlighting the cyclical nature of the reported history and giving a moral assessment of this cycle. It opens with a message from the angel of YHWH—an indictment of the people of Israel for their failure to obey YHWH's commands, and a statement of his refusal to intervene any further for them. After this opening section of reported speech mechanism, the story-line proceeds by simple narration. Israel's apostasy, and YHWH's rejection of Israel, announced by YHWH's messenger, is followed by Israel's repentance, YHWH's response and Israel's salvation; this is detailed as the cycle that will be replayed throughout the rest of the book of Judges. The simple narration that forms the body of the chapter is bracketed by reported speech, ending the same way it began, with another message of judgment from YHWH.

This section is set off from the preceding material by two clauses that are irregular for the Narrative History text-type.[3] The syntactic

---

text-types, for the significant differences between the two texts are explainable by 'text-type' alone.

2.   The full text of Judg. 2, in four-column format, is found in Appendix 1.

3.   The first, 1.35.3, is a wc + Prefix < היה clause, the second is a verbless

marker of the second episode boundary (2.23.2) is what Longacre calls a 'momentous negation' clause:[4] ולא־נתנם ביד־יהושע 'and he did not give them into the hand of Joshua'. This boundary is also marked by a topic shift in the following episode (episode boundaries need not always be syntactically marked; it is usually the combination of features, syntactic and otherwise, rather than a specific mechanism, that conveys the desired signals), and, I propose, by a change to the expository text-type.[5]

It is the material between the two judgment oracles that will require our attention at this stage. Of the 80 clauses in this episode,[6] 22 are found in reported speech; I will observe here only that, of these 22, 9 are subordinated. The remaining 58 clauses are simple narration; of these, 13 are subordinated, with the rest (45 clauses) non-subordinated.

Now, these 45 clauses include a variety of types:

1	Ellipsis (2.18.1)
1	Asyndetic Suffix clause (2.17.4)
1	Suffix clause with -ו copula (2.19.2)[7]
2	Suffix clauses with a preposed element; one with היה
5	Negated suffix clauses
35	wc + Prefix clauses; 3 with היה
45	non-subordinated clauses

A full 82% of these clauses are wc + Prefix clauses. This is clearly the form of the verb that is preferred for conveying Narrative History information. We can separate out, provisionally, the wc + Prefix clauses with היה, since they tend to indicate states rather than events

---

clause; both are common devices for indicating a break in the flow of the narrative, as we will see in the following chapter.

4. That is, a clause in which an important event is indicated by the lack or failure of an action.

5. I will discuss the Expository text-type more fully in the following pages.

6. The consideration as 'clauses' of at least two of these (2.18.1 and 2.22.3, both of which are elliptical) may cause some consternation, but I have nevertheless chosen to include them in the count as full clauses; it will be seen that this approach does not greatly influence the analysis.

7. In this, and in the preceding category, we have two examples of what Niccacci says cannot happen ('The QATAL which has first position in the sentence is distinct from a second position QATAL. The first kind occurs in discourse [my 'Reported Speech'] but never in narrative' [*Syntax*, p. 30]). My analysis will have less difficulty explaining this feature.

(and thus do not advance the main line of narration), and are often used to signal paragraph and other macro-syntactic boundaries. Even with this taken into consideration, wc + Prefix clauses (with verbs other than היה) account for 76% of the non-subordinated clauses.

It is this kind of distribution which numerous authors have noted, and which justifies reference to this form of the verb as the 'narrative' form, and the like.[8] The identification of this clause-type as the main-line Narrative History clause-type is the starting point for our research into text-types and their uses of clause-types.

Yet we are faced with approximately a quarter of the clauses in non-subordinated narration being what is termed 'off-line'. What are these doing? If the wc + Prefix clauses are main-line, advancing the narrative by consecutive events, and so on—if these are the bones of the narration, what then are these other clauses?

In brief, if the former are the 'bones', the latter are the 'joints'. We have seen in Longacre, in a variety of works on other language groups, and in his work on Hebrew (and his findings are confirmed independently by others such as Niccacci),[9] that *material in non-main-line clauses adds to the narrative, not by moving it forward, but by contributing background information and creating a setting for the narrative.* Theses studies have shown that non-main-line information impedes the flow of narration, and therefore serves the purpose of arresting the reader's progress, either to highlight a particularly significant moment in the narration, or to provide means of distinguishing one sub-section of a narrative from another which follows it.[10]

It is important to note that these non-main-line clauses are evenly interspersed through the text; they tend to occur in groups, breaking the flow of main-line clause-types. In Hebrew, as in many other

8. We have already referred to GKC's comments on this form: '*imperfect* with *waw consecutive*...serves to express actions, events, or states, which are to be regarded as the temporal or logical sequel of actions, events, or states mentioned immediately before. The *imperfect consecutive* is used in this way most frequently as the *narrative tense*...' (§111a). While GKC's description of this form is inadequate at some levels, it must be admitted that the quote above has captured almost exactly the sense of Longacre's concept of ' + Contingent Temporal Succession'.

9. See Niccacci, *Syntax*, p. 35, *et passim*.

10. See, in particular, Longacre's work, but I have also pointed out Niccacci's comments about main-line and off-line forms—see esp. my p. 29 (Niccacci, *Syntax*, pp. 71 and 107); these are but a sample of what is becoming a widely substantiated understanding of text-level features.

languages, the more off-line clauses included at a specific point in a text, the greater the focus on the division being signalled, or on the event being highlighted. It is worth graphically examining this interruption of main-line 'flow'.

In the chart on the next page, the clause numbers are indicated in the left-hand column of each section;[11] moving to the right from that, we have *main-line non-subordinated clauses*; in the next two columns we have *off-line non-subordinated clauses*, and *subordinated clauses*,[12] respectively.

Clauses 2.1.3–2.3.4 and 2.20.3–2.22.3 are the reported speech sections.[13] In this chart, they can be seen clearly to bracket the remaining material. Each clause is marked on the chart with a dot, indicating the kind of clause (with reference to the main line)—with the exception of the elliptical 2.18.1, which is marked by an empty circle.

The features that become most visible in this chart, aside from the two reported speech sections, are the groupings of main-line clauses (wc + Prefix clauses with verbs other than היה), and the clustering of off-line material between 2.16.2 and 2.20.2.[14]

Imagine that this chart is a musical score: each line (each clause) stands for one measure, and all are the same length; the first column is what the drum plays, the second is the tambourine, the third is the triangle. Now, if we were to hear this 'played', we would find that the steady, pulsing 'thump' of the drum, which predominates in the earlier part of the 'piece', is progressively more and more often interrupted by the tambourine and the triangle, as time goes on, till we hear very little of it near the end—eventually the drum-beat is nearly swallowed up by the tambourine and the triangle. If we propose that the

---

11. Throughout this study, I employ a Chapter/Verse/Clause number system, as introduced earlier: hence 'Judg. 2.18.1' refers to the first clause of v. 18 in Judg. 2; there are four other clauses in this verse (2.18.2–2.18.5).

12. I have not made a thorough study of the role played by subordinated clauses in the inter-play of 'on-line' versus 'off-line' clauses. The work I have so far done suggests strongly that subordination may have macro-syntactic significance, but I will make further comments on this at a later point.

13. Since I am not going to address issues of Reported Speech in this particular text, these sections have not been given specific clause-type treatment in the charted display.

14. The reasons for assigning 2.17.3 to the 'subordinated' column will not necessarily be clear at first glance. Further comments will follow in the text.

reported speech sections be scored for flute, the 'musical' bracketing becomes even more strongly apparent.

	ML	OL	Sub			ML	OL	Sub
2.1.1	●	I	I		13.2	●	I	I
1.2	●	I	I		14.1	●	I	I
1.3	—	—	—		14.2	●	I	I
1.4	—	—	—		14.3	●	I	I
1.5	—	—	—		14.4	●	I	I
1.6	—	—	—		14.5	I	●	I
1.7	—	—	—		15.1	I	●	I
2.1	—	—	—		15.2	I	I	●
2.2	—	—	—		15.3	I	I	●
2.3	—	—	—		15.4	I	I	●
2.4	—	—	—		15.5	●	I	I
3.1	—	—	—		16.1	●	I	I
3.2	—	—	—		16.2	●	I	I
3.3	—	—	—		17.1	I	●	I
3.4	—	—	—		17.2	I	I	●
4.1	I	●	I		17.3	I	I	●
4.2	●	I	I		17.4	I	●	I
4.3	●	I	I		17.5	I	I	●
5.1	●	I	I		17.6	I	●	I
5.2	●	I	I		18.1	I	O	I
6.1	●	I	I		18.2	I	I	●
6.2	●	I	I		18.3	I	●	I
7.1	●	I	I		18.4	●	I	I
7.2	I	I	●		18.5	I	I	●
7.3	I	I	●		19.1	●	I	I
7.4	I	I	●		19.2	I	●	I
8.1	●	I	I		19.3	I	●	I
9.1	●	I	I		20.1	●	I	I
10.1	I	●	I		20.2	●	I	I
10.2	●	I	I		20.3	—	—	—
10.3	I	I	●		20.4	—	—	—
10.4	I	I	●		20.5	—	—	—
11.1	●	I	I		21.1	—	—	—
11.2	●	I	I		21.2	—	—	—
12.1	●	I	I		21.3	—	—	—
12.2	●	I	I		22.1	—	—	—
12.3	I	I	●		22.2	—	—	—
12.4	●	I	I		22.3	—	—	—
12.5	●	I	I		23.1	●	I	I
13.1	●	I	I		23.2	I	●	I

There are four short sections of non-subordinated off-line material (2.4.1; 2.10.1; 2.14.5–2.15.1 [2 clauses]; and 2.23.2), and one long section (2.17.1–2.19.3 [14 clauses]). Remembering our hypothesis that the macro-syntactic purpose of off-line material is to signify with reference to main-line material, we begin to look for their significance: every time we hear the tambourine we must ask why it is being played at that time.[15] What are these devices signalling?

I propose that this background material functions in two ways: (1) to signal the divisions in the text, and (2) to highlight the key point of the history. The first two off-line clauses (2.4.1 and 2.10.1) signal the beginning and end, respectively, of the first section of this introduction. I would begin a new paragraph at 2.10.2; there is no reason to connect 2.10.2 to 2.10.1, syntactically, and no objection can be raised at any other level (save perhaps at the lexical level, as both clauses refer to *dwr*, but this is very weak objection—many examples can be found in the commentaries citing just such cross-boundary lexical cohesion as the height of authorial craft.[16]

I would suggest as well that 2.14.5 likewise signals the end of a section.[17] The final clause of the chapter (2.23.2), as well, signals closure. On the other hand, I would propose that the material in the longer section, flanking as it does the single main-line clause 'and he saved them from the hand of their enemies all the days of the judge' (2.18.4), serves to identify the peak event of the section. This, in fact, is the message of the book of Judges as a whole; it is the truth that is to be learned from all these histories—and it is *syntactically marked* as such by 5 preceding off-line non-subordinated clauses (with

---

15. To return for a moment to the question of subordination as a possible macro-syntactic device: this particular chart shows a remarkable frequency of alignment between [other?] off-line clauses and subordination. The fact that both *slow down* the forward movement of the main line by contributing background information suggests that they may function similarly. I will comment again on this in more detail in the treatment of Ruth in the following chapter.

16. Boundaries are often 'transition zones' rather than strongly delineative borders: 'And all וגם כל־הדור ההוא נאספו אל־אבותיו // ויקם דור אחר אחריהם אשר לא־ידעו את־יהוה that generation were also gathered to their fathers // And there arose another generation after them, who did not know YHWH... (Judg. 2.10.1-2). Compare Exod. 1.8, where a new paragraph is introduced with nearly identical wording (minus the lexical cohesion, excepting that of 'Joseph'): ויקם מלך־חדש על־מצרים אשר לא־ידע את־יוסף.

17. With v. 15 being connected closely to 2.14.5, as a sort of amplification thereof—see my further comments below on 2.17.3.

4 subordinated clauses thrown in), and by 3 following off-line non-subordinated clauses (with 1 subordinated clause).

The interaction of vv. 14-15, and v. 17, with the rest of the text requires comment. Verse 17 contains five clauses:

וגם אל־שפטיהם לא שמעו	2.17.1
כי זנו אחרי אלהים אחרים	2
וישתחוו להם	3
סרו מהר מן־הדרך	4
אשר־הלכו אבותם לשמע מצות־יהוה	5

It is 2.17.3 which is most intriguing—here we have an occurrence of a main-line Narrative clause assigned to a subordinated section. Though this may seem alarmingly out of keeping with my proposed assignment of wc + Prefix forms to the main line, this clause is clearly to be considered a continuation of the previous clause, which in itself is subordinated. It is a history within a history—or, to put it more technically, we have here *Narrative History material*, encoded as such, but set into a sentence to serve as an explanation; the fact that it is an explanation has cast it in the form of subordinated material; this in turn forces certain syntactic adaptations on the first of these two clauses: it is forced by the preceding *ky* to forsake the normal [clause-initial] wc + Prefix form, and uses the Suffix form instead; the second of the two clauses in the explanatory Narrative History continues the history, in the normal way, with the main-line form.

Although it is beyond the scope of this study to pursue identification of paragraph-types, it may be said that these three clauses (2.17.1–2.17.3) form what Longacre calls a 'narrative amplification' paragraph, about which he writes, 'Amplification paragraphs are paragraphs that consist of a Text and an Amplification, with the latter adding new information not contained in the former, while at the same time essentially incorporating the material found in it'.[18]

The second section requiring comment is 2.14.5–2.15.5.[19] The six clauses together (three non-subordinated clauses—the first a negated suffix clause, the second a clause with a suffix form of היה and a preposed subject and temporal phrase, and the third a wc + Prefix

---

18. Longacre, *Joseph*, p. 97; Here Longacre uses 'Text' in much the same way as school grammars tend to use 'Topic Sentence'. His 'Discourse' provides a skeletal introduction to this level of text-linguistic analysis (see pp. 20ff.).

19. See Appendix 1 for full text.

clause—and three אשר clauses) articulate one thought: that Israel suffered without YHWH's help.[20] This unit serves to conclude the second of the simple narration sections. The following section begins with a shift of topic, with the emphasis being on the salvation of Israel, rather than their humiliation.

So, then, this chapter is in five sections (§§I–V). It is bracketed by reported speech sections (the first of which [§I] is introduced by two main-line clauses, and the second of which [§V] is concluded by two clauses, one of which is non-main-line). The first of the simple narrative sections (§II) is set into motion by a wc + Prefix clause with היה;[21] it deals with the people's faithfulness under Joshua, and is concluded with a Suffix clause with preposed subject. The second simple narrative section (§III) is concluded by the 'amplification paragraph' discussed above. The final simple narration section (§IV) is the peak episode of this historical overview; it opens with a topic shift. It is bracketed with two main-line clauses at either end (2.16.1-2 and 2.20.1-2), and contains only one other main-line clause (2.18.4); this is set off from the surrounding main-line material by 13 non-main-line clauses on either side of it. After the reported speech section (§V), the following chapter begins with a shift in topic, and possibly a shift from the Narrative to the Expository text-type.[22] Judges 2, then, exhibits the following structure:

I   2.1.1–2.3.4   FIRST JUDGMENT SPEECH—boundaries: 2 initial main-line clauses (2.1.1-2), Reported Speech

II   2.4.1–2.10.1   ISRAEL UNDER JOSHUA—boundaries: 1 initial off-line clause, and 1 final off-line clause

III   2.10.2–2.15.5   ISRAEL WITHOUT LEADERSHIP—boundaries: initial topic shift; final 'amplification paragraph' (sequence of 7 clauses, 5 of which are off-line)

---

20. This is another amplification paragraph; v. 15 provides explanatory detail to v. 14.

21. A temporal clause, which is a frequently used device for initiating new sections (see notes on Ruth in the following chapter)—other mechanisms exist for non-macro-syntactic introduction of temporal material (e.g. בכל אשר יצאו יד־יהוה היתה־בם לרעה, from v. 15).

22. I, personally, am convinced of this. However, until I can present the whole of the book of Judges as an analysed text (as an introduction to the body of which this putative expository section serves, in the same way that wc + Prefix < היה clauses and verbless clauses may be introductory to shorter sections of narrative), I will not make this claim.

IV   2.16.1–2.19.3   ISRAEL UNDER JUDGES—initial topic shift; peak
                       event marked with 13 off-line clauses

V   2.20.1–2.23.2   SECOND JUDGMENT SPEECH—boundaries:
                       initial topic shift, final off-line clause followed by
                       topic- and text-type (?) shift

This brief overview of the macro-syntactic features of Narrative
History is the starting point for looking at other text-types. We have
seen that *the 'wc + Prefix' form is the main-line clause-type for
Narrative History, and that non-main-line clause-types function as
'break' markers or peak markers*. Next we will look at what I call the
'Procedural/Instructional' text-type, with a text sample from Leviticus
14. This will not be an exhaustive analysis, but instead will build on
the observations just made on the Judges 2 text, and will present to us
our first non-Narrative text-type.

3. *Leviticus 14.1-32*

We now look at a text of a different text-type. Lev. 14.1-32 is a text
(on more or less the same topic) of sufficient length for us to see some
internal structure; other texts offer certain features that we don't find
in this one, but are generally shorter than we would like for a starting
text. It is relatively free of textual difficulties.

This text presents instructions for the ritual cleansing of a 'leper'. It
is set, as is the overwhelming majority of legal material in the Hebrew
Bible, into a Narrative History framework.[23] The unit is introduced by
a typical speech formula;[24] the following unit also begins with a
speech formula, identical but for the inclusion of Aaron. Within these
boundaries, the text is further bracketed by an Expository introduction and summary: immediately following the introductory speech
formula is an Expository introductory clause (זאת תהיה תורה..., 14.2.1);
the final sentence in the section echoes this (...זאת תורת אשר, 14.32.1-
2), recapitulating the entire chapter. In addition, the central division
(14.21.1-2) consists of two existential clauses (one verbless [with אם],
the other with אין); this, however, is not necessarily a reflection of

---

23. It is also, it would seem, presented as an Expository text within this Narrative
History framework. This need not delay us here; my purpose is to examine the
Procedural material; see the notes on Lev. 6.1.1(Heb)–7.37.2, following the treat-
ment of Lev. 14.

24. וידבר יהוה אל־משה לאמר, 14.1.1.

some attempt to tie this material into an 'Expository framework', but is instead likely to be a syntactic marking of the paragraph division.

	ML	OL	Sub		ML	OL	Sub
14.2.1		●			16.1	●		
2.2	●				16.2			●
3.1	●				16.3	●		
3.2	●				17.1		●	
3.3		●			17.2			●
4.1	●				18.1		●	
4.2	●				18.2			●
5.1	●				18.3	●		
5.2	●				19.1	●		
6.1		●			19.2	●		
6.2	●				19.3		●	
7.1	●				20.1	●		
7.2	●				20.2	●		
7.3	●				20.3	●		
8.1	●				21.1		●	
8.2	●				21.2		●	
8.3	●				21.3a–22.1e	●		
8.4	●				22.2			●
8.5		●			22.3		●	
8.6	●				22.4		●	
9.1		●			23.1	●		
9.2		●			24.1	●		
9.3		●			24.2	●		
9.4	●				25.1	●		
9.5	●				25.2	●		
9.6	●				25.3	●		
10.1		●			26.1		●	
11.1	●				27.1	●		
12.1	●				27.2			●
12.2	●				28.1	●		
12.3	●				28.2			●
13.1	●				29.1		●	
13.2			●		29.2			●
13.3			●		30.1a–31.1d	●		
13.4			●		30.2			●
13.5			●		31.2			●
14.1	●				31.3		●	
14.2	●				32.1		●	
15.1	●				32.2			●
15.2	●				32.3			●

This chapter contains 81 clauses;[25] the first is the introductory speech formula (a wc + Prefix clause), which presents the material that follows as part of what YHWH said to Moses on the mountain.[26] Of the remaining 80 clauses, 15 are subordinated clauses, 18 are non-subordinated off-line clauses, and 47 are wc + Suffix clauses (not < היה—two clauses with wc + Suffix < היה occur, at 14.9.1 and at 14.22.3). Clearly, we have here the same kind of reliance on a main-line clause-type (in this case, wc + Suffix < non-היה verbs) as we saw in the Narrative History, Judges 2, text. In addition, we see the same kind of distribution pattern as we recognized in Judges 2.[27]

The features that I find significant in this text are relatively straightforward. In the first place, there is a predominance of wc + Suffix forms (the main-line clause-type [left-hand column of the above chart]); these 47 clauses comprise 59% of the clause totals.[28] They tend to occur in strings. Where these strings are broken by non-subordinated off-line clauses, we can propose paragraph divisions, for example:

והנה נרפא נגע־הצרעת מן־הצרוע	14.3.3
את־הצפר החיה יקח אתה ואת־עץ...	14.6.1

---

25. The reader will notice an anomaly in the above chart: the sequence of clauses runs 14.29.2 / 14.30.1a–31.1d / 14.30.2. This displacement of 14.30.2 has its root in the charting methodology that I have employed, where every clause is treated as a unit. Where a subordinated clause is embedded inside the clause to which it relates, it is removed from that clause, and follows it in the chart on a separate line.

26. It is not surprising that religious systems that derive a substantial part of their authority from direct connection with a founder (as is the case in Judaism, Christianity, Islam, Mormonism, etc.), should seek to tie their non-narrative (non-historical) material to a historically validating setting, by passing that material on in a Narrative History format. The ' + Agent Orientation' feature is as important to the authority of the text as is the ' – Projection' feature.

27. See chart of Judg. 2, p. 128.

28. The percentage of these main-line clauses may not seem like a vast majority; however, other clause-types fall significantly below this percentage: there are 15 subordinated clauses of a variety of types, 19%; there are 10 non-subordinated prefix clauses with verbs other than היה (one of these is clause-initial, 14.9.2), 12.5%; there are 3 verbless clauses, 4%; there are 2 wc + Suffix clauses with היה, 2.5%, and one each of Prefix < היה, existential clause with אין, and הנה + Suffix form (a conditional protasis).

or peak moments in the text, as in the following sequence:

ואחר יבוא אל־המחנה	14.8.5
וישב מחוץ לאהלו שבעת ימים	14.8.6
והיה ביום השביעי	14.9.1
יגלח את־כל־שערו	14.9.2
את־ראשו ואת־זקנו ואת גבת עיניו ואת־כל־שערו יגלח	14.9.3
וכבס את־בגדיו	14.9.4
ורחץ את־בשרו במים	14.9.5
וטהר	14.9.6

The proposal that these 'off-line' clauses mark the peak events of the episode offers a reasonable explanation for the fact that the *first* shaving of hair is described with a wc + Suffix clause (־ולח את־כל שערו, 14.8.1), while the *second* is encoded with the off-line 'direct object + Prefix' clause (14.9.3). The suppliant is brought back into the camp, but first only as an outsider, and finally is accepted back into society; the text marks these events as the goal of the entire procedure (cf. also 14.16.1–19.3; 14.25.2–31.3).

The off-line clauses used to mark paragraph division tend to occur singly; those which mark peak sections tend to occur in collections, and form clusters around single main-line clauses, or short strings thereof.[29]

This profile is so similar in nature to that of the Judges 2, Narrative History, text that it is difficult to understand how the existence of a Procedural/Instructional text-type has been overlooked by contemporary Hebrew text-linguists.[30]

4. *Leviticus 6.1 (Hebrew)–7.37*

We will turn our attention very briefly to another text from Leviticus. In this data sample I will present an example of complex embedding, with an overview of any other significant text-level features.

This text deals, in general, with laws of sacrifice and priestly function, and is broken up into six shorter units of differing topics. It

---

29. This is true of such a large number and variety of texts, that it can serve almost as a rule of thumb.

30. One could deny them both, of course, but would be hard pressed to explain these features in a more satisfying manner. The data demand an even more streamlined description than what we propose here, if the present explanation be rejected.

belongs to the first section of Leviticus which deals with sacrificial laws—it is difficult to say whether this section extends from the beginning of the book through to the beginning of the narrative section in chs. 8–10, or from the beginning of the book to the beginning of the 'Holiness Code' in ch. 17, with chs. 8–10 being an interpolation.[31] The initial boundary of our data sample is marked by a Narrative History speech formula, accompanied by a topic shift; it follows a summary statement of the material covered in the preceding paragraph. The terminal boundary of our sample is marked in a similar fashion, and will be discussed in greater detail below.

The material is set into a Narrative History framework, where it is recounted that Moses was commanded by God to command the people (and here we have the Hortatory text-type, which uses command forms, and wc + Suffix clauses for the main line) to do certain things. Each of these units is introduced by a verbless clause beginning with זאת:

The Narrative History and Hortatory introduction:

וידבר יהוה אל־משה לאמר	6.1.1 (Heb.)
צו את־אהרן ואת־בניו לאמר	6.2.1

the topical 'paragraph headings':

זאת תורת העלה	6.2.2
[ו]זאת תורת המנחה	6.7.1
זה קרבן אהרן...ביום המשח אתו	6.13.1
זאת תורת החטאת	6.18.2
וזאת תורת האשם	7.1.1
[ו]זאת תורת זבח השלמים...	7.11.1

the topical summary:

זאת התורה לעלה [ו]למנחה ולחטאת	7.37.1
ולאשם ולמלואים ולזבח השלמים	

and the Narrative History and Hortatory closure:

אשר צוה יהוה את־משה בהר סיני ביום	7.38.1
צותו את־בני ישראל להקריב את־	
קרבניהם ליהוה במדבר סיני	

---

31. For our purposes this mention of the larger structure of Leviticus will suffice; none of the details presented in the material which follows hinges on concerns of this sort.

These features make it clear that we should consider this section a single larger unit, for the final sentence (7.37.1–7.38.1) summarizes each of these verbless clauses, then recapitulates the Hortatory, and the Narrative History, settings into which this material is set. The narrative summary is, in fact, a conclusion to the first part of Leviticus, for it looks back to the opening statements of the book, giving a specific time reference and topic content, which can be traced only to 1.1, and refers to the material contained in the intervening chapters as 'bringing offerings', that is, summary of the whole by lowest common denominator.

Like an onion, made up of concentric layers, these Procedural/ Instructional and Hortatory texts are wrapped in Expository (the הז clauses) material, then in Hortatory, then Narrative History, layers. The hearer's 'way into' this text is by way of *story-telling*, which recounts a situation in which Moses was *commanded* to *explain* to the Israelites, *what they must do*, this latter material being the bulk of the text and taking the form of instruction and exhortation. This should not appear exaggerated, since the 'lexical cohesion' of the bracketing of this text substantiates fairly well these hypotheses.

5. *Parallel Pericopes from Exodus*

Our next texts for consideration are found in the parallel accounts of the building of the Tabernacle. The first account, Exodus 25–31, is set in the context of Moses receiving instructions on how the Tabernacle is to be built;[32] the second account, chs. 35–40, is given the form of a historical account of how the building of the Tabernacle *was accomplished*. We will look at only a sampling of these texts on the building of the tabernacle; a brief analysis will be sufficient for our purpose, which is to mount a comparison between the Narrative History text-type and the Procedural/Instructional text-type. In addition, we will take another look at the question of nature of the Expository text-type.

I have organized the material into 'pericopes' (sections exhibiting a certain semantic cohesion), in the following manner:

32. For a synoptic presentation of these two sets of texts, see 'Appendix Two: Exodus Texts Compared in Columnar Format', together with a colour-coded sample of this material (pericopes B and C), in my PhD dissertation, which is the basis of this book (University of Edinburgh, 1993). Owing to the limitations of printing these are not included here. An alternative, though in my opinion inferior, methodology for marking different clause-types has been suggested in this volume (Chapter 3).

Pericope	Narrative History Text	Instruction Text	Semantic Contents
A	37.1-9	25.10-22	The Ark
B	37.10-16	25.23-30	The Table
C	37.17-24	25.31-40	The Lampstand
D	36.8-34	26.1-30	The Structure of the Tabernacle
E	36.35-38	26.31-37	The Veil
F	38.1-8	27.1-8	The Altar of the Burnt Offering
G	38.9-20	27.9-19	The Court

The sequential order of the first set of texts (Exod. 25–27) will be followed here; this will displace some pericopes of the second set from their own literary sequence.[33] I will move somewhat freely back and forth between the texts and the Historical Account Procedural/ Instructional texts, commenting from time to time on the two as a set of 'parallel texts'.

My goal is to test the hypotheses constructed from our first examinations of data on these texts from Exodus. I will not, in this section, go much beyond reconfirming the main-line clause-type of these text-types; there will be occasions where the text throws up difficult passages, but for the most part we will have to leave these sections unattended to here (though I will comment on how the theory we are working with here would attempt to resolve these problems, or will point the way toward other possible solutions).[34]

33. I make no claims for the chronological precedence of one or the other set of pericopes (although the first [Instructional] set does appear from certain indications to be the earlier version), these concerns being largely irrelevant to the present inquiry. My decision to follow the order of the first set is more or less arbitrary, conditioned in part by the temporal relationship between the contents of the two sets, and the real-time construction of the Tabernacle.

34. The reader may well challenge me on this point—am I not just avoiding unaccomodating data? My response to this challenge is that I am proposing a detour around concerns that require more information than this text has yet been able to present. This study has never had as its goal a thorough-going description of Hebrew macro-syntax, but hopes rather merely to *initiate* the process by illustrating some very basic concepts; we will not be able to return during the present study to solve all these problems. This, too, may sound escapist. However, the purposes of this study are sufficiently broad that I will not be able to fine tune each of my identifiable text-types, in addition to presenting the assessments of other works, and the presentation of linguistic principles, theory and methodology. Such a finetuning would require further substantiation—especially as regards the finer details of each text-type—than

Our analysis of the text begins with the question of initial and terminal boundaries of the pericopes. This series of pericopes shifts abruptly from one topic to the next, and tends to mark pericope boundaries semantically rather than macro-syntactically; it does not exhibit much macro-syntactic paragraph indication (of the sort that we observed in the text of Judg. 2), that kind of indicator being largely unnecessary here, owing to explicit topic-shifts.

Since the subject matter (rather than the text-type itself), requires the inclusion of a fair number of 'measurements', we find that the Expository text-type (which focuses on 'state' rather than 'action') is often embedded into the Procedural/Instructional material and the Historical Account, as a mechanism to incorporate the measurements into the main text.[35]

We will look first at Pericope D,[36] since it is the longest of the pericopes in our selection. The Historical text has 43 clauses; the Procedural text has 51. Three clauses of the Procedural text are represented by non-clausal elements in the Historical text (26.11.3 and 26.11.4 → 36.18.1b; 26.24.4 → 36.29.3b), while one clause in the Historical text is represented by a non-clausal element in the Procedural text (36.25.1a–26.1-2 → 26.20.1g–21.1l). The remaining additional clauses in the Procedural text are not represented at all in the Narrative text.

The Historical text is relatively unexceptional, apart from a higher proportion of x + Suffix clauses[37] than we might normally expect (exactly one third of the non-subordinated clauses, and only one fewer than the wc + Prefix clauses without היה). We will return to this feature later to examine its possible significance.

There is a significant break in the pericope between vv. 13 and 14, which is marked by this pericope's only wc + Prefix clause with היה (36.13.3—ויהי המשכן אחד); this clause is followed by a clear topic shift

---

space permits if I am to present a taste of the linguistic systems under examination. At the end of the day, the reader will, I hope, concur with me: the material omitted from discussion will be minimal—though, I grant, not inconsequential—in contrast with that with which we will actually engage.

35. As was pointed out in the preceding chapter, the concept of embedding is central to this approach to the language; it is advisable that the reader understand this principle well before going further into the data, for it will feature highly in this chapter and the next.

36. 36.8.1–36.34.3; 26.1.1–26.30.2.

37. Where 'x' represents any clause element(s) coming before the verb; cf. Niccacci, *Syntax*, p. 13, *et freq.*

(from the curtains of linen to the curtains of goats' hair), and can therefore be said clearly to mark a paragraph boundary. This is consistent with the function of such היה clauses in other Narrative History texts (cf. Judg. 2).

There is another interruption of the more common forms at verses 29 and 30, where three non-subordinated Prefix < היה clauses occur—this distribution is remarkably similar to the peak-marking devices we saw in our earlier, Narrative History, text-samples.[38]

36.29.1	והיו תאמים מלמטה
2a	ויחדו יהיו [mlt Mss, היו] תמים
b	על־ראשו אל־הטבעת האחת
3a	כן עשה לשניהם לשני
b	המקצעת
30.1a	והיו שמנה קרשים ואדניהם כסף ששה
b	עשר אדנים שני אדנים שני אדנים
c	תחת הקרש האחד

Verbless clauses are 9, in total (21% of non-subordinated clauses), and occur in three clusters of three clauses each. Each cluster comes after the introduction of a new topic (i.e. an item is reported as made, then described by measurement; the details of manufacture and/or installation follow),[39] and, in fact, since there are only the three topic shifts in this pericope, the verbless clauses add directly to the macro-syntactic identification of new paragraphs. This format is repeated in a large number of the pericopes in our material.[40]

---

38. I follow the proposed emendation in 36.29.2 from יהיו to היו; the 'ketib' is easily explained as a borrowing from the form in the parallel text (26.24.2), and that יהיו resembles closely the preceding, clause-initial, ויחדו. One might wonder why the making of the two frames for the rear corners of the Tabernacle should be considered the peak event of the episode, yet a very plausible case could be made for exactly this—for this *is* the last set of instructions concerning the building of the Tabernacle itself, rather than its furnishings.

39. 36.8.1, topic shift from the contributions for building, to the construction of linen curtains, followed by three verbless clauses (36.9.1-3);

36.14.1, topic shift to goat's hair curtains, followed by three verbless clauses (36.15.1-3);

36.20.1, topic shift to the boards for the Tabernacle, followed by three verbless clauses (36.21.1-2, 36.22.1).

40. I concede that it is 'logical' to find such descriptive material where we do, and that we are not required to posit macro-syntactic significance in order to justify

The Procedural text shows similarity to other texts of the same text-type. It, too, shows the same slightly higher percentage of clauses with Prefix forms of verbs other than היה as did the Historical text just examined.[41] This is not surprising, for where there is clause-to-clause correspondence between the two pericopes,[42] only the following 4 (or 5) clauses render their material with a change of syntax as well as form:

ואת־המשכן תעשה עשר יריעת שש משזר	26.1.1
ותכלת וארגמן ותלעת שני	
ויעשו כל־חכם־לב בעשי המלאכה את־	36.8.1
המשכן עשר יריעת שש משזר	
ותכלת וארגמן ותלעת שני	
חמש היריעת תהיין חברת אשה אל־אחתה	26.3.1
ויחבר את־חמש היריעת אחת אל־אחת	36.10.1
וחמש יריעת חברת אשה אל־אחתה	26.3.2
וחמש יריעת חבר אחת אל־אחת	36.10.2

and,

כן יהיה לשניהם // לשני המקצעת יהיו	26.24.3-4
כן עשה לשניהם לשני המקצעת	36.29.3

Verbless clauses appear to have the same function of marking topic shifts as do those in the parallel, Narrative History, text.

Clauses with היה appear to mark boundaries (26.6.3; and 26.11.4 and 26.13.1), and may mark peak events (26.24.1-4—again it would appear that the completion of the structure of the Tabernacle is marked as the peak event).[43]

---

its presence; but equally good logic can be summoned for their distribution elsewhere in the text, where they might have no macro-syntactic function. The fact that their presence in the text at this particular juncture can be tied to other facets of the text than its macro-structure does not negate the possibility of macro-syntactic significance, and merely underscores my presupposition of the interrelatedness of many different ways of approaching text-level features.

41. Non-היה clauses: wc + Suffix clauses occur 17 times and comprise 35% of the non-subordinated clauses; x + Prefix clauses, 13, and 26%; verbless clauses, 10, and 20%.

42. 42 clauses—97% of the Historical text, and 82% of the Procedural text.

43. A possible exception to this is 26.3.1 (noted in the preceding table), which may mark the beginning of action in the pericope, or may not. It is an odd clause: its

Looking at other pericopes in this material continues to confirm our hypotheses, and we will see in our analysis of Pericopes A through C, below, the same general patterns we have seen elsewhere. We look first at Exod. 37.1.1–9.3; 37.10.1–16.3; and 37.17.1–24.1. These exhibit macro-syntactic patterns similar to those discovered in the Judges 2 text and in Exod. 36.8-34 (Pericope D).

Pericope A (37.1.1–9.3), the description of the building of the Ark, has 22 clauses, which are distributed as follows:

> 10 of these are wc + Prefix clauses (of which one is a clause with היה);
> 9 are verbless clauses;[44]
> the remaining three are Suffix clauses (of which one is with היה).

The pericope ends with a sequence of 6 clauses off-line (37.7.2–37.9.3); the only other off-line clauses are three groups of verbless clauses (37.1.2-4; 37.3.2-3 and 37.6.2-3). The layout of this pericope is as follows: the opening clause (wc + Prefix) introduces the topic, the building of the Ark; this is followed by the measurements of the Ark (3 verbless clauses) and eight clauses describing the various processes involved in the building of the Ark, interrupted by two putative verbless clauses, which may serve to separate the construction of the Ark itself from the construction of the various secondary features of it; the section concludes with seven off-line clauses which have to do with the placement of the cherubim. The initial and terminal boundaries of this pericope are clearly marked by off-line clauses, and off-line clauses may also serve to articulate an internal structural division.

היה existential statement is followed immediately by another clause, a verbatim repetition of the first, minus the היה form. The same thing occurs in the parallel text (36.10.1-2), where the wc + Prefix form of הבר is transmuted into the Suffix form (both finite forms replace the participles found in the Procedural text); this is less strange, in that it does not require comment as a macro-syntactic feature at the basic level with which we are now working, but it, too, is curious.

44. 37.3.2 and 37.3.3 contains material that could be considered appositional phrases, and which do not stand on their own as full clauses, but which I have chosen to consider full 'verbless clauses', largely because they are introduced by the copula (which suggests that they be taken as on a par with other sequential clauses). If we accept them as full clauses their presence here may mark a division between the construction of the Ark itself and the construction of the items associated with it. If we accept them as appositional phrases the structure of the pericope is simplified, and verbless clauses appear only at the beginning and end of the pericope. From the standpoint of macro-syntax, I find the latter preferable, but owing to microsyntactic considerations, I am more comfortable with the former.

The distribution of the 17 clauses in Pericope B (37.10.1–16.3) is as follows:

> 10 wc + Prefix clauses (none with היה);
> 3 are non-subordinated verbless clauses;
> one is a Suffix clause with היה;
> three more are subordinated, two of these being verbless, and one
>   containing a Prefix form.

The pericope ends with two subordinated clauses (37.16.2-3). The ten wc + Prefix clauses are broken in only two places—with three verbless clauses (37.10.2-4) at the initial boundary of the pericope, and with a subordinated verbless clause followed by a Suffix < היה clause (37.13.3–14.1); here again, the off-line clauses appear to mark a 'paragraph division'.

In Pericope C (37.17.1–24.1), we find 16 clauses. Here, however, we find a very different distribution of clause-types:

> there are 10 verbless clauses (two of which include a participle);
> there are four Suffix clauses (two of these with היה);
> and there are two wc + Prefix clauses.

The chiastic structure here is unmistakable. One might be inclined to see this pericope as artistically structured to highlight the central clause,[45] but there is little logic—and I, to date, have seen no precedent—for such an intensive highlighting. It is no doubt cleverly devised, and no doubt the central clause *is* being highlighted, but this explanation alone is unsatisfactory. The placement of these clauses is fascinating:

17.1	1	wc + Prefix clause עשה	A
17.2	1	Suffix clause < עשה	B
17.3	1	Suffix clause < היה	C
18.1	1	Verbless clause, with Ptc. < יצא	D
18.2–21.2	8	Verbless clauses	E
21.3	1	Verbless clause, with Ptc. < יצא	D'
22.1	1	Suffix clause < היה	C'
23.1	1	wc + Prefix clause < עשה	A'
24.1	1	Suffix clause < עשה	B'

---

45. 37.19.2: כן לששת הקנים היצאים מן־המנרה, 'thus [it was] for the six branches going out of the lampstand'.

Our theoretical base suggests the possibility that the group of 'static' clauses (the two היה clauses, and the ten verbless clauses,[46] 37.17.3–37.22.1)—as an embedded Expository unit, with its own aperture, body of material, peak statement, and closure, inserted into an otherwise unexceptional narrative history text. This also produces a much more streamlined ('elegant') description.

Returning our attention to the larger text, we will find it helpful to look at these counts from a different angle, to get a bird's-eye view of the clause distribution. The clause distribution chart opposite shows, in a condensed form of my previous charting technique, the clause count of Pericopes A through C; as in the earlier chart, the main-line clauses are in the left-hand column, non-subordinated off-line clauses are in the center, and subordinated clauses are in the right-hand column.[47]

There are 85 clauses in these five pericopes, of which 37 are wc + Prefix clauses with verbs other than היה. This may seem like a severely weakened 'Narrative History', with so few main-line clauses, but an alternative view of this distribution gives results more in line with expectations of this text-type. If we regard clusters of verbless clauses and היה clauses as embedded 'Expository' material, the clause counts regain some equilibrium.[48] From our tally of Narrative History, non-subordinated off-line material, we may then exclude those sections where two or more of these 'Expository-type' clauses occur in sequence,[49] and find this distribution:

37   13   4

---

46. The latter of which Longacre proposes to be the main-line clause-type for expository texts (Longacre, *Joseph*, pp. 111ff.; 'Perspective', pp. 88-89).

47. I have included in this chart, for the sake of comparison, the clause counts of 37.25.1–38.8.2 (two pericopes, 31 clauses; the first pericope has 12 clauses, the second, 19). Although I will not examine them in depth, this glance at their structure gives an idea of the kinds of forms that predominate in these contiguous texts.

48. This may seem dangerously close to 'doctoring the data', but the reader must permit me, at least temporarily, this hypothesis. Other material will be presented, in due course, which will help to substantiate this position.

49. A moment's consideration of these sections of the data (31 clauses) will show that they tend to be corroborative descriptive material, and are only loosely tied to the main-line material. The exclusion of the data from these clause-counts is intended merely to show more clearly the similarities between these pericopes and other 'Narrative History' texts; we still recognize the text-level function of intrusive material (it serves to highlight a break in the text, or a peak), even if we seek to identify the text-type of that material.

	wc + P (ML)	Other (OL)	Sub
Pericope A	1		
		3	
	3		
		2	
	4		
		2	
	1		
		6	
Pericope B	1		
		3	
	6		
			1
		1	
	3		
			2
	1		
Pericope C	1		
		1	
		1	
		10	
		1	
	1		
		1	
(Exod. 37.25.1–37.29.1)	1		
		4	
		1	
	2		
		1	
	3		
(Exod. 38.1.1–38.8.2)	1		
		4	
	1		
		1	
	2		
		1	
	5		
		1	
	1		
			1
Clause Totals	37	44	4

Clause Distribution Chart

This is what we would *expect* to find in such a text, and the explanation given of embedding satisfies both logic and theory.

However, we find *considerable* mixing of clause-types in these pericopes; and although there is sufficient presence of wc + Prefix clauses to warrant proposing that these texts are related in text-type to the Judges 2 'Narrative History' that we examined earlier, we need to consider another option as well. Longacre writes that

> procedural/instructional discourse looks very similar to predictive. Both, for instance, have a mainline which consists of *waw*-consecutive perfects. But while in predictive discourse imperfects can occur both in VSO clauses to mark a secondary storyline and in NV clauses [Noun–Verb clauses] to mark an action/event relative to a noun, in procedural discourse the imperfect occurs only in NV clauses.[50]

What does he mean? Another look at the matrix of text-types will elucidate the question:

	+ Agent Orientation	– Agent Orientation	
	NARRATIVE	PROCEDURAL	
	Prediction	How-to-do-it	+ Proj.
+ CTS	———	———	
	Story	How-it-was-done	– Proj.
	BEHAVIOURAL	EXPOSITORY	
	Exhortation Promisory Speech	Budget Proposal Futuristic Essay	+ Proj.
– CTS	———	———	
	Eulogy	Scientific Paper	– Proj.

If 'Predictive discourse' (which I prefer to call the 'Narrative Prediction' text-type, to preserve its close ties with Narrative History) is so similar to the Procedural/Instructional text-type that they share, for example, main-line clause-types, then it is possible that our 'Historical' text is not an example of the 'Narrative History' text-type, but rather of a related one. It stands to reason that, if Narrative Prediction and Procedural/Instructional text-types are similar, then

---

50. Longacre, 'Perspective', p. 183.

Narrative History and 'Procedural/Lab Report' (as I shall call it) may likewise differ in no more than subtle ways.

It is worth juggling the idea, then, that both of these Exodus texts may be, in fact, Procedural—the one being the Procedural/Instructional, the other being Procedural/Lab Report, text-type.

The set of parameters from Longacre's theoretical base provide us with a means to analyse the 'deep-structure' differences between the two texts. The most obvious of these is *Projection*: one text puts the doing of these things into the future, and, therefore, according to Longacre's terminology, is 'plus', with reference to 'Projection', whereas the other text places the doing of these events in the past, and is therefore 'minus,' with reference to 'Projection' (cf. chart on p. 138):

Parameter	Exod. 35–40	Exod. 25–31
Projection	–	+

The texts of instructions are clearly 'minus Agent Orientation' and therefore Procedural, or Expository; the second set of texts be 'plus Agent Orientation', as the agent/actor is mentioned by name on more than one occasion (Exod. 35.30-35, 36.1, 37.1, etc.), or it, too, may be 'minus Agent Orientation', as the agent/actor references are very few, and the sense of the text does not hang in any way on interplay between the agent/actor and event (as it so clearly does in 'pure' Narrative History).

Parameter	Exod. 35–40	Exod. 25–31
Projection	–	+
Agent Orientation	+ (–)	–

On the other hand, it can be said with confidence that both sets of texts are 'plus' with reference to 'Contingent Temporal Succession'; that is to say, both texts emphasize a certain 'following on' from one event to the next: one thing leads to another, and each event tends to be connected in some way with its (immediate) predecessor. Thus, we have:

Parameter	Exod. 35–40	Exod. 25–31
Projection	–	+
Agent Orientation	+ (–)	–
Contingent Temporal Succession	+	+

or, to return to Longacre's matrix:

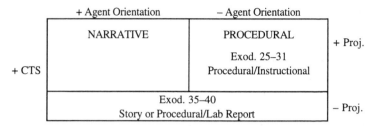

So then, we have two sets of texts, the texts from Exodus 25–31 are clearly

 + CTS / – Agent Orientation / + Projection, or '*Procedural/Instructional*',

and the texts from Exodus 35–40 are either

 + CTS / + Agent Orientation / – Projection, or '*Narrative History*',

or they are

 + CTS / – Agent Orientation / – Projection, or '*Procedural/Lab Report*'

The jargon of the preceding paragraphs is a technical way of saying that—in addition to being nearly identical at the micro-syntactic, lexical and semantic levels—Exodus 25–27 and Exodus 35–38 are a 'minimal' pair of texts[51] which belong to different (yet very similar) linguistic text-types, and that we see here two sets of texts whose very few differences are largely traceable to their *difference of text-type*. This pair of texts allows us to examine text-type differences without the confusions of working with unrelated texts.

Yet another possibility that we must consider is that Hebrew does not significantly distinguish the Narrative History text-type from the Procedural/Lab Report text-type. In a majority of languages studied to date by linguists, these two text-types are distinguished from one another by language-specific features[52]—and it may be that the same is true of Classical Hebrew. Likewise, it may be that in Classical Hebrew these text-types form a 'porte-manteau' category (two halves folded into one), where both receive the same encoding treatment.[53]

---

51. Or perhaps, what is termed an 'analogous pair', in which the differences between the two compared items are not so great as to throw doubt on the analysis, but are slightly greater than the single difference required for the term 'minimal pair'.

52. In English, for example, the Procedural/Lab Report text-type relies heavily on passive forms, which are rare in Narrative History.

53. There is ample precedent for the coalescing of two logical categories into one

Our data here present no conclusive evidence with regard either to the text-type identification of these 'Historical' texts or to the question of whether the two text-types under discussion are differentiated in the surface-structure of Classical Hebrew. (The differences observable between other Narrative History texts and the texts under discussion here may be occasioned by stylistic factors, for example; but we may yet find that these two different text-types[54] encode their information with subtle differences in choice of clause-types, as Longacre proposes with reference to Narrative Prediction and Procedural/Instructional texts.)

With the current state of research, however, we must content ourselves simply to note the similarity between these 'Historical' pericopes with the material we examined from Judges 2, and to note that if these texts are evidence that Hebrew *does* distinguish these two text-types, then we must conclude that it does so at a fairly subtle level. Further research on this question will permit us to comment on this issue with greater confidence. We may proceed in spite of this insecurity, however, to gain as much ground as we can at this early stage in our description, for little in the way of further text-linguistic description in this volume will be hindered by the relative insecurity of these particular observations.

The consistent similarity to each other of the two columns requires little further comment. The texts in the two columns are very nearly identical. Apart from certain lacunae (at both the word- and the clause-levels), there are few changes in vocabulary, and only minimal changes in syntax. In the samples given (pericopes A through G), the Exodus 25–31 account contains 191 clauses (of which 46 are omitted from, or replaced by non-clausal elements in, the other), and the Exodus 35–40 account contains 161 clauses (of which 16 do not occur in the Exod. 25–31 account).

'less logical' one—one has only to look at the verbal 'themes' of Classical Hebrew, where the nine-cell chart has two 'holes', whose functions are adopted by other forms. Despite these holes, the language continued to function without apparent difficulty. In English the Hortatory/Exhortation text-type often overlaps with the Procedural/Instructional text-type, due to socio-linguistic patterns of mitigation—we exhibit a reluctance to frame exhortations to bluntly, and often modify our presentation of them to 'tone down' their bluntness.

54. That is, different at a deep-structure level.

Historical material	both accounts	Procedural/Instructional
alone		material alone
16	145	46

These clause totals do not require closer attention; they represent the same kind of shifts and omissions that were commented upon above, in the notes on Pericope D.

Before we leave the Exodus texts, we will examine one more pericope (the others included in the appendix provide no new surprises). Pericope G[55] begins as one would expect, given the data we have so far surveyed, with a 'wc + the appropriate conjugation' clause, and is marked as well by a topic shift (to 'the court of the Tabernacle'). The terminal boundaries of the two texts are marked by topic shifts.

The exceptional feature of this pericope is that these are the only clauses with finite verbs; all others are verbless clauses. In the future-oriented text the *only* distinctive feature of the remaining clauses is that two of them contain participles (27.16.1 and 27.17.1); the same is true of the historically-oriented text (here the corresponding clauses occur in the opposite order—38.17.4 and 38.18.1). These texts are clearly neither Narrative History (or Procedural/Lab Report) nor Procedural/Instructional; following clues from their semantic content and their macro-structure, we are led to conclude that we have here another instance of an embedded Expository text (cf. Longacre's matrix).

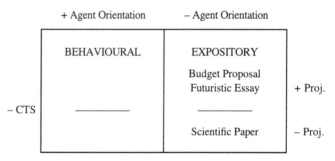

The proposed 'embedded Expository texts' from Pericope C can be added to these data, and some conclusions can be ventured, based on the kinds of things we have seen in other text-types.[56] These texts are,

55. 27.9.1–27.19.1 and 38.9.1–38.20.1.

56. Owing to the small amount of data currently reviewed, I offer these only as a tentative working hypothesis, although I do not believe they will require much

in my view, clear representatives of the Expository text-type. Although long stretches of this text-type are not frequent in the Hebrew Bible, the text-type is seen frequently as smaller pieces embedded in other text-types.

The main-line clause-type of this text-type appears to be the verb-less clause, and its principal off-line clause-types, x + Participle clauses, and clauses with finite forms of היה (which identify, where necessary, the temporal reference ['plus- ' or 'minus- Projection'] of the material)—our data so far have shown us only x + finite forms of היה, and I would suggest that clauses with wc + finite forms of היה will be even less common, for they move further away from the stative sense of the main-line clauses.[57]

In the preceding pages we have examined a variety of texts, and

alteration as more data is processed. The existence of this as a logical, 'notional' (deep structure) category, attested often enough in other languages to qualify as a language universal, and the fact that this text-type is encoded in relatively consistent ways in other languages, permits us to 'borrow in' the category for the description of Classical Hebrew, despite the limited amount of data available for analysis. We accept this 'borrowing in,' as a working hypothesis, looking to language universals for possible characteristics, and we rely on the data 1) to deny us this hypothesis; 2) to force us to admit that our data are insufficient to the task of proving or disproving the hypothesis; or 3) to confirm the existence of the category proposed. Leaving out this text-type considerably complicates our description, where including it as a feature of the language enables us to formulate a more elegant description.

57. On the clause-types one can expect in Expository texts, Longacre writes: '...it is sufficient to note that as the inverse of narrative discourse (and to some degree of predictive as well), expository discourse can be defined as discourse in which the most static verb forms of a language predominate and have the highest ranking. For this reason, elements at the bottom of the clines for Narrative, Procedural, and Hortatory discourse (cf. Chapters 3 and 4) have the highest ranking in Exposition.

'Thus the nominal (verbless) clause is the static clause par excellence. Clauses with *yēš*, 'there is', and *'ên* 'there isn't', (also the negative of nominal clauses) have about the same ranking as nominal clauses. Clauses with copulative uses of *hāyâ*, 'be', rank a step lower; by virtue of having any sort of verb at all they are not as completely static as verbless clauses. Possibly, clauses with stative/denominative perfects rank next; these verbs are essentially adjectival in function. Below all of these rank clauses with participials [i.e., participial clauses]—since these encode activities in whatever discourse type they are found. Finite verbs rank lowest... Not that the sort of clauses that predominate in expository discourse are the typical stuff, for example, of Setting in narrative paragraphs. Clearly, what is off-the-line in narrative is on-the-line in exposition' [Longacre, *Joseph*, pp. 111-12].

these have shown us at least three text-types: Narrative History, Procedural/Instructional, and Expository. Other text-types which have been hinted at, but which we have not yet examined are Narrative Prediction and Hortatory; in addition, a possible Procedural/Lab Report text-type may come into play in the 'minus Projection' texts of the Exodus pericopes we looked at.

In the next chapter, we will continue our examination of macro-syntactic features, and will apply our theory and methodology in the analysis of a complete text to test our initial working hypotheses, and the hypotheses derived from this chapter's analyses. In brief, these latter are:

1. The main-line clause-type of the Narrative History text-type is the wc + Prefix clause-type; its off-line forms are wc + Prefix clauses with היה, Suffix clauses, and verbless clauses, with or without Participles.

2. The main-line clause-type of the Procedural/Instructional text-type is the wc + Suffix clause-type; its off-line forms are wc + Suffix clauses with היה, Prefix clauses, and verbless clauses, with or without Participles.

3. The main-line form of the Expository text-type (whether '+ Projection' or '– Projection') is the Verbless clause; '+ or – Projection' will be indicated in this text-type by some of its off-line clauses (those with finite verbs will show the temporal orientation of the texts); its off-line clause-types are verbless clauses with Participles, clauses with היה, and clauses with other finite verbs.

4. A shift from the main-line clause-type to an off-line clause-type is indicative of a break in the flow of the text; this can serve three functions (though usually not all three at the same time): (a) to indicate the introduction of background information; (b) to signal a change of scene; and (c) to indicate the peak event, most important fact, and so on, of the text.

5. Texts may be embedded in other texts; just as a Participle can 'fill the slot' or 'perform the function' of *Subject* in a clause (e.g. '*Typing* is fun'), so also can a Verb Phrase, or Sentence (e.g. '*To be or not to be* is not the only question'), that is, items from the next lower structural level are the expected constituents of a construction, but items from other levels may in fact be the constituents.

6.   Material of one text-type may be imported into another by means of embedding; the embedded material becomes part of the incorporating unit in the same way as does any other functional part of that unit. The identity (e.g. the text-type) of the embedded material is not altered by the embedding process.

Chapter 5

JEPHTHAH AND RUTH—REFINING AND TESTING THE HYPOTHESES

1. *Introduction*

In this chapter, I will present two texts in detail (Judg. 10.6–12.7, 'the Jephthah story', and the book of Ruth), building on observations made in the last chapter, with the intent of working our way towards a balanced presentation of Hebrew macro-syntax, as descriptive of what is seen in the data.

My main purpose, as I turn to the Jephthah story, is to underline a principle which will be received with scepticism by some hebraists, and which, therefore, will require more thorough explanation. The principle is this: Features that are characteristic of specific text-types will be found in material of that text-type, whether in Reported Speech sections or not.[1]

To this end we will look at the non-subordinated narrative, and compare it to five Reported Speech sections of the Jephthah story. Here I will be confronting directly Niccacci's thoughts on this passage, for he comes to very different conclusions from my own. We will need to till the soil fairly deeply in this section—moving slowly in order to prepare the ground upon which to work in the analysis which follows.

We will also need to wrestle once again with the principle of embedding; many of the examples of individual text-types that I identify in the analyses that follow occur in combination with other text-types, and unless the concept of embedding is well-understood, the reader will not be able to judge accurately my results and proposals. Here again we will move at a fairly deliberate pace.

When we have completed our examination of the Jephthah story's

---

1. As is asserted by hypothesis 6 (see previous page).

Narrative History sections, which will serve to illustrate and clarify certain theoretical points, we will turn to the book of Ruth. Here I hope to leave aside, as much as possible, apologetic and explanatory material about theoretical issues, in order that we may examine a single text with all our tools at hand, to see what results.

2. *The Jephthah Story: Judges 10.6–12.7*

2.1 *The Main Narrative*
In the Jephthah story, we will look first at the patterns found in non-subordinated narrative (chiefly those created by the shifts away from the main line), and will then focus our attention on the selected sections of Reported Speech. This material will permit us to examine the Narrative History text-type in Reported Speech, to see whether, in fact, it does obey different rules, as Niccacci claims.[2]

I have found it most helpful thus far to arrange these clauses in the format described for Judges 2 in ch. 4, with subordinated material set apart from un-subordinated, and 'narration' set apart from Reported Speech. This gives us the following distribution of the clauses[3] in this story (see next page).

A large proportion of the text is Reported Speech (54%);[4] this is, in fact, fairly standard in Hebrew Narrative History.[5] It is common to accomplish a large proportion of the story-telling by recording the interaction of the participants.

In early parts of a Narrative History, however, the scene is being set for what follows, and Reported Speech is not used[6]—we will look at this again in the 'Jephthah Story' at a later point, and will examine the role of Reported Speech in much greater detail in the book of Ruth.

---

2. §§28 (p. 49) and 75 (pp. 102ff.), esp. p. 107.

3. A total of 228 clauses, not including the elliptical clause proposed for 11.13.2; this 'empty' clause is proposed on the basis of the fact that the clause that 'follows it' is syntactically subordinated, and requires something to be understood: ויאמר מלך בני־עמון אל־מלאכי יפתח [...] כי־לקח ישראל את־ארצי..., 11.13.1, [2], 3. This empty clause does not figure in any of the clause counts presented.

4. See chart, following page.

5. Cf. Ruth, where 56% of the clauses are Reported Speech; see chart below in this chapter (p. 176).

6. This is the most fitting explanation for the relative lack of reported speech in Judg. 1, and especially, 2—it is introductory to the remainder of the book, and as such its job is not so much to describe *events* as to establish *setting*.

D	C	B	A
(subordinated rep'd speech)	(un-subordinated rep'd speech)	(subordinated narration)	(un-subordinated narration)
42 clauses	80 clauses	7 clauses	99 clauses
19%	35%	3%	43%
Reported Speech		Narration	
54%		46%	

As with most of the Judges stories, the boundaries of this pericope are marked primarily with semantic features: most often the report of the death of a particular judge marks the end of one pericope, as is the case in this instance (12.7.2-3); and the inception of a new section is marked either by the introduction straightaway of a new judge (if the judge's reign is dealt with only cursorily [e.g. Shamgar, 3.31]), or by the formula, 'And the people [again] did evil in the eyes of YHWH' (e.g. Gideon: ויעשו בני־ישראל הרע בעיני יהוה [6.1]), as in this case (10.6.1, with אסף). There is no heavy macro-syntactic marking, since the pericopes are clearly distinguishable on the basis of semantic content.[7]

With the borders of our passage thus secured, we will first examine so-called 'narration' (that material which is not related as Reported Speech). Distribution of the clause-types in this material is shown below:

(Column B)	(Column A)	(Column A)
Subordinated Clauses	Non-main-line Clauses	Main-line Clauses
7	18	81

The total of these clauses is 106, the percentages being 6.6%, 17% and 76.4%, respectively. The clause-type distribution for non-subordinated, non-Reported-Speech clauses (column A in the 'columnar' text) is:

wc + Prefix	81
wc + Pref of חיה	6
Suffix	5 (3 negated)
Suffix of חיה	2
Verbless Clauses	3
Clause with אין	1
Prefix	1[8]

---

7.   It may be that this identification by contents rather than by syntax is merely a matter of the author's choice, and therefore 'stylistic'; on the other hand Classical Hebrew may betray a preference for one or the other of these across the board, or in certain contexts. No strong pattern has emerged from the data so far evaluated.

8.   Since these figures total 99 clauses, the percentages are self-evident.

This indicates once again a decided preference for wc + Prefix clauses to tell the story. The thread of wc + Pref forms in column A is broken by eighteen clauses (not counting subordination and Reported Speech), producing 12 breaks in the main line of the story—most of these clauses occur singly, but at three places the off-line clauses occur in 'clumps',[9] forming the major hinges in the story.

Following macro-syntactic clues (with minimal reference to other [e.g. semantic] clues), we can make the following outline of the story, as it is told by the clauses in Column A.

1			10.6.1–18.4	Introduction
	1.1	/*	10.6.1-4	General Introduction: Israel's apostasy
	1.2		10.7.1–18.4	Specific Introduction: YHWH's response, and Israel's oppression
2			11.1.1–12.7.3	Jephthah's Life
	2.1	**/	11.1.1–3.4	The Introduction of Jephthah
	2.2		11.4.1–33.2	Jephthah and the Ammonites
	2.2.1	*/	11.4.1-2	The Ammonites Wage War on Israel
	2.2.2	*/*	11.5.1–28.2	Jephthah's Defence
	2.2.3	**/	11.29.1–33.2	Jephthah's Offence
	2.3		11.34.1–40.1	Jephthah's Daughter
	2.3.1	****/	11.34.1–38.2	Jephthah's Daughter— the Victory Sacrifice
	2.3.2	*/***	11.39.1–40.1	Jephthah's Daughter Returns
	2.4		12.1.1–7.3	Jephthah and the Ephraimites
	2.4.1		12.1–5.1	The Conflict
	2.4.1	*/*	12.5.2–6.7	The Aftermath
3			12.7.1-3	Concluding Formula

Outline of the Jephthah Story

9. These occur at (1) 11.1.1-2 (2): ‏והוא בן־אשה‏ // ‏ויפתח הגלעדי היה גבור חיל‏
    ‏זונה // ויולד גלעד...‏
    (2) 11.34.2–35.1 (4): ‏ורק היא יהידה // אין־לו ממנו בן‏ // ...‏והנה בתו יצאת‏
    ‏או־בת // ויהי כראותו אותה // ויקרע את־...‏; and
    (3) 11.39.5–40.1 (3): ‏מימים ימימה‏ // ‏ותהי־חק בישראל‏ // ‏והיא לא־ידעה איש‏
    ‏תלכנה בנות ישראל... // ויצעק איש...‏

The asterisks in the chart mark non-subordinated off-line clauses: '*/' indicates one off-line clause at the beginning of a section, '/**' indicates two off-line clauses at the end of a section, and '*/**' indicates one off-line clause at the beginning, and two at the end, of a section).

There is nothing very new about this division of the text, based on its macro-syntax and its semantic content; it is a fairly standard outline of the unit. The significant point is that the macro-syntax points to the same structure as do other features of the text.[10] I will comment only briefly on the more important features of this text.

I have mentioned above breaks in the stream of main-line clauses; I have specifically mentioned, so far, only those places where the main line is broken by off-line, non-subordinated clauses.[11] I will shortly be looking as well at breaks in the main line created by subordination and by Reported Speech. First, however, we return to the question of off-line clauses in column A.

These clauses have a distribution similar to those we looked at in Judges 2; that is, those which occur singly appear to indicate minor paragraph breaks; those that occur in larger blocks appear to indicate a major break, or a peak in the episode. Applying this observation to the text at hand, we find that there are 9 such 'minor breaks', and (as previously mentioned) 3 'clumps'.

These are found in the text as follows:

10.6.4	neg'd Suffix cl.	end of intro. to the Jephthah history
11.1.1-2	Subj. + חיה cl. verbless cl.	introduces Jephthah episode
11.4.1	ויהי + N Phr	introduces episode of Jephthah and Ammon
11.5.1	ויהי + sub'd cl.	introduces (embedded) episode of the Elders of Gilead and Jephthah
11.28.1	neg'd Suffix cl.	concludes episode of Jephthah's messages to Ammon
11.29.1	ותהי + Subj. + PrepPhr.	introduces episode of Jephthah's battle with Ammon

---

10. Scholars have long followed both guidelines in constructing outlines of their texts; I am not claiming anything that has never before been noticed—rather I am trying to collate it into a new form of description.

11. I.e. remaining within the confines of 'Column A' in our formatted text.

11.29.4	Suffix cl.	concludes 'aperture' section of episode of Jephthah's battle with Ammon
11.34.2–35.1	והנה + Ptc. cl. Verbless cl. אין cl. ויהי + InfPhr.	marks peak event (the appearance of Jephthah's daughter)
11.39.1	ויהי + PrepPhr.	introduces closure section of (embedded) episode of Jephthah's daughter
11.39.4-5	Subj. + Neg'd Suffix cl. ותהי + NPhr	concludes closure section of episode of Jephthah's daughter
12.5.2	והיה + sub'd speech fmula	introduces 'Shibboleth' episode
12.6.4	neg'd Prefix cl.	concludes 'Shibboleth' episode

The deployment of these clauses is not uniform; for example, there is no off-line clause (or series of them) at the end of ch. 10, where we might expect one, to indicate that the 'introduction' has ended and the 'main episode is about to begin. This should not be perceived as a failure of the system; such features as lexical and participant strings suggest such a division even where no off-line clauses are employed.[12] Yet this is not the final word on the matter; other features (such as subordination, Reported Speech, and longer stretches of main-line clauses) also contribute to the 'text-map' given to the reader/hearer.

Subordination from the main-line (or rather from 'Column A') occurs only 7 times in this story. In the previous chapter, I examined the distribution of subordinated clauses and strings of clauses, in the texts under study, and commented on the possibility of a text-level function for subordinated material.[13] Here again, the distribution of subordinated clauses arouses suspicion, for they occur only at boundary or peak sections:

---

12. Cf. my comments on Judges in the previous chapter, and on the Exodus pericopes, where episodes are not distinguished so much macro-syntactically as semantically.

13. This is not surprising at a logical level—subordinated clauses constitute, by their very nature, a break in the main line of the text-type. It is not inconceivable that they serve here, in Narrative History, as do היה clauses, for example, to alter the rhythm of the text to indicate a 'high point' or a juncture in that text.

10.8.3-4   '...all the people of Israel, אֲשֶׁר were beyond the
           Jordan in the land of the Amorites, אֲשֶׁר is in Gilead'
11.5.2   'And when (כַּאֲשֶׁר // וַיְהִי) the Ammonites made war',
11.28.2   'the message of Jephthah אֲשֶׁר he sent to him'
11.39.4   'according to the vow אֲשֶׁר he had made'
12.4.4   'for (כִּי) they had said, "..."'
12.5.3   'And when (כִּי היה ...) any of the fugitives of
           Ephraim said, "..."'

The first two clauses (10.8.3-4), and the next (11.5.2), form part of
the aperture sections of the episodes in which they occur. 10.8.3-4
may seem a bit too distant from the first clauses of the section to be
considered 'aperture', but examination of the flow of this episode
indicates that the action of the section is contained in the Reported
Speech (YHWH's message to Israel—10.11.1–14.4—is the peak
moment of the episode); the clauses in question occur in the build-up
to that action, rather than being part of it. 11.5.2 likewise is part of
the build-up section of its episode.

The next two clauses occur at the end of their respective episodes:
11.28.2 concludes the episode of Jephthah sending and receiving messages from the King of Ammon; 11.39.4 is part of the closure of the
episodes about Jephthah's daughter.

The remaining two subordinated clauses bracket what appears to be
the peak clause of the final (and post-peak) episode of the Jephthah
story, which clause reads וַיִּלְכֹּד גִּלְעָד אֶת־מַעְבְּרוֹת הַיַּרְדֵּן לְאֶפְרָיִם 'And Gilead
took the fords of the Jordan against Ephraim' (12.5.1). The peak (in
terms of the modern reader's interest is usually considered to be the
Ephraimites' dialect betraying their identity, but *syntactically*, the
marked peak is the geographical detail.[14] It is understandable that our
attention be drawn more vividly to the material that follows, with its
fascinating revelation of contemporary Hebrew dialectal phonology,
than to this section—but the warfare and victory against Ephraim (in
particular, the taking of the fords of the Jordan), may well have been
the more significant detail for the contemporary reader.[15]

Another reading of this would be to consider this sequence of
clauses (12.4.1–5.3) a rather complicated initial boundary marker for

---

14. 12.5.1.

15. I grant that, had the phonological detail no interest value for the original
reader, it would not have been included. I maintain, however, that it is more on the
line of 'added colour' than 'peak event'.

this episode. This appears to me less likely, as this section, and other Judges material studied to date, tends toward simplicity, rather than complexity, for boundary marking.

A case may be made for seeing this section as focusing on the detail of the pronunciation of שִׁבֹּלֶת; this is done more by default than by intention, it would seem, since it is accomplished by discounting the significance of the taking of the fords. Most commentators write at length on the linguistic security procedures employed at the fords of the Jordan, but little mention is made of the actual taking of the fords, except to remark that the taking of the fords was a measure taken to cut off the retreating Ephraimites.[16] Boling's comments, however, are instructive:

> The account of Ephraim's expedition against Jephthah sustains the implicit comparison of Jephthah and Gideon (7.24–7.3). Gideon's problem with the Ephraimites stemmed from his being a west bank judge who had become an east bank feudalist. Jephthah's problem with the Ephraimites no doubt stemmed from his east bank prominence and the consequent threat to Ephraim's prior west bank influence within the confederation. Given the widespread devastation and power vacuum which Abimelech created in a few years at Shechem, it is not surprising that the center of early resistance to the Ammonite challenge shifted to Gilead, with tribal politics taking on a whole new configuration.[17]

This underlines the geographical importance of this victory, which is hinted at in the macro-syntax of the text. Webb writes:

> The diplomacy of vv. 1-3 was superficially like that between Jephthah and the Ammonites, but with significant differences. The same applies to the report of the battle, only here the contrasts are more striking than the similarities. This time there is no mention of divine charisma, nor does Yahweh give the victory. Indeed, as far as we know Yahweh is not involved in any way. This battle is not presented as a holy war, but with wry humour as a rather squalid tit-for-tat feud. The Gileadites answer the taunt of the Ephraimites ('you are fugitives of Ephraim', 4e) by putting them to inglorious rout and thereby making them the *true* 'fugitives of Ephraim', (v. 5)—פְּלִיטֵי אֶפְרַיִם again. The pronunciation test of vv. 5-6 adds a further sardonic touch to the scene. The tactic of seizing the fords of the Jordan (v. 5) previously used to such effect by Israelites against Moabites (3.27-30) and by Israelites against Midianites (7.24-28) is now

---

16. Cf. Martin, *The Book of Judges*, p. 148.
17. Boling, *Judges*, pp. 213-14.

used by Israelites against Israelites. The slaughter is prodigious (v. 6). The intertribal feud under Jephthah is part of a thematic development (progressive internal disintegration) which reaches its climax in the civil war involving the whole of Israel at the end of the book (chs. 19–21).[18]

I find both hypotheses convincing—on the one hand, that these off-line clauses bracket the peak *clause*; and on the other, that they merely introduce the whole episode—but not equally so. I favour the former, for the reason (in addition to that cited above) that, while both hypotheses are justifiable on the basis of plot structure, the former has the added merit of conforming more closely to expected macro-syntactic behaviour: we have seen that single main-line clauses flanked by off-line clauses tend to stand out as the peak clause of a unit.[19]

Reported speech also appears to serve a sort of text-level function. The developing and releasing of tension in a story, for example, can be described as a curve like that of a camel's hump. At the aperture of an episode, the tension has not been introduced; at the closure, the tension has (in theory, at least) been resolved—thus, at both ends of the curve there is little tension. At the peak, the tension is at its highest.

The techniques for creating, maintaining, or resolving tension in a story are language-specific. A feature which is commonly used for increasing tension in the story would, very likely, be out of place at the end of a story (and therefore might be placed there intentionally by the word-smith, or avoided altogether). So, those things which have a function in developing the story-line in a particular way are generally distributed according to a discernible plan.

In Classical Hebrew, Reported Speech tends to function as a *tension-maintaining device*. So, for example, in Judg. 10.6-15, once the stage is set, and a certain amount of tension has been created,[20] Israel and YHWH have a conversation.[21] The end result of this conversation is

18. Webb, *The Book of Judges*, p. 72.

19. For example, at Judg. 2.18.4; we have seen similar features in other text-types as well, in our examinations of Leviticus and Exodus texts; see ch. 4 above.

20. The apostasy of Israel and their subjugation (10.6.1–9.2), though a formulaic theme in the book of Judges, nevertheless introduces a significant tension to the story-line.

21. Verses 10-15; we will return shortly to look at the Reported Speech material of this section in greater depth.

recorded in the seven main-line clauses that follow: Israel puts away its foreign gods, and YHWH's heart is turned again to them. But they are still under oppression—and the Reported Speech device is employed again to *maintain the tension* during the transition to the next episode: 'Who is the man who will fight for us? He shall be our chief'. This maintaining of tension is reiterated by the use of a question introducing a new topic—the quest for a leader.

Reported Speech serves this purpose of maintaining tension throughout the text.[22] It is used extensively to detail the several obstacles Jephthah must overcome in his life: the rejection by his people is highlighted in 11.1-10; the intractability of the King of Ammon in 11.12-27; the stark exigency of his vow to YHWH, and its outcome in 11.30-31 and 11.35-38; the aggression of the Ephraimites in 12.1-3 and 12.4-6. In most of these cases little is added which has not already been recounted on the main line of the story, or which will not be retold on the main line at a later point.

Conversation exhibits a tendency to bracket peak events.[23] I cannot yet afford to make a solid proposal about this, as the data offer too little evidence for such conclusions. We will, however, encounter the same concerns as we look at more data. The reader may find this hypothesis less suspect after our examination of Ruth.

Before moving away from the text we have been examining, I would like to make another tentative observation: it would appear that 'aperture' and 'closure' sections of text have an affinity for unbroken chains of main-line clauses. The opening 'Israel and YHWH' section, 10.7.1–18.4 (1.2 in the outline above), opens and closes with stretches of these main-line clauses, as do 11.1.1–3.4 (2.1.1 'Jephthah's Early Life'), 11.29.1–33.2 (2.1.4, 'Jephthah's Offense') and 12.1.1–6.7 (2.3,

---

22. We will look at this feature only in passing here, but will return to it again in our analysis of the book of Ruth. It is worth noting in passing, at this point, that the book of Jonah *ends* with Reported Speech, which seems to vitiate my hypothesis that it has a text-level function. Yet, if we hold to our idea that it maintains tension over transitional sections of text, we can propose that the unusual occurrence of Reported Speech at the end of Jonah actually serves to strengthen the purpose of the book—it leaves the reader hanging—the final resolution is, in a sense, the reader's/hearer's own responsibility. The point of the tale is hammered home all the more firmly by this lack of resolution of carried-over tension.

23. Cf. the treatment, above, of the subordinated clauses 12.4.4 and 12.5.3, both of which, in fact, introduce Reported Speech sections.

'Jephthah and the Ephraimites'). The story as a complete unit in itself likewise opens, and is concluded, with sequences of main-line clauses (10.6.1-3 and 12.7.1-3). In addition, other episodes conclude with stretches of main-line clauses although their apertures are handled differently: the subsections (embedded narratives) of 'Jephthah and the Elders' (11.11.1-3), 'Jephthah's Daughter Goes to the Hills' (11.38.3-5), and 'Jephthah's Daughter' (11.39.2-3).

One section of text does not fit this pattern: 12.4.1-3. The sequence of clauses here is followed immediately by the two subordinated clauses (which may mark the peak of this episode), and therefore is not likely to be episode-marginal. This entire section raises difficult questions, and I hesitate to draw any conclusions from it.

2.2 *Narrative History in Reported Speech*

In this section I will present five samples of Reported Speech. For the sake of simplicity I have restricted the data we will examine to Narrative History texts in Reported Speech. The conclusions I reach in this brief section will be applied to other text-types in Reported Speech when we turn to the analysis of Ruth.

Judges 12.2.1–3.6

This text is actually the last, sequentially within Judges, of the five we will examine; it is, however, also the least difficult. The text is presented, below, like most of the other sample texts, in a format that permits comparison between *narration* and *Reported Speech*, on the one hand, and between *subordinated material* and *non-subordinated material*, on the other. Columns A and B, on the right hand side of the page, contain narration, that is, material that is *not* Reported Speech; the left half of the page contains columns C and D: Reported Speech material. In each of these two halves, the right-hand column contains non-subordinated material, and the left, subordinated.[24]

---

24. Owing to formatting restrictions of this volume, Column B is not fully independent of Column A, nor is Column D of Column C. This should, however, occasion no difficulties.

	D	C	B	A	
			ויאמר יפתח אליהם		12.2.1
	איש ריב הייתי אני ועמי ובני־				2a[25]
	עמון מאד				b
	ואזעק אתכם				3
	ולא־הושעתם אותי מידם				4
	וארא‌ה				3.1
כי־אינך [אין] מושיע					2
	ואשימה נפשי בכפי				3
	ואעברה אל־בני עמון				4
	ויתנם יהוה בידי				5
	ולמה עליתם אלי היום הזה				6a
	להלחם בי				b

The speech formulae, in this as in all other Reported Speech units examined in this book, are included as part of those units. In an instance such as we have above, the text reported to have been spoken is an embedded direct object of the verb of speech; the direct object 'slot' may be filled by anything from a single word or particle (e.g. 12.5.7-8 ויאמר לא) to a fully developed, complex text (e.g. 11.15.1–27.3—43 clauses—we will examine this in depth after dealing with the shorter texts). Therefore the above quotation from Judges is but a single, complex sentence. (The same could be said of vast sections of the Pentateuch, where whole series of chapters are introduced by a single speech formula [thus making the series of chapters merely an embedded Direct Object of the speech formula]; however, beyond acknowledgement that this is, indeed, the case, there is little to be gained from considering such sections as single clauses.) This text contains, apart from its speech formula, 9 clauses:

1 Subordinate clause with אין	12.3.2
3 Suffix clauses	12.2.2 (with היה), 12.2.4 (negated);
	12.3.6 (in an interrogative clause)
5 wc + Prefix clauses	

In examining Reported Speech sections, we must be on the lookout for clues as to why the text was spoken; this gives us our principal clues

---

25. Where a single clause spans more than one line in these charted texts, the device 'a', 'b', and so on will be employed to so indicate; this will be true as well of clauses which span more than one verse (cf. Judg. 11.39.6–11.40.1, one clause which spans four lines).

for analysing the 'constituent structure' of the text. In this case, we may say that Jephthah is repudiating the right of the Ephraimites to challenge his behaviour—the final clause reads: ולמה עליתם אלי היום הזה להלחם בי, 'Why then have you come up against me this day, to fight against me?' The earlier material is his justification for his choice not to request Ephraim's help; he accomplishes this by explaining the historical background of that decision. This historical background is presented in an embedded Narrative History text.

Internally, the Narrative History text is composed of two episodes: the first is a description of the circumstances in which Jephthah found himself (12.2.2-4), the second, his response to those circumstances (12.3.1-5). The boundary between the two episodes is marked by the negated clause (12.2.4), and the repetition of that material in the sentence ואראה כי־אינך מושיע // (12.3.1-2).

The most significant point here is that *there is nothing out of the ordinary about this Narrative History text*. It opens, as do many Narrative History texts, with the stage-setting device of a היה clause;[26] its boundaries are marked by the same sort of features as we have noted in other Narrative History texts. This begins to call into doubt the conclusions voiced by Niccacci on Judges 11: that somehow 'narrative discourse' has a different shape to it from narrative proper.[27]

Judges 10.10.1-4
We move now from the last sequentially, of our sample texts, to the first. This one is brief, but still permits analysis:

	ויזעקו בני ישראל	10.10.1a
	אל־יהוה לאמר	b
חטאנו לך		2
וכי עזבנו את־אלהינו		3
ונעבד את־הבעלים		4

---

26. We will see the same device employed in the book of Ruth on more than one occasion. Logic as well gives us a rationale for such a function and device: do we not say that a story has to 'start somewhere?' We expect a story to start with some kind of anchor into space and time—this kind of anchor is provided by such things as Verbless, and היה, clauses—and if such a setting slot were filled by an embedded text of more than one clause in length, we would expect it to be an Expository one, which has as its main line just such clauses.

27. Niccacci, *Syntax*, pp. 102ff.

The formulaic opening is one of a sequence of main-line, wc + Prefix forms, and requires no particular comment. The content of the Reported Speech is a text of three clauses.

Let us, for the record, describe this unit in terms of its constituents; we have:

an Intransitive Clause:[28]

DirObj   ויזעקו בני ישראל אל־יהוה לאמר

with the following construction:

PredComplement ← IndObj ← Subj ← Predicate,

where

> Pred = Finite Intransitive Verb
> Subj = NounPhr
> IndObj = PrepPhr
> PredComplement = InfPhr,

and

> InfPhr = Infinitive + DirObj,

and, finally,

> DirObj = Embedded Narrative History Text.

10.10.3-4 is an embedded Narrative History text, filling the Direct Object slot in the speech formula. The second clause in this embedded text begins with a wc + Prefix form, but the first begins with כי, which *must* be clause-initial; so the verb form in this first clause (and therefore the clause-type) must accommodate it—this is the only reason we need to seek for the Suffix clause replacing a wc + Prefix clause.[29]

Here we have an embedded three-clause historical unit, in which the first clause gives the general material, and the two remaining give the

---

28. It may seem odd, at first blush, that I consider a verb of speech 'Intransitive', for I am arguing that the speech material is an embedded Direct Object of the speech verb; yet in this case the speech material is the Direct Object of the infinitive לאמר, *not* of ויזעקו; the latter is the defining feature of the main clause, and its syntax defines it here as an Intransitive verb.

29. We are, of course, speaking of non-entities; there is no 'wc + Prefix clause', and therefore we can only posit that it 'would otherwise have been there'. It is clear, however, that if it 'wanted' to be there, it nevertheless could not be there, owing to the restrictions placed on the clause by the subordinating conjunction.

specific reason for the statement of the first. The latter two give, first, the specific reason with regard to YHWH, and second, that reason with regard to other gods.

Judges 10.11.1–14.4

YHWH's response to the speech we have examined above comprises 12 clauses (including the speech formula). The speech formula is a transitive clause (in this case, without the Predicate Complement = Imperative), where the Direct Object slot is filled by an embedded text. The text itself is rather complex:

ויאמר יהוה אל־בני ישראל	11.1
הלא ממצרים ומן־האמרי ומן־בני	2a
עמון ומן־פלשתים	b
וצידונים ועמלק ומעון לחצו אתכם	12.1
ותצעקו אלי	2
ואושיעה אתכם מידם	3
ואתם עזבתם אותי	13.1
ותעבדו אלהים אחרים	2
לכן לא־אוסיף להושיע אתכם	3
לכן	14.1
וזעקו אל־האלהים	2
אשר בחרתם בם	3
המה יושיעו לכם בעת צרתכם	4

YHWH's response begins with a question (an elliptical one, at that). Questions are features only of Reported Speech in Classical Hebrew narrative, and seem to play a part in the establishment of participant roles, and the like. There seems to be an element of protest, scorn, condescension, and/or anger, to rhetorical questions in our data; their purpose appears to be to establish the order of precedence and deference between speaker and addressee, as well as to highlight to the address information that the addressee should take (or should have taken) into account.[30]

30. Each instance of rhetorical questions in the Hebrew Bible will need to be analysed in terms of its sociolinguistic setting (inferior → superior, equal → equal, superior → inferior, to name but a few of the possible settings we might have to deal with in this sort of description), the degree of intensity of communication, the text-type of the material (if any) which follows the rhetorical question, the position of the rhetorical question in the Reported Speech, and many other issues. The nature of the topic precludes us from examining it even briefly during this study, though we are

The purpose of our text is essentially that of exhortation:

לכו // וזעקו אל־האלהים // אשר בחרתם בם // המה יושיעו לכם בעת צרתכם‏[31]

The reason for this exhortation is that YHWH will no longer deliver them (לכן לא־אוסיף להושיע אתכם, 'Therefore I will deliver you no more', 10.13.3); and in turn the reason for this state of affairs is that YHWH had delivered them but they have turned away from him to serve other gods. This latter section is expounded by a Narrative History text of five clauses' length.

This Narrative History text is introduced by a Suffix clause (providing, along with the rhetorical question preceding it, a setting for the text that follows), and a second episode of it is signalled by another of the same. This text presents us with no surprises. We can, therefore, divide it into its constituent parts:

Judges 10.11.1–14.4:

Speech Formula (a main-line NH cl.)		ויאמר יהוה אל־בני ישראל	11.1
NH text Aperture?		הלא ממצרים ומן־האמרי ומן־ בני עמון ומן־פלשתים‏[32]	2a b
NH text		וצידונים ועמלק ומעון לחצו אתכם	12.1
		ותצעקו אלי	2
		ואושיעה אתכם מידם	3
		ואתם עזבתם אותי	13.1
		ותעבדו אלהים אחרים	2
	Narr. Prediction Text	לכן לא־אוסיף להושיע אתכם	3
	Hortatory Text	לכו	14.1
		וזעקו אל־האלהים	2
		אשר בהרתם בם	3
		המה יושיעו לכם בעת צרתכם	4

We have not so far looked at Hortatory text types—for the time being, however, they will occasion little comment, for two reasons: (1) their

impoverished for our lack of understanding of its functions and purposes.

31. 'Go // Cry to the gods // whom you have chosen // Let them deliver you in the time of your distress'.

32. This section of text poses some textual difficulties, but they need not delay us here; I have already stated my intention to bypass rhetorical questions in the current study.

simplest features are relatively obvious—they are composed of
cohortatives, imperatives and jussives, on the main line, with Prefix
forms running close to the main line; their off-line clauses would
require greater attention, but since we are not looking yet at any
longer texts, this can be postponed; and (2) this text-type is
considerably influenced and shaped by the sort of sociolinguistic
factors that I mentioned above in reference to rhetorical questions—
deference to one of higher rank, for example, precludes the use of
command-forms, and such mitigation can have a variety of nuances.[33]
This will be yet another area that we must leave relatively unexplored,
although where the data require us to give this issue our attention, we
will do so. The lack of in-depth attention to this text-type will not
seriously hinder us, however; I will rely on Longacre's 'Verb Rank
Cline' for this text-type[34] to provide us with working hypotheses, and
will deal only cursorily with questions of mitigation.

Judges 11.7.1-5
This short text also contains an embedded Narrative History text.

11.7.1   ויאמר יפתח לזקני גלעד

הלא אתם שנאתם אותי	2
ותגרשוני מבית אבי	3
ומדוע באתם אלי עתה	4
כאשר צר לכם	5

Its introductory formula is unexceptional and requires no extended
comment. The opening clause is again a rhetorical question about
historical fact; it is followed by a wc + Prefix clause. Another rhetorical question with a subordinated clause concludes the Reported Speech.

Despite my disclaimers above about rhetorical questions, I will toy
with them a little here. If we were to render the first rhetorical
question as a statement, the result would be 'you hated me'—or

---

33. Longacre writes, 'The presence of mitigation (making a command more
mollified and socially acceptable) and deference (e.g., of commoner to monarch)
make the analysis of hortatory discourse the more difficult' (*Joseph*, pp. xif.); he
devotes 21 densely reasoned pages to an examination of this concern (ch. 5,
pp. 119-40). It is well beyond the limits of this study to 'unpack' and render that
material here. I will content myself with the occasional elucidation from other data.

34. I will do the same for the Narrative Prediction text-type (which Longacre calls
Predictive).

perhaps, more emphatically (acknowledging the nuance of the negative structure of the rhetorical question), 'you hated me greatly' (perhaps with an infinitive absolute construction in Hebrew?)—in any case, a simple statement of a past event.

The second rhetorical question, however, would require a more complex structure: the resulting unit would be either a Narrative Reason Paragraph (to use Longacre's terminology: 'You come to me now, because...'), or a Narrative Result Paragraph ('You come to me now, in order to/that...').[35]

Thus, I consider 11.7.2 to be a Narrative History clause, turned inside out to express annoyance, or superiority, or some other such nuance. It serves the purpose of introducing the historical setting (and first event) of a brief Narrative History text.

Judges 11.15.1–27.3

This text-sample contains 43 clauses (with a short and unexceptional introductory speech formula); Niccacci has examined this in *Syntax*, and makes a number of observations—I will take exception to some of these, and concur with others.

First, however, we will examine the data for ourselves; later, we will return to compare our findings with Niccacci's.

11.15.1	ויאמר לו
2	כה אמר יפתח
3a	לא־לקח ישראל את־ארץ מואב ואת־
b	ארץ בני אמון
16.1	כי בעלותם ממצרים
2	וילך ישראל במדבר עד־ים־סוף
3	ויבא קדשה
17.1a	וישלח ישראל מלאכים אל־מלך
b	אדום לאמר
2	אעברה־נא בארצך
3	ולא שמע מלך אדום
4	וגם אל־מלך מואב שלח
5	ולא אבה
6	וישב ישראל בקדש

35. This sort of 'back-formation' gives us a clearer idea of the underlying structure of the unit; however, due to the tentative nature of such analyses at the present time, these results will not be used as the basis for further speculation.

וילך במדבר	18.1
ויסב את־ארץ אדום ואת־ארץ	2a
מואב	b
ויבא ממזרח־שמש לארץ מואב	3
ויחנון בעבר ארנון	4
ולא־באו בגבול מואב	5
כי ארנון גבול מואב	6
וישלח ישראל מלאכים אל־	19.1a
סיחון מלך־האמרי מלך חשבון	b
ויאמר לו ישראל	2
נעברה־נא בארצך עד־מקומי	3
ולא־האמין סיחון את־ישראל	20.1a
עבר בגבלו	b
ויאסף סיחון את־כל־עמו	2
ויחנו ביהצה	3
וילחם עם־ישראל	4
ויתן יהוה אלהי־ישראל את־	21.1a
סיחון ואת־כל־עמו ביד	b
ישראל	c
ויכום	2
ויירש ישראל את כל־ארץ	3a
האמרי יושב הארץ ההיא	b
ויירשו את כל־גבול האמרי	22.1a
מארנון ועד־היבק ומן־המדבר	b
ועד־הירדן	c
ועתה יהוה אלהי ישראל הוריש את־	23.1a
האמרי מפני עמו ישראל	b
ואתה תירשנו	2
הלא+++++תיריש	24.1
+++ את אשר יורישך כמוש	2a
אלהיך אותו +++	b
+++++ אותו נירש	3
+++ ואת כל־אשר הוריש יהוה	4a
אלהינו מפנינו +++	b
ועתה הטוב טוב אתה מבלק בן־צפור	25.1a
מלך מואב	b
הרוב רב עם־ישראל	2
אם־נלחם נלחם בם	3
בשבת ישראל בחשבון ובבנותיה	26.1a
ובערעור ובבנותיה ובכל־הערים	b

+++++ שלש מאות שנה	c
+++ אשר על־ידי ארנון +++	2
ומדוע לא־הצלתם בעת ההיא	3
ואנכי לא־חטאתי לך	27.1
ואתה עשה אתי רעה להלחם בי	2
ישפט יהוה השפט היום בין בני	3a
ישראל ובין בני עמון	b

This unit constitutes Jephthah's final message to the King of Ammon, who had ordered Jephthah's people to restore his land to him, accusing them (unjustly, it would seem) of having taken it, on their coming up from Egypt.[36] Jephthah responds in the negative. After the Narrative History speech formula, Jephthah's speech employs another speech formula (a formal one—11.15.2), and is followed by a denial of the accusation (11.15.3) and a justification for that denial (a Narrative History text, embedded within a subordinated clause—11.16.1–22.1); this denial and justification is followed by a summary of the historical justification, and a series of questions and statements on the subject of 'take what your god has given you'. It concludes with a jussive: בני עמון ישפט יהוה השפט היום בין בני ישראל ובין, 'Let YHWH, the Judge, judge this day between the Israelites and the Ammonites' (11.27.3).[37]

There are two negated indicative clauses in this unit, both of which deny the King of Ammon's claims of injustice:

לא־לקח ישראל את־ארץ מואב ואת־ארץ בני־עמון, 'Israel did not take the land of Moab and the land of Ammonites' (11.15.3)

ואנכי לא־חטאתי לך, 'I have not sinned against you' (11.27.1)

These clauses form the aperture and closure of the speech unit; the second of which initiating a closure paragraph, composed of 3 clauses (neg'd Suffix cl., Verbless clause with Ptc. and Jussive clause).

The boundary between the first section (11.15.2–11.22.1) and the second section (11.23.1–11.27.3) is clearly marked: not only is there a shift from wc + Prefix forms to Prefix forms, there is a shift to a

36. 11.13.1-4.

37. This section combines all the difficulties of rhetorical questioning with those of mitigated Exhortation; in short, the body of the second section is awkward. We can analyse the bracketing of this section with the opening of the speech, but any actual identification of the text-type(s) of the second section would be, at best, provisional.

predominant use of the verb root יֵרשׁ, which occurs in this next section six times (in six contiguous clauses).[38] Although other features of the second section of this text could be noted here, my real interest in this passage—for this study—is the first, Narrative History, section of the Reported Speech material (11.16.1–22.1).[39]

The text commences with a quote from the King's message to Jephthah: בעלוֹתוֹ ממצרים, 'In his coming up from Egypt' (11.13.3), becomes בעלוֹתם ממצרים, 'In their coming up from Egypt' (11.16.1). It is followed by 17 wc + Prefix clauses, which are from time to time interrupted by eight off-line subordinated, or Reported Speech clauses. These eight clauses occur in three groups: 11.17.2–17.5, 11.18.5-6 and 11.19.3-4.

The middle group of these three (11.18.5-6—a neg'd Suffix clause, and a subordinated Verbless clause) marks a text division; this division is emphasized by the use of similar events at the initial boundaries of both sections. The first section commences with Israel's arrival at the borders of Edom, and their sending a request to Edom's king, which is refused (11.16.3–17.3); the second takes place at the borders of the Amorites, and commences with their sending a request to their king, which is likewise refused (11.19.1–20.1). These features serve to create two distinct episodes: 11.16.1–18.6, with 15 clauses, and 11.19.1–22.1, with 11 clauses.

The other two groups of off-line clauses each contain a Reported Speech 'request for right of passage' to a king, followed by negated Suffix clause(s). I identify these as the syntactically marked peaks of the two Narrative History episodes.

2.3 Conclusions from Analysis of the Jephthah Story

At no point in my examination of the material in the Jephthah Story have I seen evidence that would lead me to conclude that Narrative History in Reported Speech behaves differently from that in non-Reported Speech, as Niccacci concludes. What little evidence Niccacci

---

38. This latter feature, combined with a shift from, primarily, Prefix forms, to Verbless clauses and Suffix forms, leads me to suspect a subdivision at 11.25.1.

39. Admittedly, I am inclined to see 11.23.1—...הורישׁ ישׂראל אלהי יהוה ועתה, 'And now, YHWH, God of Israel, has given...'—as a hinge that functions both to conclude the first section and to introduce the second, but we will deal with it here as extraneous to the embedded Narrative History text, since it is clearly not to be considered subordinated under the כי in 11.16.2, as is the Narrative History text.

cites in favour of his proposal is more elegantly explained by two, somewhat overlapping, principles.

First, Narrative History texts I have so far examined (and here I am referring not only to those texts in Classical Hebrew) tend to begin with a stage-setting section, in which clause-types that are off-line for Narrative History predominate. This is a normal, and logically justifiable, state of affairs—a story requires background and setting. The only consistent exception to this trend is where the text in question is too short to employ such a device, or where previously introduced material obviates the necessity for such a device.

Second, even where a text might conceivably employ a clause-initial, main-line for Narrative History, wc + Prefix clause, this does not happen. The language prefers to underscore the relationship between the embedded Reported Speech material, and the speech formula into which it is embedded as Direct Object.

This may sound very like what Niccacci has proposed; it is, in fact, radically different. Niccacci proposes that 'narrative discourse' is a different 'type of narrative';[40] I propose that Narrative History texts are formulated according to the same principles whether in Reported Speech or non-Reported Speech—there is no 'different type of narrative' for Reported Speech. Material in Reported Speech *is*, however, subject to restrictions with regard to its initial clause—in order to call attention to the fact of its being embedded—as if to say 'this is not actually the beginning of the clause; rather, it is the Direct Object of another clause'.

3. *The Book of Ruth*

3.1 *Basic Facts and Statistics*
The boundaries of this text are clearly marked. Aside from the obvious ones—the beginning and end of a self-contained book—there are clear macro-syntactic markers. The opening boundary is marked by two ויהי clauses;[41] the terminal one is marked by two verbless clauses and a genealogical appendix (an embedded text of a different type).[42]

---

40. Niccacci, *Syntax*, p. 102.

41. ויהי בימי שפט השפטים, 'In the days when the judges were judging' (1.1.1), and ויהי רעב בארץ, 'there was a famine in the land' (1.1.2).

42. 4.17.4–22.2.

The book of Ruth contains 399 clauses, by my accounting; ten of these form the genealogy at the end of the book. For the percentages given in our discussion, however, I omit these genealogical clauses, giving a working total of *389 clauses.*[43] The distribution of these clauses in the four columns is as follows:

D	C	B	A
(Subordinated Reported Speech)	(Un-subordinated Reported Speech)	(Subordinated Narration)	(Un-subordinated Narration)
74 clauses	146 clauses	13 clauses	156 clauses
(19%)	(38%)	(3%)	(40%)[44]

Reported Speech	Narration
220 clauses	169 clauses
(57%)	(43%)

We will first examine the non-Reported Speech material. After I have commented on the structure and constituents of that portion of the text, I will analyse the Reported Speech sections.

3.2 Ruth—The Non-Reported Speech Text

I will be examining here the interplay between main-line clauses (by which I mean 'main-line for the Narrative History text-type', for which I propose the wc + Prefix clause), off-line clauses, subordinated clauses, and Reported Speech sections.[45] As we have come to expect, these interruptions of the main line are not spread haphazardly through the text, but function as indicators of episode divisions and as peak markers.

Where concentrations of off-line clauses occur, the significance of the break, or of the peak event, is the greater. There are six places in

43. For some statistical purposes, the genealogical clauses would weight the proportions too much in one direction or another; for example, the ratio of main-line clauses to off-line clauses in the main Narrative History would look significantly different if these clauses were allowed to influence it—for example, if we figure the percentage of Suffix forms in the main Narrative History (non-subordinated, non-Reported Speech clauses), the difference is noticeable (4%, calculated with the lesser number; 11%, when calculated with the greater number).

44. Percentages are given in round figures.

45. These last will be dealt with as individual units on pp. 187ff.; here they will be examined only as deviations from the main line of the narration.

the text where concentrations of more than one off-line clause occur (1.1.1-2; 1.2.1-3; 1.4.2-3; 1.22.2–3.1.2, 4 clauses; 4.8.1-4; and 4.17.4–18.1, 2 clauses). If we allow for the possibility that subordination may have some macro-syntactic significance, 3 more clause-groups present themselves (2.3.4–2.4.1, 2 clauses; 2.17.3-4; and 4.1.3-4); in addition, several of the features we are looking at can be found separated by only one or two main-line clauses (e.g. 3.6.1 and 3.6.4).[46]

3.2.1 *Ruth 1.1.1–5.2*

I have already spoken briefly about the initial and terminal boundaries of this text; we now return to look more closely at the initial boundary. As was said above, there can be no question of this not being the initial boundary; however, there is much yet to be said on the nature of this boundary, and its extent.

The text opens with two ויהי clauses (1.1.1–1.1.2). Two ויהי clauses in succession is in itself very unusual. One search of the Hebrew Bible using a CD-ROM data-base indicated 918 occurrences of ויהי.[47] I found, among these 918, only 17 pairs of ויהי clauses in succession (e.g. Job 1.3 and Exod. 12.41), and two triplets (Gen. 39.2 and Josh. 17.1-2). This gives a percentage of less than 4%.[48] This is a very rare feature.

Some of these occurrences are clearly paragraph-initial if not episode-initial (e.g. Ruth 1.1, Gen. 39.2 and Job 1.3); others may either be episode-initial, or they may require to be divided, thus marking one boundary each (initial/terminal). Gen. 27.30 is an example of a 'maybe'—this pair may *initiate* the section wherein Esau seeks a blessing from Isaac (which Jacob has just 'stolen'), or the first of the two ויהי clauses may serve to conclude the previous section, while the second clause opens the following section.[49]

---

46. Rather than list these occurrences here in some kind of indecipherable short-hand form, I will identify them as we come upon them in the text.

47. I make no claim to absolute accuracy with these figures, but I estimate the margin of error to be no greater than 1–2%.

48. There are six ויהי pairs of Gen. 1—the formulaic...ויהי־ערב ויהי־בקר יום—which I have excluded from my examination, rightly or wrongly; if these are added into the count, the percentage is raised to just over 4%.

49. This function appeared fairly frequently among the ויהי pairs which were separated by one or two clauses not containing ויהי (e.g. Gen. 39.10-11), and may be normative, or at least common, for contiguous pairs as well.

In any case, the Ruth passage is unquestionably text-initial, and cannot be a bridging mechanism, as may be suspected of other occurrences of multiple ויהי clauses.[50]

And yet, not only do we have two ויהי clauses here, but they are also separated from six other off-line clauses by only four main-line clauses. 1.6.1 introduces the journey back to Bethlehem, and begins a new section; we can extend this opening section to the end of v. 5;[51] this gives us an opening section of 16 clauses. The ratio of main-line clauses to off-line clauses in 'Column A' of this opening section of Ruth is 1 : 1, whereas the ratio for the remainder of the text is roughly 15 : 2. This opening section clearly does not reflect the standard pattern of clause distribution for Narrative History.

Yet, on a larger scale, this is fairly normal, as has been pointed out above; story-telling usually starts from nothing, and the most basic information must be given at the outset, in order that the hearer/reader can make sense of the text. All but the very shortest of our sample texts have had a sort of 'setting the stage' section at their beginning.[52]

3.2.2 *Ruth 1.6.1–19.1*

The next section—the return to Bethlehem—begins with four main-line clauses, interspersed by three subordinated clauses (1.6.1–7.4), which are followed by a sequence of 58 clauses, interrupted in three places by 31 clauses of Reported Speech, and again by an off-line clause (1.14.5), and by one subordinated clause (1.18.2).

A more detailed look shows the introductory section (1.6.1–7.4) to be followed by the first Reported Speech (Naomi advising her daughters-in-law to return to their own culture and families, 1.8.1–9.2). Three more main-line clauses follow this (the reaction of the daughters-in-law, 1.9.3-5), and two speech sections (their intention to

---

50. I did find, however, one other feature of these clauses which is of interest: in several of the clause pairs I have examined, the first provides general background information, which the second narrows into a specific context (often with a temporal function; cf. 1 Kgs 17.12)—these two clauses are a textbook case of this pattern. How frequently this is the case, however, I cannot yet say. This feature, however, strengthens the case for reading these as inseparable pairs.

51. 1.5.2—the conclusion of the 'death' motif, the first motif of the story.

52. Judg. 2.4.1:...ויהי כדבר מלאך יהוה; Lev. 14.2.1:...זאת תהיה תורה; etc.; the Jephthah story, on the other hand, does not have a *syntactically* marked 'stage', but nevertheless begins with one—see commentary above on Judg. 10.6.1-5.

accompany Naomi, 1.10.1-3, and Naomi's response, 1.11.1–13.6). Another set of four[53] main-line clauses (Orpah's decision to leave Naomi, 1.14.1-4 [or 1.14.1-3]) comes to an end with a Suffix clause: ורות דבקה בה, 'and [but] Ruth clung to her' (1.14.5). This off-line clause marks the peak, in my opinion, of this first episode; either the clause itself is the peak, or it signals that the following interchange between Naomi and Ruth (two speech sections, 1.15.1-3, Naomi reiterating her advice that Ruth leave her, and Ruth's refusal, 1.16.1–17.6) is the peak—this latter is the more likely, I believe.[54] The remainder of the episode contains three main-line clauses, broken by one subordinated clause, which describe the journey itself (1.18.1–19.1, 1.18.2 being the subordinated clause).

The string of main-line clauses, in addition to being interrupted by Reported Speech and a subordinated clause, is broken by a second off-line clause. The first off-line clause, the peak-marking 1.14.5, occurred within the text, the second occurs as the initial boundary of the following section (1.19.2).[55]

Thus the first episode is bounded, initially and terminally, by strings of main-line clauses interrupted by subordination, initially by a clear topic shift, and terminally by the off-line clause marking the initial boundary of the following section. The peak is marked by a Suffix clause.

This is the first instance of Reported Speech in this text, and it will be helpful to explore here its role in Narrative History texts.

Without exception, Reported Speech material can be 'translated' into main-line Narrative History wc + Prefix clauses, but something is lost in so doing. For example, Naomi's first exchange with her daughters-in-law could be re-cast as, 'Ruth told her daughters-in-law to return to their families, and blessed them; and she kissed them and they raised their voices and wept, and refused to go'. Yet to reduce this and the remaining interchanges between these characters to such a

---

53. Or three, if one does not accept the reintroduction from the LXX of 1.14.4—ותשב אל־עמה—whose omission by haplography is easily explained on the basis of 14.3—ותשק ערפה לחמותה—and whose sense and syntax fit easily into the text. Neither their inclusion in, nor their deletion from, the text alters its macro-syntactic structure.

54. I have not come across any obvious Narrative History peaks encoded as off-line clauses; off-line clauses generally serve to *point* to something else.

55. See below.

Narrative History text would shear them of much of their power and nuance. We would fail to capture a sense of Naomi's stoic attitude and bitterness, and of Ruth's deep love and unyielding commitment. Such nuances could not be conveyed in simple Narrative without a laboured proliferation of clauses and relative material—other text-types, however, convey these things better, and can be introduced by way of Reported Speech.

Such a proliferation of clauses in the narration would have the additional effect of 'distancing' these events from the reader/hearer. Reported Speech has the opposite effect—the reader/hearer is deposited, as it were, into the very place and time of the interaction, heightening the 'presence' of the events.

This movement into and out of the interchanges is part of the 'breathing' of the text—part of the increasing and decreasing plot-tension. These moments of immersion in the actual event are vital to the development of characters and plot.

3.2.3 *Ruth 1.19.2–22.3*

This episode, dealing with the arrival of the two women at Bethlehem, begins with the aforementioned off-line clause: ויהי כבאנה בית לחם, 'As they entered Bethlehem', 1.19.2. This is a short episode; after the initial clause, there are one main-line clause (1.19.3), two speech sections (1.19.4-5, and 1.20–21.5—Naomi's interchange with the women of Bethlehem[56]), another, single main-line clause, and the terminal boundary. The terminal boundary is marked by two off-line clauses (a verbless clause, 1.22.2, and a Suffix clause, 1.22.3). The final three clauses summarize the return to Bethlehem, and the last, in addition, points forward toward the next section by indicating that they returned 'at the beginning of the barley harvest'. The summary material indicates that this break concludes not only the most recent sub-section but also the general section which began with 1.6.1, if not the whole of this first chapter.[57]

---

56. The function of this section of Reported Speech appears to be to carry the tension of the 'widowhood' (with all its attendant insecurities in that culture) section into the following section, where Ruth meets Boaz—this is no joyous homecoming, but a retreat toward at least marginal security.

57. The mention of 'Ruth, the Moabite, her daughter-in-law' points to an intentional inclusion of the material in 1.1.1–5.2.

3.2.4 *Ruth 2.1.1–17.3*

This next section of the text likewise has a syntactically marked boundary of two clauses, which, when taken alongside the previous two clauses, form one of the most significant 'hinges' in the story. No other boundary in Ruth (apart from the opening of the book as a whole, and the terminal genealogy) is marked by so many off-line clauses.

These boundary clauses introduce the other main participant of the story, Boaz. The episode is composed of 15 main-line clauses, with 12 Reported Speech sections (in five groups), two subordinated clauses, and one off-line clause.

This episode contains a great deal of Reported Speech material, maintaining the tension created in the main-line clauses (and, of course, contributing to it through the speech contents themselves) through this section and into the next. This gets underway immediately, with two short speech sections on the subject of Ruth going out to glean (2.2.1-4 and 2.2.5-6); it is followed by a section of non-Speech clauses reporting her finding a place to glean. Here, we have four main-line clauses (2.3.1-4), followed by a subordinated clause (2.3.5), which in turn is followed by a Suffix clause beginning with והנה (2.4.1). This והנה + Suffix clause identifies the peak of this episode.[58]

It is followed by three speech sections (2.4.2-3, 2.4.4-5 and 2.5.1-2), one main-line clause (2.5.3), and two more longish speech sections (2.6.2–7.6 and 2.8.1–9.8)—these cover Boaz's exchange of greetings with his workers, his question to his foreman about Ruth, the foreman's response, and Boaz's first words to Ruth. Ruth's response contains two main-line clauses and one speech (2.10.1-2 and 2.10.3-5).

Boaz addresses himself again to Ruth (one main-line clause, 2.11.1, and a Reported Speech section, 2.11.2–12.3); this is followed by two more speech sections (Ruth's gratitude to Boaz, 2.13.1-4, and Boaz's invitation to the meal, 2.14.1-4). A series of six main-line clauses (2.14.5–15.1) describes Ruth's meal.

---

58. This claim is likely to be met with some scepticism. However, the clause marking the peak is not to be equated with the peak itself (the meeting of Boaz and Ruth), which follows, and is expounded in conversation. That this comes so early in the episode is no less understandable: this is a peak without complete resolution, and the tension thereof is carried through the remainder of the story, and is built upon, until the main peak of the episode is reached (the agreement at the city gate between Boaz and the *go'el*).

The episode comes to an end with a speech section (Boaz's instructions to his young men, 2.15.2–16.4), two main-line clauses and a single subordinated clause (2.17.1-2 and 2.17.3—which describe Ruth's gleaning). The Reported Speech material in this episode is concerned mainly with character development. The terminal boundary is marked by a ויהי clause, indicating the measure of her gleaning: ויהי כאיפה שערים, 'And there was about an ephah of barley' (2.17.4).

3.2.5 *Ruth 2.17.4–3.7.7*

The initial boundary of this episode is not syntactically marked, but rather is identifiable on the basis of the previous, off-line, clause, and on the basis of the topic shift from 'gleaning' to 'returning home'. The episode contains 17 main-line clauses, eight speech sections (in three blocks) and four subordinated clauses.

The first seven clauses contain five main-line clauses, broken by two subordinated clauses; these describe Ruth's return home to her mother-in-law. Naomi questions her about her day (Reported Speech: 2.19.1-4); Ruth's response is introduced by a single main-line clause, with a single subordinated clause (2.19.5-6), then the speech formula; the five speech sections that follow (2.19.7-9; 2.20.1.3; 2.20.4-6; 2.21.1-7; 2.22.1-4) recount Ruth's day, and Naomi's amazement. Then follow two main-line clauses describing Ruth's gleaning throughout the harvest, and then two speech sections where Naomi instructs Ruth on the right way to approach Boaz (2.23.1-2; 3.1.1–4.8; 3.5.1-3).

Ruth 3.6.1–7.8 contains nine main-line clauses, and one subordinated clause, and describes Ruth's actions in fulfilling her mother-in-law's instructions.

The Reported Speech material in this section reflects the tension developed in the previous material and hints at a possible resolution.

I am intrigued by the presence of the four subordinated clauses. I am tempted to propose that their presence here serves to underscore the concern with stability and security in this story (a decisive majority of the subordinated clauses in this text occur in sections occurring at home, or in some way connected with economic or domestic security). A wider sampling of material will be necessary however, before any more secure hypotheses may be proposed.

There appears to be no syntactic marking of the peak in this episode, unless we consider the repeated speech formula without change of speaker, in 20.20.4, to be performing this function.[59] Some would make an episode division at 3.1.1, owing to the semantic content, and owing to the fact that the preceding two verses summarize an elapsed period of time. I am not averse to this; the preponderant majority of texts that I have so far examined mark episode boundaries and the like syntactically, but not all. It must be pointed out, however, that the lack of syntactic marking—in a text which has demonstrated a tendency to mark boundaries syntactically— does indicate that the break, if any, is fairly understated.

The end of the episode is marked once again by the following episode-initial ויהי clause.

3.2.6 *Ruth 3.8.1–18.6*

This episode, introduced by another ויהי clause, deals with the night-scene at the threshing floor, and Ruth's return afterward to her mother-in-law. After the opening (temporal) clause, we find two main-line clauses, then a verbless clause with a participle, introduced by והנה. This, I would say, introduces the peak event of the episode.

This is followed by a conversation between Ruth and Boaz (three sections: 3.9.1-2; 3.9.3-6 and 3.10.1–13.9) concerning her redemption; this is followed by two main-line clauses and a subordinated clause, and two Reported Speech instructions to Ruth about her return home (3.14.1-2; 3.14.3; and 3.1.4.4–15.4, both by Boaz). This is followed by Ruth's return, and report, to Naomi (five main-line clauses, 3.15.5–16.1, and three speech sections, the middle one of which is introduced with a main-line clause + subordinated clause + speech formula, 13.16.2-3; 3.17.1-4; and 3.18.1.6). The terminal boundary is once again indicated by the initial-boundary-marking devices of the next episode.

3.2.8 *Ruth 4.1.1–13.1*

The initial boundary here is marked by a Suffix clause. The episode contains seven main-line clauses, interrupted by nine Reported Speech sections, five off-line clauses and two subordinated clauses.

The Suffix clause is followed by a single main-line clause (4.1.2), then a verbless clause with participle (which is introduced by והנה— 4.1.3), a subordinated clause (4.1.4), and a speech section (4.1.5-7). The action continues with three main-line clauses, a speech section and

---

59. This would appear to be the logical peak of the episode, as well. See below.

another main-line clause (4.1.8-2.1; 4.2.2-3; 4.2.4). The participants are all now present at the city gate: Boaz, the *go'el*, and the ten elders of the city.

I do not find it surprising that a clause which I have consistently considered to be a peak-marking device (the והנה + ptc, verbless clause—4.1.3) is found so early in this episode. First, we have seen it used fairly early on other occasions (see commentary above), and secondly, this is the Peak Episode of the entire story; and thirdly, little additional material needs to be added to this episode (additional material which would normally form the 'stage-setting' section of the episode)—any such stage-setting has been accomplished in earlier episodes. The author is free to launch immediately into the peak event. If we propose that this clause-type serves to mark the *opening of the peak scene*, then we can find ample logic for its use where we have found it.[60]

Then follow four Reported Speech sections alternating between Boaz and the *go'el*, fine-tuning the details of the redemption of Naomi and of Ruth (4.1.3–4.10; 4.4.11-12; 4.5.1-2; and 4.6.1-6). The next four clauses are intriguing: a verbless clause (4.7.1); two verb-initial Suffix clauses (4.7.2-3); and another verbless clause (4.7.4, a résumé of the first). These clauses occur at the precise moment of Boaz's receiving the right of redemption.[61]

The mechanisms of peak-marking devices are language specific, as we have noted before. The language may have a preference for saturating the text with verbs (thus increasing the speech of the events), or with adverbials and relative material (thus increasing the detail of the events); it may work to slow down the forward march of events, giving a kind of 'slow-motion' effect to the text. Classical Hebrew appears to have a preference for the latter. Texts marked clearly for peak events show the tendency to interrupt the flow of events, just at the point where the tension is at its peak. It is not surprising to me, therefore, that we find this set of four clauses where we find it.

---

60. In 2.4.1, it begins the scene of Ruth's first encounter with Boaz. In 3.8.1, it begins the scene of Ruth's second (recorded) encounter with Boaz. Both of these scenes are the keys to the building up toward this, the final, key scene.

61. E.F. Campbell, *Ruth* (AB; Garden City, NY: Doubleday, 2nd edn, 1975), p. 148. On the question of whether or not this verse is intrusive—a later addition which does not blend into the surrounding material—see my own notes below.

The question of its integrity in the text could be argued either direction, in my opinion, without impact on our assessment of this section's macro-syntactic function. If it *is* intrusive, it was added in such a way as to serve the purposes of the text admirably well (taking into consideration its effect as a peak marker); if it is part of the original story, its contribution is the same. The question will have to be addressed without reference to its having 'broken up the flow of the text', for that is what it would have been intended to do, whether as an original part, or as an added part, of the text.

The speech of the *go'el* resumes (4.8.1-2), and he performs the ceremony mentioned in v. 7 (4.8.3). The story continues with two speech sections (Boaz addresses the witnesses, 4.9.1–10.3, and the witnesses respond, 4.11.1–12.3); the latter of these two is introduced by a speech formula containing a subordinated clause. The episode concludes with a single main-line clause (ויקח בעז את־רות, 'And Boaz took Ruth', 4.13.1), and a ותהי clause ('and she became his wife', 4.13.2).

3.2.8 *Ruth 4.13.2–17.4*

What follows now in the text is a pair of what may be called 'post-peak episodes'[62] (4.13.2–16.2 and 4.16.3–17.4), whose role is to unravel the tension of the story; they perform the function of a dénouement. The first has no syntactically marked initial boundary, but is identifiable on the basis of the preceding ותהי clause, and on the basis of a topic-shift, from the marriage, to the marriage bed. The second follows another ותהי clause (terminating the first alleged post-peak episode), in which Naomi becomes nurse to her grandson. While both do contain speech sections, they contain a lesser proportion to narrative than we have seen in the major episodes of the story; nor is this surprising if we maintain our hypothesis that conversational material in Hebrew has a tendency to maintain or strengthen tension in the text—the opposite effect of what is desired here.

In the first of these episodes, we find three main-line clauses, then a speech of blessing on Naomi by the townswomen; this is followed by two main-line clauses, in which Naomi takes up the child (4.13.2;

---

62. We need to examine the option that these are not actually separate episodes; this question will be addressed in depth after the present hypothesis has been commented on.

4.13.3-5; 4.14.1–15.4; and 4.16.1-2), and is concluded by the 'Naomi as nurse' ותהי clause (4.16.3).

The second of these contains a speech section, and another main-line clause, and concludes with a verbless clause (4.17.1-2; 4.17.3; and 4.17.4—these acclaim Naomi, name the child, and indicate his significance in history).

It is worth noting that the speech materials in these last two sections are fairly static in nature—even though the first is '+ Projection' and the second is historical, both are concerned more with *state* than with *action*. Further work will enable hypotheses to be constructed with regard to specific tension-building capacities of different text-types.

The question arises as to whether היה clauses that translate into English as 'become' clauses have different macro-syntactic significance. I have strong doubts about this, for the real issue seems to have more to do with the semantic domains of the English words 'be' and 'become' than with the *function* of the Hebrew clause-type(s).

Nevertheless, the question presents itself, and the more so here because the semantic content of the passages in which they are found does not admit altogether readily to their identification as episode-boundary features. In 4.13.1-3 (ויקח בעז את־רות // ותהי־לו לאשה ויבא אליה //, 'And Boaz took Ruth, and she became his wife, and he went in to her...'), for example, the clauses all deal with the same subject, and flow on from one another without looking much like a break of any sort.

And in 4.16.1–17.1 (ותקח נעמי את־הילד // ותשתהו בחיקה // ותהי־לו לאמנת ותקראנו לו השכנות שם לאמר... // 'And Naomi took the child, and laid him in her lap, and became to him a nurse; and the neighbour women gave him a name, saying...) the same thing is the case, although the case becomes stronger here for assigning the ותהי clause the role of episode-terminal boundary indicator. Further work on this verb will give us more freedom to draw conclusions about its various functions.

3.2.9 *Ruth 4.18.1–22.2*

The remaining ten clauses do not require much comment. They conclude the book, as is obvious; they are not of what we have described as the Narrative History text-type. They are introduced by a single verbless clause (4.18.1), which also ties the section (loosely) to the preceding material (by mention of the name 'Perez', also found in 4.12.1).

3.3 *Ruth—The Reported Speech Material*

In this section, I will examine the individual texts embedded, as Reported Speech, into other clauses. I cannot hope to do this justice— each text deserves, if not requires, the same kind of attention we have paid to the other portions of Ruth examined above, and both time and space impose rather strict demands. In addition, not much has been contributed towards description of non-Narrative History text-types in Classical Hebrew. Therefore the scope of the following analyses will be restricted to (1) general identification of text-type(s) involved in each text, and (2) comment on internal structure, where this is possible without undue speculation.

I will go through Ruth from start to finish[63] and will comment on every speech unit, even if only to remark on why I cannot pursue analysis of it at this point. Those sections where analysis is limited by the size of the text, or where the text admits no description without a far greater commitment of energy, will be relegated to footnotes.[64] I will not hesitate in this section to be succinct in, and to forego extended justification of, my analyses of these texts, once the reader has been introduced to my approach to the data.

In each case, clause counts of the texts will include the speech formula, to reiterate the embedded nature of the Reported Speech matieral in the speech formula.

3.3.1 *Ruth 1.8.1–9.2*

Naomi's advice to her daughters-in-law to return to their homes. This is a text of seven clauses: 1 Speech Formula (1.8.1), 3 Imperative (1.8.2-3, 1.9.2), 2 Jussive (1.8.4, 1.9.1) and 1 Subordinated (Suffix) (1.8.5).

1.8.1	ותאמר נעמי לשתי כלתיה
2	לכנה
3	שבנה אשה לבית אמה
4	<Q> יעשׂ יהוה עמכם חסד
5	כאשר עשיתם עם־המתים ועמדי
9.1	יתן יהוה לכם
2	ומצאן מנוחה אשה בית אישה

---

63. Though it is strongly tempting to analyse these texts by grouping them first according to text-type, this approach, and its attendant benefits, must await a less restricted study.

64. Eleven such sections will be addressed only in footnotes.

As can be seen from the clause-types, this text is readily identifiable as a Hortatory text. We can propose another Hortatory text embedded in the first (1.8.4–9.1)—a blessing, since there is a shift to third person—bracketed by the two, and one, imperative clauses.[65]

Ruth 1.11.1–13.6[66]

This text allows us much more freedom to explore. It contains 18 clauses: a speech formula, and an embedded text of 17 clauses—the last eleven of these are subordinated—I will outline this section more fully below; the first six contain: 3 Imperative clauses (1.11.2, 1.12.1-2), 1 Prefix (question) (1.11.3), 1 Verbless (question) (1.11.4) and 1 wc + Suffix < היה (1.11.5), followed by a subordinated clause (1.12.3), into which the remaining material in this Reported Speech section is embedded by another subordinated clause, a speech formula (1.12.4).

	ותאמר נעמי	11.1
	שבנה בנתי	2
	למה תלכנה עמי	3
	העוד־לי בנים במעי	4
	והיו לכם לאנשים	5
	שבנה בנתי	12.1
	לכן	2
כי זקנתי מהיות לאיש		3
כי אמרתי		4
	יש־לי תקוה	5
גם הייתי הלילה לאיש		6
וגם ילדתי בנים		7
הלהן תשברנה		13.1

---

65. As I intimated while working on Judg. 10.6.1–12.7.3, I am adopting Longacre's proposed verb-rank 'clines' for Narrative Predictive (see his *Joseph*, p. 107, and above) and Hortatory (*ibid.*, p. 121, and above).

66. (1.10.1-3) This unit is composed of a speech formula, and a subordinated clause for which we must supply an ellipsis: ותאמרנה־לה כי אתך נשוב לעמך. I can offer no further comment on this regarding text-type—its subordinating conjunction enforces a non-initial verb form, so we cannot know its true text-type. As it is in response to Naomi's advice, and as the verb is a Prefix form, we may guess it to be from the Narrative Predictive text-type (allowing for the fact that the context, and the content, would suggest that this response would be '+ Agent Orientation').

עד אשר יגדלו	2
הלהן תעגנה לבלתי היות לאיש	3
אל בנתי	4
כי־מר־לי מאד מכם	5
כי־יצאה בי יד־יהוה	6

The structure of this unit, and the text-types involved here, are complex. It is clear that there is a break at 1.12.3, at the subordinating conjunction; the section preceding the subordination is clearly another Hortatory text, with another embedded text within it (the embedded material being a sort of sub-text within the paragraph, bracketed by the repeated שבנה בנתי clauses). I will not at this time comment further on this text, owing to the difficulties of sifting through the implications of the questions. (The second and third clause, being a Verbless clause and a 'wc + Suffix < היה' clause, point us in the direction of an Expository/'What-it-will-be' text-type.)

The remaining section (1.12.3–13.6) likewise leaves us few clues to text-types. The subordinating conjunctions, adverbials and question formats make identification of text-types nearly impossible (we can identify 1.12.5, of course, as belonging to one of the Expository text-types, but this is hardly an improvement). On the other hand, we can explore the internal structure of this second section with more success. We can assign the two questions and their intervening subordinated clause (1.13.1-3) to a single subsection; and I propose that the כי אמרתי of 1.12.4-7, which immediately precedes it, is a sort of protasis, to those questions. The questions are answered by the speaker (they are obviously rhetorical) in the negative and reasons are given (1.13.4-6).

3.3.3 *Ruth 1.15.1-3*
A simple speech formula introduces this unit of two clauses: the first clause (a Suffix clause) is introduced by הנה; the second is an Imperative clause.

ותאמר	15.1
הנה שבה יבמתך אל־עמה ואל־אלהיה	2
שובי אחרי יבמתך	3

This is a Hortatory text, where the reason for the command is given; this arrangement is called by Longacre a Hortatory Reason Paragraph.[67]

---

67. See Longacre, *Joseph*, p. 92, also p. 125 *et passim*.

Ruth 1.16.1–17.6

This masterful section, introduced by a simple speech formula, contains 13 clauses, only one of which (a negated Imperative clause [1.16.2], occurring first in the sequence of Reported Speech clauses) does not occur as subordinated text. The subordinated clauses (1.16.3–1.17.6) include 8 Prefix clauses, broken by 3 Verbless (1.16.7-8, 1.17.5 [w/ Ptc.]) and 1 Jussive (1.17.4).

ותאמר רות	16.1
אל־תפגעי־בי לעזבך לשוב מאחריך	2
כי ++++++ אלך	3
+++ אל־אשר תלכי +++	4
++++++ אלין	5
+++ ובאשר תליני +++	6
עמך עמי	7
ואלהיך אלהי	8
++++++ אמות	17.1
+++ באשר תמותי +++	2
ושם אקבר	3
כה יעשה יהוה לי	4
וכה יסיף	5
כי חמות יפריד ביני ובינך	6

The same configuration prevails here as in the last unit analysed: this is another Hortatory Reason Paragraph. The reason in this case is an extended list of Narrative Predicative clauses, many of which are paired by subordination. I am tempted to propose that two of the Verbless clauses (1.16.7-8) are peak-markers. This, of course, is speculative, since we cannot be certain of the nature of the text for which we are proposing the peak.

The text concludes with an oath (1.17.4-6—the oath formula itself [a Prefix clause, and Verbless clause w/ Participle], and the attendant restriction [a subordinated Prefix clause]).

Ruth 1.20.1–21.5[68]

The contents of this section are: 1 Speech formula (1.20.1), 2 Non-subordinated Suffix clauses (1.21.4-5), 3 Subordinated Suffix clauses (1.20.4–21.2), 4 Prefix (1.20.2 [negated], 1.21.3 [a question]) and 1 Imperative (1.20.3).

ותאמר אליהן	20.1
אל־תקראנה לי נעמי	2
קראן לי מרא	3
כי המר שדי לי מאד	4
אני מלאה הלכתי	21.1
וריקם השיבני יהוה	2
למה תקראנה לי נעמי	3
ויהוה ענה בי	4
ושדי הרע לי	5

The first two clauses are clearly Hortatory; the remainder is less easy to place. This is poetic in style, and we have very little to go on in terms of studies of *poetic syntax*.[69]

3.3.7 *Ruth 2.2.1-4*

This unit comprises four clauses; the speech formula contains one, the remainder are two Cohortative clauses, and one Prefix clause (2.2.4, embedded by subordination). The text is clearly Hortatory.

ותאמר רות המואביה אל־נעמי	2.2.1
אלכה־נא השדה	2
ואלקטה בשבלים	3
אחר אשר אמצא־חן בעיניו	4

68. (1.19.4-5) This is a very brief speech section, containing only three words: a speech formula, and a two-word Verbless clause in question format (התאמרנה הזואת נעמי). It is a non-rhetorical 'yes-or-no' question, which allows us to speculate on the kind of form it would take if it were not a question; it is likely that this is a representative of the Expository text-type.

69. My feeling is that poetic concerns displace text-type features sufficiently that text-type identification of highly poetic passages is nearly impossible, or at best, irrelevant. Dr Longacre tells me (personal communication, 1992) that very little application of his theory and methodology to poetic texts has been made to date.

Ruth 2.4.2-3[70]

This unit contains one speech formula clause, and one Verbless clause.

4.2	ויאמר לקוצרים
3	יהוה עמכם

Although the embedded text contains Verbless clause, it is Hortatory (it contains a blessing, not a command) rather than Expository. Here is a case where semantics, rather than syntax, identifies for us a text's type. As I have repeatedly noted, evaluation by means of one rarely excludes the other.

Ruth 2.5.1-2[71]

This unit contains one speech formula clause, and one Verbless clause (a question).

5.1	ויאמר בעז לנערו הנצב על־הקצרים
2	למי הנערה הזאת

This embedded text is Expository.[72]

Ruth 2.6.1–7.6

This speech unit contains nine clauses: 2 Speech formula clauses (2.6.1-2, both wc + Prefix), 3 wc + Prefix (2.7.1, a speech formula, introducing the next two, embedded clauses, and 2.7.4-5), 1 Verbless clause (2.6.3), 1 Cohortative (2.7.2) and 1 wc + Suffix (2.7.3) and the final, 'badly disrupted',[73] clause, whose precise syntax will, unfortunately, very likely remain a mystery.

6.1	ויען הנער הנצב על־הקצרים
2	ויאמר
3	נערה מואביה היא השבה עם־נעמי משׂדה מואב
7.1	ותאמר

70. (2.2.5-6) This unit contains one speech formula clause and one Hortatory (Imperative) clause: ותאמר לה לכי בתי.

71. (2.4.4-5) This unit contains one speech formula clause and one Jussive clause. The latter is a Hortatory text (ויאמר לו יברכך יהוה).

72. The question is not rhetorical, which simplifies understanding its purpose, and enables us to determine more easily its nature.

73. Campbell, *Ruth*, p. 96.

אלקטה־נא   2
ואספתי בעמרים אחרי הקוצרים   3

ותבוא   4
ותעמוד מאז הבקר ועד־עתה   5
זה שבתה הבית מעט   6

This is the first instance in Ruth of a coordinated speech introduction; this phenomenon intrigues me greatly but I will not comment on it here. It is a feature which surely imports unique detail into the text, yet without study of all such occurrences I cannot draw any conclusions.[74]

Despite the great variety of clause-types, and the textual difficulties with the final verse,[75] this text is fairly easy to sort out. The initial clue is the 3 wc + Prefix clauses; these, and the semantic content, secure the identification of this text as an embedded Narrative History text. The first of these clauses is another speech formula, which introduces an embedded Hortatory text (2.7.2-3). The first and last clauses in the embedded Narrative History text look very like the sort of things we have begun to expect at the initial, and terminal, boundaries of Narrative History texts.[76]

Ruth 2.8.1–9.8

This speech sections contains 13 clauses: 1 Speech formula clause (2.8.1), 5 Prefix clauses (2.8.3-4 [negated], 2.9.2 and 2.9.8 [subordinated]), 4 wc + Suffix (2.9.3, 2.9.5-7), 2 Suffix (negated) (2.8.2, 2.9.4) and 1 Verbless (2.9.1).

---

74. The exhaustive treatise of Meier (*Speaking of Speaking: Marking Direct Discourse in the Hebrew Bible*) is the best starting place for a fuller treatment of this phenomenon. Although he does not devote a specific section to the question of multiple-clause introductions to Reported Speech, he makes several comments on sections containing such speech formulae.

75. For further comments on these textual difficulties, see Campbell, *Ruth*, pp. 94ff.

76. Both the difficult MT reading (in essence, a Verbless clause with a substantival Infinitive), and the apparently derivative LXX reading (a negated Suffix clause), could fit easily into the role expected of a terminal clause.

ויאמר בעז אל־רות	8.1
הלוא שמעת בתי	2
אל־תלכי ללקט בשדה אחר	3
וגם לא תעבורי מזה	4
וכה תדבקין עם־נערתי	5
עיניך בשדה	9.1
אשר־יקצרון	2
והלכת אחריהן	3
הלוא צויתי את־הנערים לבלתי נגעך	4
וצמת	5
והלכת אל־הכלים	6
ושתית	7
מאשר ישאבון הנערים	8

This section, though it, too, looks somewhat difficult at first glance, is relatively straightforward. The questions (2.8.2 and 2.9.4) are difficult, but do not impede us from analysis of the rest of the text. 2.8.3–9.2 are clearly Hortatory clauses; 2.9.3 and 2.9.5-8 are clearly Procedural/Instructional. Both units conclude with a subordinated clause.

Ruth 2.11.1–12.3[77]

This text begins with a two-clause introductory speech formula; it continues with 4 Suffix clauses (2.11.7 [negated], 2.11.3-4, 2.12.3), 2 wc + Prefix (2.11.5-6) and 2 Jussives (2.12.1-2, the second with היה).

ויען בעז	11.1
ויאמר לה	2
הגד הגד לי	3
כל אשר־עשית את־חמותך אחרי	4a
מות אישך	b
ותעזבי אביך ואמך וארץ מולדתך	5
ותלכי אל־עם	6
אשר לא־ידעת תמול שלשום	7

---

77. (2.10.3-5) This unit is comprised of 3 clauses (מדוע מצאתי הן בעיניך להכירני ואנכי נכריה): a speech formula, a Suffix clause (a question) and a Verbless clause. Once again, we have a non-rhetorical question, which—in combination with the Verbless clause—permits us to determine this as an embedded Expository text.

ישלם יהוה פעלך	12.1
ותהי משכרתך שלמה מעם יהוה	2a
אלהי ישראל	b
אשר־באת לחסות תחת־כנפיו	3

This is the second instance of a coordinated speech formula.[78]

Leaving aside 2.11.3, whose text-type affiliation is elusive, I turn to the next four clauses (2.11.4-7), which are clearly Narrative History (note once again the concluding subordinate clause); the following three clauses (2.12.1-3) are another blessing text (Hortatory, with a yet another concluding subordinate clause).

Ruth 2.13.1-5

This speech unit contains a simple speech formula, and four other clauses—two Suffix clauses (subordinated), bracketed by two Prefix clauses (the latter negated and of היה).

ותאמר	13.1
אמצא־חן בעיניך אדני	2
כי נחמתני	3
וכי דברת על־לב שפחתך	4
ואנכי לא אהיה כאחת שפחתיך	5

The first section of this unit remarks on the unexpected kindness of Boaz (which in this text is followed by two subordinated clauses); the second is a statement of identity. This is similar in structure to 2.10.3-5;[79] the specific paragraph- and text-types of these units are difficult to ascertain.

Ruth 2.14.1-4

This speech unit contains a speech formula and one Imperative clause, followed by two wc + Suffix clauses.

ויאמר לה בעז לעת האכל	14.1
גשי הלם	2
ואכלת מן־הלחם	3
וטבלת פתך בחמץ	4

---

78. See comments on 2.6.1–7.6 above.
79. See note 77 above.

The embedded text appears to be a command, and its result; this may fall under the category of Hortatory, or it may be a combined Hortatory and Narrative Predictive paragraph.

Ruth 2.15.2–16.4

The unit contains one speech formula clause, and 4 Prefix clauses (2.15.4, 2.16.4 [negated]; and 2.15.3, 2.16.1) and 2 wc + Suffix clauses (2.16.2-3).

15.2	ויצו בעז את־נעריו לאמר
3	גם בין העמרים תלקט
4	ולא תכלימוה
16.1	וגם של־תשלו לה מן־הצבתים
2	ועזבתם
3	ולקטה
4	ולא תגערו־בה

The embedded text appears to be a solid stretch of Procedural/ Instructional material, much of it in secondary (off-line) forms owing to negation or fronting of emphasized clausal elements. The repetition of גם at 2.15.3 and 2.16.1 may indicate the onset of paragraphs; this suggests two units—2.15.3-4 and 2.16.1-4—both of which are terminated by negated clauses. That this material is intentionally structured as the two units proposed here is further substantiated by a shift from, on the one hand, forbidding the workers to harass Ruth, to, on the other hand, requiring them to be intentionally generous with the grain left for her.

Ruth 2.19.5-9[80]

The response to Naomi's questions (2.19.1-4) comes in the form of a Narrative History text, and of a Reported Speech section. We can see the former as part of a composite introductory speech formula. The remaining clauses are two: a Verbless clause, and a subordinated Suffix clause. The speech text is Expository.

---

80. (2.19.1-4) The unit consists of 1 speech formula, 2 Suffix clauses (in question format), and 1 Jussive (blessing) clause. I cannot comment any further at this point, since the difficulties of question texts, and of Suffix clauses unaccompanied by contextual material to help with identification, preclude greater precision (ותאמר לה חמותה איפה לקטת היום ואנה עשית יהי מכירך ברוך).

19.5	ותגד לחמותה	
6	את אשר־עשתה עמו	
7	ותאמר	
8	שם האיש ++++++ בעז	
9	+++ אשר עשיתי עמו היום +++	

Ruth 2.20.1-3

The following text is composed of a simple speech formula, a Verbless clause, and a subordinated negated Suffix clause.

20.1	ותאמר נעמי לכלתה
2	ברוך הוא ליהוה
3	אשר לא־עזב חסדו את־החיים ואת־המתים

This embedded text can be described as a Hortatory unit, despite its similarity of clause-types to the preceding text; the Verbless clause, in this case, presupposes a Jussive form of היה.

Ruth 2.20.4-6

This unit consists of one speech formula and two Verbless clauses. The embedded text is Expository.

20.4	ותאמר לה נעמי
5	קרוב לנו האיש
6	מגאלנו הוא

This text is unique in Ruth in that the speech formula is repeated, without a change of speaker and/or addressee. This phenomenon occurs at the point where connections are being made (i.e. that Boaz is a near relative who can serve as a redeemer) which will be integral to the resolution of the story—whether this is coincidence or artifice is unclear at this point.

Ruth 2.21.1-7

This section contains 1 Speech formula clause (2.21.1), 2 Suffix clauses (2.21.3 [subordinated], 2.21.6), 3 Verbless clauses (2.21.5, 2.21.7 [both subordinated]) and 1 Prefix clause (2.21.4).

ותאמר רות המואביה		21.1
	גם [...]	2
כי־אמר אלי		3
עם־הנערים +++++ + תדבקין		4
+++ אשר־לי +++		5
עד אם־כלו את כל־הקציר		6
אשר־לי		7

The rather disjointed embedded text commences with an elliptical—or rather, defective—clause (does this reflect excited speech?), to which is subordinated a speech formula; the remainder amounts to an embedded Procedural/Instructional or Hortatory text, with an appended temporal clause.

Ruth 2.22.1-4
This section contains four clauses, in order: one speech formula, one Verbless clause and two Prefix clauses (one negated).

ותאמר נעמי אל־רות כלתה		22.1
טוב בתי		2
כי תצאי עם־נערותיו		3
ולא יפגעו־בך בשדה אחר		4

The embedded text in this unit is Expository, with the reason for the Expository statement being expounded by an embedded (by subordination) Narrative Predictive text.

Ruth 3.1.1–4.8
This unit contains 19 clauses: 1 Speech formula (3.1.1), 8 wc + Suffix clauses (3.3.1-4, 3.4.2, 3.4.4-6), 6 Prefix (3.1.2-3, 3.3.5 [both negated]; 3.4.3, 3.4.7-8), 2 Verbless (3.2.1 [a negated question], 3.2.3 [w/ הנה + Ptc]), 1 Suffix < היה (subordinated) (3.2.2) and 1 Prefix < היה (negated) (3.3.5).

3.1.1	ותאמר לה נעמי חמותה
2	בתי הלא אבקש־לך מנוח
3	אשר ייטב־לך
2.1	ועתה הלא בעז מדעתנו
2	אשר היית את־נערותיו
3	הנה־הוא זרה את־גרן השערים הלילה
3.1	ורחצת
2	וסכת
3	ושמת שמלתיך \<Q> עליך
4	וירדת \<Q> הגרן
5	אל־תודעי לאיש עד כלתו לאכל ולשתות
4.1	ויהי בשכבו
2	וידעת את־המקום
3	אשר ישכב־שם
4	ובאת
5	וגלית מרגלתיו
6	ושכבת \<Q>
7	והוא יגיד לך
8	את אשר תעשׂין

The first two clauses are difficult, again owing to the 'question of questions'; they appear to be introductory to the remainder of Naomi's speech. The two Verbless clauses, and their intervening subordinated היה clause, provide the setting for the following Procedural–Instructional text (3.3.1–4.6); this text is divided into two episodes, the first terminating with a negated Prefix clause, the second beginning with a Prefix clause < היה. The subordinated clause (3.4.3) *may* function to introduce the peak.[81] The final two clauses are Narrative Predictive (3.4.7-8), forming a Procedural Result sort of paragraph.

Ruth 3.9.3-6[82]
This speech section is composed of a speech formula clause, 2 Verbless clauses (1 subordinated), and 1 wc + Suffix clause.

81. 'Peak' is perhaps an inappropriate term for Procedural/Instructional material; what is being referred to here is the clause or sequence of clauses which form the focal set of instructions.
82. (3.5.1-3) This unit, composed of a speech formula clause, and 2 Prefix

9.3	ותאמר
4	אנכי רות אמתך
5	ופרשׂת כנפך על־אמתך
6	כי גאל אתה

The embedded text I would identify as Procedural–Instructional—or an Expository unit and a Procedural–Instructional unit. The former explanation considers the Verbless clause at the commencement of the speech unit to be a background 'setting' for the Instruction section; the latter explanation sees the two sections as more on an equal footing, or even that the first is of greater 'weight' than the second. I lean slightly toward the latter explanation, but consider the two sections more or less equal.

Ruth 3.10.1–13.9
This unit contains 20 clauses: 1 Speech formula (3.10.1), 7 Verbless clauses (3.10.2 and 3.11.4 [w/ Ptc];3.11.5, 3.12.2-3), 6 Prefix (3.11.1 [negated], 3.11.2-3, 3.13.4-6 [the last functioning as a Jussive]), 2 Imperative (3.13.1, 3.13.9), 2 wc + Suffix (3.13.3 [< היה], 3.13.7), 1 Suffix (3.10.3), 1 Clause with ישׁ (3.12.4) and 1 Elliptical clause (omitted from the clause count) (3.12.1).

10.1	ויאמר
2	ברוכה את ליהוה בתי
3a	היטבת חסד האחרון מן־הראשון לבלתי־
b	לכת אחרי הבחורים אם־דל ואם־עשיר
11.1	ועתה בתי אל־תיראי
2	אעשה־לך ++++++
3	+++ כל אשר־תאמרי +++
4	כי יודע כל־שער עמי
5	כי אשת חיל את
12.1	ועתה [...]
2	כי אמנם

clauses (one of which is subordinated), contains a Narrative Predictive text (ותאמר אליה כל אשר־תאמרי אלי <Q> אעשׂה).

(3.9.1-2) This unit contains 2 clauses: a speech formula, and a Verbless clause. The embedded text (a question), appears to be Expository (ויאמר מי־את).

כי גאל אנכי	3
וגם יש גאל קרוב ממני	4
ליני הלילה	13.1
והיה בבקר	2
אם־יגאלך	3
טוב	4
יגאל	5
ואם־לא יחפץ לגאלך	6
וגאלתיך אנכי	7
חי־יהוה	8
שכבי עד־הבקר	9

The embedded text opens with a Hortatory Reason Paragraph (a blessing text—3.10.2-3); it is followed by another of the same, but this time the second part is expounded by a Predictive text, rather than a historical one. This latter contains a reason for the reason, as it were (two Verbless clauses).

The third section (a complex Hortatory text, 3.12.1–13.9) is divided from the second by ועתה, as was the second from the first. The initial clause of the third section is defective; an Expository text is subordinated to it (3.12.2-4); this is followed by the body of the Hortatory text, which itself has several layers of embedding.[83] Suffice it to say that there is Predictive material, and there is Hortatory material, as well as Expository material, embedded in this unit.

Ruth 3.14.4-5
This speech section consists of three clauses: the speech formula, a negated Jussive clause and a subordinated Suffix clause. There is no difficulty in identifying the embedded text as Hortatory, on the basis of the single main clause.

	ויאמר	14.4
אל־יודע		5
כי־באה האשה הגרן		6

Ruth 3.15.1-4
This unit comprises a speech formula and two Imperative clauses separated by a subordinated Verbless clause. This text is likewise Hortatory.

---

83. I would risk going too far with this analysis, were I to attempt to describe closely each clause in this section; any suggestions would be no more than provisional. This, too, I will leave unattended.

ויאמר	15.1
הבי המטפחת	2
אשר־עליך	3
ואחזי־בה	4

Ruth 3.16.4–17.4[84]

This section contains 6 clauses: 3 speech formula clauses and 2 Suffix clauses (one of which is subordinated), followed by a negated Prefix clause.

ותגד־לה	16.4
את כל־אשר עשה־לה האיש	5
ותאמר	17.1
שש־השערים האלה נתן לי	2
<Q> כי אמר אלי	3
אל־תבואי ריקם אל־חמותך	4

This composite speech formula is very similar to the one we saw at 2.19.5-7, which occurs—as does this one—in the context of Ruth recounting to Naomi an important encounter with Boaz. The 'past tense' parts of the embedded text hint at Narrative History, but the evidence is not sufficient to secure an identification; the subordinated clause, however, is a speech formula clause, and introduces an embedded Hortatory text.

Ruth 3.18.1-6

The six clauses of this speech unit include 1 Speech formula (3.18.1), 1 Imperative clause (3.18.2), 3 Prefix (all subordinated) (3.18.3-5 [the last is negated]) and 1 Suffix (3.18.6).

ותאמר	18.1
שבי בתי	2
עד אשר תדעין	3

---

84. (3.16.2-3) This section is identical in structure to 3.9.1-2 (see note above; the same comments apply), apart from the vocative added to the end of the question.

איך יפל דבר	4
כי לא ישקט האיש	5
כי־אם־כלה הדבר היום	6

The text is an embedded Hortatory Reason Paragraph, the second half (3.18.5-6) being a Predictive text with a temporal (Suffix) clause.

Ruth 4.1.5-7

This unit contains a speech formula clause and two Imperative clauses; the embedded text is Hortatory.

ויאמר	5
סורה	6
שבה־פה פלני	7

Ruth 4.3.1–4.10[85]

This unit contains 13 clauses: 1 Speech formula clause (4.3.1), 4 Prefix (3.4.5 and 3.4.7 [subordinated; the latter is negated], 3.4.2, 3.4.8), 3 Imperative (3.4.3-4, 3.4.5), 2 Suffix (3.3.2, 3.4.1), 2 Verbless (3.3.3, 3.4.10), 1 Clause with אין (3.4.9).

ויאמר לגאל	3.1
חלקת השדה ++++++ מכרה נעמי	2
השבה משדה מואב	
+++ אשר לאחינו לאלימלך +++	3
ואני אמרתי	4.1
אגלה אזנך לאמר	2
קנה נגד הישבים ונגד זקני עמי	3
אם־תגאל	4
גאל	5
ואם־לא יגאל <תגאל>	6
הגידה לי	7
ואדעה <Q>	8
כי אין זולתך לגאול	9
ואנכי אחריך	10

---

85. (4.2.2-3) This unit contains 2 clauses—a speech formula and an Imperative clause (ויאמר שבו־פה); its embedded text, like that in the previous one, is Hortatory.

The embedded text contains a speech formula (4.4.1-2), which introduces an embedded Hortatory text (4.4.3-10)—the latter part of this (4.4.8-10) is an amplification of 4.4.7; the earlier section (4.3.2–4.2) is unclear, though I take it to be a stage-setting device for the Hortatory text that follows it.

Ruth 4.4.11-12
This unit contains a speech formula, and a Prefix clause; the embedded text is Predictive.

ויאמר	11
אנכי אגאל	12

Ruth 4.6.1-5[86]
This speech unit contains 5 clauses: a speech formula clause, 3 Prefix clauses (2 negated; 2 subordinated) and 1 Imperative clause (3.6.5).

ויאמר הגאל	6.1
לא אוכל לגאול־לי	2
פן־אשחית את־נחלתי	3
גאל־לך אתה את־גאלתי	4
כי לא־אוכל לגאל	5

The embedded text is composite: the opening clause is Predictive, and is followed by a result statement (Predictive?); the second section (4.6.4-5) is a Hortatory Reason Paragraph, the second half being a summary of the first (Predictive) clause.

Ruth 4.9.1–10.3[87]
There are 8 clauses in this unit; after a single clause speech formula, we find: 4 Verbless (4.9.4-5 [subordinated], 4.9.2, 4.10.3), 2 Suffix (4.9.3, 4.10.1), 1 Prefix (negated) (4.10.2).

---

86. (4.5.1-2) This section is composed of a speech formula and a Suffix clause. Identification of the text-type of the embedded clause is not possible (ויאמר בעז ביום־ קנותך השדה מיה נעמי ומאת רות המואביה אשת־המת קניתה <Q> להקים שם־המת על־נחלתו).

87. (4.8.1-2) This unit is composed of a speech formula and an Imperative clause—ויאמר הגאל לבעז קנה־לך; the embedded text is Hortatory.

9.1	ויאמר בעז לזקנים וכל־העם
2	עדים אתם היום
3	כי קניתי ++++++ ++++++ מיד נעמי
4	+++ את־כל־אשר לאלימלך +++
5	+++ ואת כל־אשר לכליון ומחלון +++
10.1	וגם את־רות המאביה אשת מחלון קניתי לי לאשה להקים שם־המת על־נחלתי
2	ולא־יכרת שם־המת מעם אחיו ומשער מקומו
3	עדים אתם היום

The embedded text is bracketed by two Verbless clauses (identical); these identify the incorporating text as Expository; the material contained in the subordinated clauses is some sort of historical/expository material.[88]

Ruth 4.11.1–12.3

This speech section is introduced by a composite speech formula containing 2 clauses, and includes a further 8 clauses. These are: 3 Prefix clauses (4.11.4 [Jussive], 4.12.1 [< היה], 4.12.3), 2 Suffix (subordinated) (4.11.5, 4.12.2), 2 Imperative (4.11.6-7), 1 Verbless (4.11.3).

11.1	ויאמרו כל־העם ++++++ והזקנים
2	+++ אשר־בשער +++
3	עדים
4	יתן יהוה את־האשה הבאה אל־ביתך כרחל וכלאה
5	אשר בנו שתיהם את־בית ישראל
6	ועשה־חיל באפרתה
7	וקרא־שם בבית לחם
12.1	ויהי ביתך כבית פרץ ++++++ מן־הזרע
2	+++ אשר־ילדה תמר ליהודה +++
3	אשר יתן יהוה לך מן־הנערה הזאת

---

88. This appears to be formal speech; we simply do not have enough data processed to be able to venture conclusions about its text-linguistic features.

In response to Boaz's formal speech to them as witness of the trans-
action, the ten elders respond with an Expository 'we are witness', and
continue on with a blessing of the couple; this divides into two units
(semantically, the first section dealing with Boaz, the second with
Ruth), which both conclude with subordinated clauses.

Ruth 4.14.1–15.4

This section contains 8 clauses: 1 Speech formula (4.14.1), 3 Suffix
clauses (subordinated) (4.14.3 [negated], 4.15.2-3), 2 Verbless
(4.14.2, 4.15.4), 1 wc + Suffix < היה (4.15.1), 1 Prefix (possibly as
jussive) (4.14.4).

ותאמרנה הנשים אל־נעמי	14.1
ברוך יהוה	2
אשר לא השבית לך גאל היום	3
ויקרא שמו בישראל	4
והיה לך למשיב נפש ולכלכל את־שיבתך	15.1
כי כלתך +++++ ילדתו	2
+++ אשר־אהבתך +++	3
אשר־היא טובה לך משבעה בנים	4

This embedded text is Hortatory (a blessing)—it has a historical
section (4.14.2-4) giving the reason for the praise.

Ruth 4.17.1-2

The final Reported Speech section of the book is composed of two
clauses: a speech formula and a Suffix clause. The embedded text does
not admit to any more precise description than 'historical'.

ותקראנה לו השכנות שם לאמר	17.1
ילד־בן לנעמי	2

3.4 Summary and Conclusions

The conclusions we may draw from this examination of Reported
Speech material in Ruth are hindered by three factors:

1. Although I have, throughout this volume, cited the need to test our conclusions against further data, here the need is the greater; in short, the data-sample has been too small to make any but the most obvious, and the most tentative observations, for a variety of reasons. Nonetheless, here more than elsewhere we need to process more texts.

2. The first of these reasons for needing a larger data-base is that text-types within Reported Speech material shift rapidly, and it is not common to find long stretches of material in a single text-type. Broadening our data-base would bring to us more texts of a greater length, which are a better starting point for research than shorter ones.

3. It is clear that subordination (which is more common in Reported Speech than in non-Reported Speech), specifically, and embedding, more generally—by reason of their cohesion with other units within their context—both limit the kinds of clauses that can occur at the outset of any text unit in such a section. This immediately means that we have a greater number of clauses than we would like whose surface-structure signals as to text-type have been obscured by such permutations.

On the other hand, however, there have been encouraging results as well. One of my working hypotheses[89] was that the constituent structure of a text would be marked by divergences from the main-line form in all text-types, and that the 'off-line marking of constituent structure will be confirmed by other types of marking devices'. Where the text has been ample enough to examine both main-line and off-line clauses in a single text-type, we have seen this hypothesis substantiated: Ruth 2.15.2–16.4 is a good example of this, where syntactically marked divisions are confirmed by a shift in topical focus.

It was also found that the data I have examined follow the patterns established for their individual text-types; any disruptions of the expected pattern can be seen to be consistent with the hypothesis that these were conditioned by syntactic relationships between the embedded (Reported Speech) text and the clause into which it is embedded.

89. See p. 117.

We have seen in our examination of Ruth strongly consistent tendencies, both within the book itself and in comparison with other texts. In particular, the Narrative History text-type and the Procedural–Instructional text-type (being the two text-types with which the reader will now be most familiar) were shown to have consistent boundary, main-line and peak-marking features throughout the data, whether in simple narration or in Reported Speech. The treatment of Reported Speech in Ruth has shown that the kinds of features observed in other texts examined occur equally when the material is conveyed as Speech. I anticipate that this hypothesis will be found the more solidly substantiated as more data are processed.

Chapter 6

SUMMARY, CONCLUSIONS AND IMPLICATIONS

1. *Summary*

In this study, I have examined five currently influential works on the text-linguistic description of Classical Hebrew, a theoretical base and methodology for such description was presented, and several texts were worked according to this theoretical model. *My goals have been to underline the need in such undertakings for good theory and methodology, and for clear and direct communication of findings.*

To this end, in the first two chapters, I surveyed Niccacci's *Syntax*, Eskhult's *Studies*, Andersen's *Sentence*, Khan's *Studies*, and Longacre's *Joseph*. Each of these contributes to our growing understanding of text-level features in Classical Hebrew. Each of them also fails to achieve our ideal standards of theoretical–methodological integrity and clarity of presentation.[1] It is claimed (1) that the Hebrew language can be described elegantly and helpfully at the level of 'text', and (2) that this cannot be accomplished if the researcher's theoretical starting point does not allow for the possibility of a variety of text-types, or if the write-up does not explain itself so that linguistically astute, but non-linguistically trained, hebraists can both trace the procedures and comprehend the results.

Of the five works we examined, it was claimed that *Joseph* offered the greatest steps forward in the description of the language—that is, its description of text-types by a matrix with three distinctive parameters, and the description of each text-type in terms of its own specific scale of clause-type distribution (which Longacre terms 'clines'); and since Longacre does not offer much theoretical explanation, the third chapter attempted this task. Since space was limited, it was decided that attention should be given primarily to that

---

1. With the exception of Khan, whose topic is so restricted, and is so alone in its class, that its usefulness is limited, even if it is a model of scholarly work.

portion of the theoretical basis which would permit the reader quickest access to the most significant contributions of *Joseph*; this has meant that we worked toward an understanding of certain basic features of 'tagmemics' which are particularly important for an understanding of the matrix and the clines.

This presentation of the theoretical base also entailed discussing methodological principles, and in the end led to the proposal of some working hypotheses with which we could give the theoretical base a 'road-test'.

This road-test consisted in asking of several texts whether text-types and main-line forms did in fact appear to be linked, and whether the patterns created by the alternation between main-line and off-line forms coincided with other features to reveal the internal structure of the texts. In addition, we looked at 'Reported Speech' to determine, if possible, whether this kind of text had the same text-type and cline characteristics as non-Reported Speech. The final analysis attempted to step away from self-conscious theoretical explanation and to apply the theory and methodology, more freely, to a single, unified text.

Thus, the organization of this volume is as follows:

Chapter 1: Introduction, and Examination of Three Texts: Niccacci, Eskhult and Andersen
Chapter 2: Examination of Khan and Longacre
Chapter 3: A Summary Introduction of the Tagmemic Linguistic Model of Text Analysis, and Resultant Principles of Methodology, Including a Set of Working Hypotheses with which to Test the Model
Chapter 4: Analysis of Hebrew Texts—Taking Text Samples from Judges, Leviticus and Exodus
Chapter 5: Analysis of More Texts—Samples from Judges and the Book of Ruth
Chapter 6: Summary, Conclusions and Implications

It is merely happenstance that the central chapter of this study focuses on theory and methodology, yet it is nonetheless significant. In fact, I might loosely apply the term 'chiastic' to the structure of this work—the central chapter lays out for the reader the details of the theory and methodology with which I have approached the data; those preceding it examine modern works with reference to their theory and methodology (at a fairly basic level)—and, generally, find them less than ideal; those following it apply the proposed theory and methodology to a set of biblical texts.

2. *Conclusions*

In our survey of other works (chs. 1 and 2), we found each of these to contain solid contributions to our field of interest, but also to exhibit specific weaknesses. In Niccacci and Eskhult, we found that the binary opposition between 'Narrative', on the one hand, and 'Discourse', on the other, which both relied upon, was inadequate to describe what is happening in Hebrew at the text level, particularly within their category of 'Discourse'. In Andersen, the difficulty encountered was one of readability; simply, valuable data is obscured by 'jargon' and idiosyncratic abbreviations, to the extent that few hebraists really tackle the work at all.

Khan's topic is very narrow, and therefore is limited in its applicability; yet it stands out as a model of controlled, balanced scholarship, and clarity of communication; little can be said by way of complaint about this work.

Longacre suffers somewhat from the same 'jargonal' deficiencies as Andersen; this is not simply a characteristic of this model of analysis, because Khan, for all his lucidity, cites Longacre as one of his strongest influences; rather, it is merely a feature of scientific studies that 'process' is highlighted over communicability, with the result that some obfuscation of the results is not uncommon. On the other hand, Longacre imports unique insight to the treatment of Hebrew texts, and his contributions are extremely valuable.

I would like to stress here that chs. 1 and 2 are *not* simply introductory, providing background for the study at hand; rather, these chapters contribute a major part of the substance of this work. I have provided an evaluation of theory and, more importantly, methodology, in a variety of text-linguistic undertakings, and a recommendation for a particular theory and methodology for further analysis of biblical Hebrew. Therefore, examination of these works is not merely required as a setting for my own project; it *is* my project.

Many authors give some attention to text-linguistic research without entering fully into it, and many others supply confirmation of the reality of text-level features by approaching texts from a completely different angle, yet arriving in the end at very similar conclusions. Moreover, there are those authors who have consciously eschewed the realm of text-linguistic description, even while acknowledging, on occasion, its value. Waltke and O'Connor's *Introduction to Biblical*

Hebrew Syntax was singled out as a particularly significant example of this, and was addressed in an excursus; for though they process an enormous amount of theoretical and otherwise difficult material, for the benefit of the less well-read user of their book, yet they bluntly refuse to do this same kind of processing when it comes to text-linguistics.

Since Longacre's insights are so significant, I have introduced some necessary complications of theoretical linguistics in order to make these contributions more readily accessible, and to equip the reader to a small degree to engage in his or her own text-linguistic research using this model. I have claimed strongly that this theory is a significantly better starting point for analysis than many others because it has been immersed, since its inception, in the problems and intricacies of real language data; few other models have had this kind of exposure to the world's languages, and fewer still are as innately responsive to the nuances of the data, and as respectful of the primacy thereof, as the tagmemic model.

So, at the risk of oversimplification, I have offered a brand of 'tagmemic' theory that will equip the reader to work more effectively with the contributions of Longacre, Andersen and Khan (*et al.*), and in particular, to appreciate the integrity of this kind of scholarship. It serves, in addition, the purpose of laying the groundwork for the methodology that I have applied to the texts examined here. The theoretical groundwork is closely linked with the methodology, which was presented with explanation of the formats employed for examining the data. Chapter 3 is the core of this study, and it is hoped that the reader will thus have available enough theory to do first hand evaluating of the data.

In the presentation of the methodological principles in this chapter, I proposed a general working hypothesis, and several 'sub-hypotheses', which space limitations would permit us to take to the data. These were:

> Main-line clause-types are text-type specific, and can be described as such; they will predominate in the text, and text-types can be identified by the predominant clause-type.
>
> The main-line clause-type for the Narrative History text-type is the wc + Prefix clause.
> The main-line for the (Narrative) Predictive text-type is the wc + Suffix clause.

The main-line clause-type for the Hortatory text-type is built on a 'command' form.

The main-line clause-type for the Expository text-types is the Verbless clause.

Other text-types, whose clines have not been described nor intimated by Longacre in *Joseph*, will be identified first by features other than 'main-line' clause-types (since these have not yet been proposed), and then clause distribution within those texts for which we have been able to posit a text-type identity, will be examined with a view toward proposing their main-line forms.

The constituent structure of texts will be marked by divergences from the main-line form in all text-types; off-line marking of constituent structure will be confirmed by other types of marking devices, and will reflect a comprehensible underlying notional structure.

The results of the above analyses will be expected to hold true for Reported Speech as well.

I applied these hypotheses first to Judges 2, with the assumption that the reader would find the results easiest to assimilate; since many have already undertaken studies of the text-level features of Narrative History prose, these features will be more familiar to the reader. I examined this text's clause distribution statistics and proposed that they fit with our hypothesis that the wc + Prefix clause is the main-line form for this text-type, and that other clauses fit the pattern as off-line forms. Some sort of text-level function in the distribution of subordinated clauses began to look plausible.

The next text examined was a section of Leviticus 14. In this sample we found that the wc + Suffix form predominated, and that this appeared to be the main-line form for Procedural–Instructional texts; off-line clause types were posited as well. We looked briefly at another text from Leviticus (from chs. 6–7), which encouraged us with regard to these identifications. Here we addressed the question of texts being embedded in other texts. Here it was seen that the Procedural–Instructional material (wrapped, albeit minimally, in Expository material) was set into a Hortatory framework, which was itself set into the over-arching Narrative History structure of the Pentateuch.

We moved from these texts to a comparison of portions of the two series of pericopes concerning the building of the Tabernacle. These two were shown to be, on the one hand, Procedural–Instructional—

with a similar distribution of features to that which we saw in the Leviticus samples—and on the other, Narrative History, or Procedural–Lab Report. The second set was difficult to identify precisely; it exhibited many of the same features that we had seen in the Judges material, but there were enough ambiguities to withhold assignment to a particular text-type identity. Longacre has stated that Procedural–Instructional texts look very similar to Narrative Predictive texts, sharing the same main-line clause types, and so on. It stands to reason, then, that Procedural–Lab Report texts might likewise share main-line clause-types with Narrative History texts. Our data at this stage are inconclusive.

The Exodus pericopes provided opportunities to try our hand at identifying the Expository text-types, with their clause distributions, as well. Longacre's suspicions about the verb ranking which one would expect to find in these text-types (stative clause-types occupying the main-line slots, etc.) were found to be good guidelines.

With these data under our belt, so to speak, we were able to add some more working hypotheses (rather, 'sub-hypotheses') to those we started with; these were not so much different from the former, as simply more specific.

Chapter 5 introduced two new texts: the story of Jephthah (Judg. 10.6–12.7), and the book of Ruth. In the first of these, I focused on the Narrative History text-type. Here, however, the intent was to examine Niccacci's view that historical texts in Reported Speech are a different text-type from those in non-Reported Speech. To this end, I examined first the non-Reported Narrative History text, then compared it with five Narrative History texts found in Reported Speech. These were found to conform significantly to patterns we had seen in earlier Narrative History material, with one slight exception: the first clause in the embedded Narrative History material never took a wc + Prefix form. However, rather than following Niccacci's lead in defining this as a different type of Narrative, I proposed that the first clause in any Reported Speech unit always indicates its status as an element in the (speech introduction) clause in which it is embedded, and therefore it is never, in terms of surface structure, clause initial. This allows us to maintain the symmetry of the matrix, and yet accounts for the distinctive features noticed in the texts so far examined, while remaining consistent with the theoretical base, and permitting a less cluttered description of the data.

Our final engagement with the data involved the book of Ruth, where we attempted to work through the text with all our tools in concert. Allowing for the development of hypotheses as we went along, we examined Ruth, first, in terms of the main-line and off-line clause-types, subordinated clauses, and embedded speech texts. These were seen to work remarkably closely with one another to show forth a 'plot' structure for the book as a whole and for individual episodes within it.

When our examination of the constituent structure of Ruth was completed, we turned our attention to analysing the internal structure of the individual speech units. Each Reported Speech section was addressed, even where the text was too short, or too complex to permit conclusions. It was found, however—these short, or difficult passages aside—that what we proposed as a result of our study of the Narrative History sections in Reported Speech in the Jephthah story was true as well here. That is to say, *once the hypothesis had been permitted that opening clauses of Reported Speech units reflect their non-initial status as embedded units, we found no reason to suggest that text-types encode any differently in Reported Speech than in non-Reported Speech.*

In the long run, this study has shown that text-types other than Narrative History have features as particular to themselves as those which have come to be recognised as features of Narrative History. In addition, these text-types show a strong preference for a particular clause-type, and this serves as the backbone of the text. Off-line clauses are also identifiable, and the two—main-line and off-line—serve with other features to mark the constituent structure (breaks in the flow, and peaks) of the text; each text-type deploys clause-types in a characteristic fashion. In addition, apart from requiring that the embedded material shows its cohesion with the text in which it is embedded, Reported Speech does not appear to challenge any of these hypotheses significantly. As a by-product of this research, strong hints surfaced that subordination plays a role in the constituent structure marking of Narrative History at least (principally occurring at the ends of episodes), and that Reported Speech does likewise (though its distribution leads us to the conclusion that its function is to sustain tension in the story or to develop it slightly).

3. *Implications for Progress*

I believe that it is in turning to fully productive linguistic models that progress will be made in assessing and describing features of Classical Hebrew. What has been presented here is merely a start along the way. What is needed is solid linguistic study of the language, written in such a way that it makes a difference to those who use the language on a day-to-day basis, that is, rabbis and pastors, teachers and students, and so on.[2]

I do not want to imply that it is linguistic scientists who should be doing this work; true, their contributions are singularly welcome (write in reasonable lucid English, or other modern language, please), but to exclude linguistically astute hebraists with no formal linguistic training would be a grave mistake, for these are often the people with the most intimate understanding of the Hebrew text. Though they lack formal tools, their knowledge is irreplaceable. What is needed is a bridge between abstruse scientific theory and the reader who would like to work on his or her own text-level analyses, that is, something that allows those who cannot—or do not want to—undertake study of linguistic theory in a university setting (and even were they to do so, what is the likelihood of finding someone to teach grammar discovery procedures, and the like?), to bring their considerable skills to the text with a high level of scientific integrity. Hebraists need to be provided with the tools of the trade, without requiring them to *give up the trade* to acquire them. It has been my goal, in this volume, to justify, and to make a beginning at, this effort; it has also been my goal to show that this task is *not* unmanageable, and that—even with a minimum of good text-linguistic theory—much can be discovered without undue mental gymnastics.

This, of course, will be easily recognizable as my *idée fixe*, my hobby-horse. The principles have been underlined time and again in this book: good theory—good methodology—good communication. Anything less does not constitute effective scholarship.

That said for the last time, what can we say about specific areas of progress?

I have made much of Longacre's observations. His matrix of text-types and his verb-rank clines are significant improvements. Other

---

2.   Not to exclude linguists, and other students of language, of course.

scholars are also contributing. Much new material is coming out, which has the potential of changing radically the way Hebrew is taught and studied. This will require careful monitoring, of course; much can seem helpful that is not. The most important measure of a description is how well it deals with *all* the language, especially the difficult data.[3]

Loose ends in this study (and Longacre's as well) include: further work in identifying text-types and their characteristics (especially Expository), further analysis of Reported Speech, examination of more texts with a view toward understanding specific functions of specific features,[4] and so on. Certain other endeavours should very likely be undertaken only by those with an intimate knowledge of the language, and at least some awareness of linguistic methodology; these include: the question of text-linguistic features in poetic material, and the question of text-linguistic features in formal language. Further to these, little has been done to examine syntax (micro- *or* macro-) in poetic material—O'Connor's *Hebrew Verse Structure* does this at the level of micro-syntax, but suffers from the same plague as do Andersen and Longacre in varying degrees and different ways—that is, it is so difficult to make sense of that it is off-putting; Watson's *Classical Hebrew Poetry* is easier to work with, but includes little real syntax.[5]

It may be taken nearly for granted that greater precision in text-linguistic description of Classical Hebrew is to be desired because such description is of value in and of itself. The relevance of this increase in knowledge for other facets of biblical studies may not be so obvious.

---

3.   I am aware that the final part of this work does not measure up well on this front; yet it does not purport to be a 'description'; rather, it is very brief introduction to the application of one promising linguistic model. It should be evaluated as such.

4.   I must stress, however, that studies like Khan's and Eskhult's will never be able to give us full answers. For this we need more studies of full texts, looking at stories, etc., as units, and describing the patterns that emerge as we compare hundreds of these to each other. Only then will we be able to see whether subordination (for example) has a specific text-level function, or whether ויהי has a strong preference for episode-initial contexts.

5.   Professor J.C.L. Gibson has observed to me that poetry appears to be governed *syntactically as well as 'stylistically'* by *parallelism* (personal communication, 1992); this feature may be a governing factor like the 'embedding/cohesion' one which I allege controls first clauses in Reported Speech. Such hypotheses as these will require long and data-intensive study.

Text-level analysis can contribute significantly to text exegesis; for example, the results of my analysis of off-line clauses led me to propose that Judges 12.5.1 is marked as the peak of the last episode of the story. It is easily overlooked that our interest in the pronunciation of the word Shibboleth would not necessarily have been shared by the earliest hearers of the account; text-linguistic research helps objectify such elements of the text-to-reader and reader-to-text relationships. In a different vein, a more thorough examination of the book of Ruth than I have been able to present in this work would allow us to trace the themes and purposes of the book, as reflected in the peak marking, topic continuity and shifts, participant reference, and the deployment of tension-maintaining devices in the text.

Text-linguistics may also contribute to text-critical discussions; assessment of emendations according to text-linguistic, in addition to other, criteria makes enormous sense.

However, it is clear that the most immediate—if not the greatest—benefit from text-linguistic research will be for students and teachers of the language. In the same way that checking the cards in a deck to determine which (if any) are missing is far easier if the cards are arranged in numerical order by suits, so also learning (and therefore teaching) *any* language is greatly simplified if its forms are systematized—all the more so if it is a dead language.[6] If the system of text-types were presented to students (I do not mean the theoretical parameters, but rather the simple existence of these text-types), and their associated main-line forms, then this much, in one stroke, would give the learner a handle to begin sorting through the various distributions and functions of the Hebrew verb.[7]

I have endeavoured to convince the reader of this volume that text-linguistic analysis and description offers significant insights into the structure of the language and the function of its forms. I have attempted as well to elucidate one model of text-linguistics that is at the same time relatively approachable and exceptionally acute in the results it leads to. This was illustrated by applying the model in seven

6.   I am not a supporter of the inductive method of learning a dead language, since inductive learning requires a deep saturation in that language in order to bring lasting success, i.e., one must hear it without ceasing, and in all manner of contexts; this is, of course, denied students of Classical Hebrew, Ugaritic, Sanskrit, Latin, etc.

7.   I recognize that this approach alone would not cover the material which a student needs to cover; however, it is a *very* good starting point.

medium- to large-scale analyses of biblical texts. Although results from these analyses could not hope to be precise, they do in fact demonstrate the distinctive features of specific text-types, and confirm several of the hypotheses that were suggested by the model.

Text-linguistic analysis of Classical Hebrew, and other ancient languages, is still in its early years; we can look forward to significant developments in the understanding of our texts as more of this research takes place.

Appendix 1

THE TEXT OF JUDGES 2 (BHS) IN COLUMNAR FORMAT

ויעל מלאך־יהוה מן־הגלגל אל־הבכים	2.1.1
ויאמר	2
אעלה אתכם ממצרים	3
ואביא אתכם אל־הארץ	4
אשר נשבעתי לאבתיכם	5
ואמר	6
לא־אפר בריתי אתכם לעולם	7
ואתם לא־תכרתו ברית ליושבי הארץ	2.1 a
הזאת	b
מזבחותיהם תתצון	2
ולא־שמעתם בקלי	3
מה־זאת עשיתם	4
וגם אמרתי	3.1
לא־אגרש אותם מפניכם	2
והיו לכם לצדים	3
ואלהיהם יהיו לכם למוקש	4
ויהי כדבר מלאך יהוה את־הדברים	4.1 a
האלה אל־כל־בני ישראל	b
וישאו העם את־קולם	2
ויבכו	3
ויקראו שם־המקום ההוא בכים	5.1
ויזבחו־שם ליהוה	2
וישלח יהושע את־העם	6.1
וילכו בני־ישראל איש לנחלתו	2 a
לרשת את־הארץ	b
ויעבדו העם את־יהוה כל ימי	7.1
יהושע וכל ימי הזקנים	2

3	אשר האריכו ימים אחרי יהושע
4	אשר ראו את כל־מעשה יהוה הגדול
5	אשר עשה לישראל
8.1 a	וימת יהושע בן־נון עבד יהוה
b	בן־מאה ועשר שנים
9.1 a	ויקברו אותו בגבול נחלתו בתמנת־
b	חרס בהר אפרים מצפון להר־געש
10.1	וגם כל־הדור ההוא נאספו אל־אבותיו
2	ויקם דור אחר אחריהם
3 a	אשר לא־ידעו את־יהוה
b	וגם את־המעשה
4	אשר עשה לישראל
11.1	ויעשו בני־ישראל את־הרע בעיני יהוה
2	ויעבדו את־הבעלים
12.1 a	ויעזבו את־יהוה אלהי אבותם המוציא
b	אותם מארץ מצרים
2	וילכו אחרי אלהים אחרים מאלהי העמים
3	אשר סביבותיהם
4	וישתחוו להם
5	ויכעסו את־יהוה
13.1	ויעזבו את־יהוה
2	ויעבדו לבעל ולעשתרות
14.1	ויחר־אף יהוה בישראל
2	ויתנם ביד־שסים
3	וישסו אותם וימכרם ביד אויביהם מסביב
4	ולא־יכלו עוד לעמד לפני אויביהם
15.1	בכל +++++ יד־יהוה היתה־בם לרעה
2	+++ אשר יצאו +++
3	כאשר דבר יהוה
4	וכאשר נשבע יהוה להם
5	ויצר להם מאד
16.1	ויקם יהוה שפטים
2	ויושיעום מיד שסיהם
17.1	וגם אל־שפטיהם לא שמעו

כי זנו אחרי אלהים אחרים	2
וישתחוו להם	3
סרו מהר מן־הדרך	4
אשר הלכו אבותם לשמע מצות־יהוה	5
לא־עשו כן	6
[...]	18.1
וכי־הקים יהוה להם שפטים	2
והיה יהוה עם־השפט	3
והושיעם מיד איביהם כל ימי השופט	4
כי־ינחם יהוה מנאקתם מפני לחציהם ודחקיהם	5
והיה במות השופט ישבו	19.1
והשחיתו מאבותם ללכת אחרי אלהים	2 a
אחרים לעבדם ולהשתחות להם	b
לא הפילו ממעלליהם ומדרכם הקשה	3
ויחר־אף יהוה בישראל	20.1
ויאמר	2
++++++ גם־אני לא אוסיף להוריש איש	21.1 a
מפניהם מן־הגוים	b
+++ יען אשר עברו הגוי הזה	20.3 a
את־בריתי	b
אשר צויתי את־אבותם	20.4
ולא שמעו לקולי +++	20.5
אשר־עזב יהושע	21.2
וימת	21.3
למען נסות בם את־ישראל	22.1 a
השמרים הם את־דרך יהוה	b
ללכת בם	c
כאשר שמרו אבותם	2
אם־לא	3
וינח יהוה את־הגוים האלה לבלתי	23.1 a
הורישם מהר	b
ולא נתנם ביד־יהושע	2

Appendix 2

THE TEXT OF RUTH (BHS) IN COLUMNAR FORMAT

1.1.1 a	ויהי בימי שפט השפטים
2	ויהי רעב בארץ
3 a	ויל איש מבית לחם יהודה לגור
b	בשדי מואב הוא ואשתו ושני בניו
2.1	ושם האיש אלימלך
2	ושם אשתו נעמי
3	ושם שני־בניו מחלון וכליון
4	אפרתים מבית לחם יהודה
5	ויבאו שדי־מואב
6	ויהיו־שם
3.1	וימת אלימלך איש נעמי
2	ותשאר היא ושני בניה
4.1	וישאו להם נשים מאביות
2	שם האחת ערפה
3	ושם השנית רות
4	וישבו שם כעשר שנים
5.1	וימותו גם־שניהם מחלון וכליון
2	ותשאר האשה משני ילדיה ומאישה
6.1	ותקם היא וכלתיה
2	ותשב משדי מואב
3	כי שמעה בשדה מואב
4 a	כי־פקד יהוה את־עמו
b	לתת להם לחם
7.1	ותצא מן־המקום
2	אשר היתה־שמה
3	ושתי כלתיה עמה
4	ותלכנה בדרך לשוב אל־ארץ יהודה
8.1	ותאמר נעמי לשתי כלתיה

לכנה	2
שבנה אשה לבית אמה	3
יעש ⟨Q⟩ יהוה עמכם חסד	4
כאשר עשיתם עם־המתים	5 a
ועמדי	b
יתן יהוה לכם	9.1
ומצאן מנוחה אשה בית אישה	2
ותשק להן	3
ותשאנה קולן	4
ותבכינה	5
ותאמרנה־לה	10.1
[...]	2
כי־אתך נשוב לעמך	3
ותאמר נעמי	11.1
שבנה בנתי	2
למה תלכנה עמי	3
העוד־לי בנים במעי	4
והיו לכם לאנשים	5
שבנה בנתי	12.1
לכן	2
כי זקנתי מהיות לאיש	3
כי אמרתי	4
יש־לי תקוה	5
גם הייתי הלילה לאיש	6
וגם ילדתי בנים	7
הלהן תשברנה	13.1
עד אשר יגדלו	2
הלהן תעגנה לבלתי היות	3 a
לאיש	b
אל בנתי [...]	4
כי־מר־לי מאד מכם	5

כי־יצאה בי יד־יהוה	6
ותשנה קולן	14.1
ותבכינה עוד	2
ותשק ערפה לחמותה	3
ורות דבקה בה	4
ותאמר	15.1
הנה שבה יבמתך אל־עמה ואל־אלהיה	2
שובי אחרי יבמתך	3
ותאמר רות	16.1
אל־תפגעי־בי לעזבך לשוב מאחריך	2
כי +++++ אלך	3
+++ אל־אשר תלכי +++	4
ובאשר +++++ אלין	5
+++ תליני +++	6
עמך עמי	7
ואלהיך אלהי	8
+++++ אמות	17.1
+++ באשר תמותי +++	2
ושם אקבר	3
כה יעשה יהוה לי	4
וכה יסיף	5
כי המות יפריד ביני ובינך	6
ותרא	18.1
כי־מתאמצת היא ללכת אתה	2
ותחדל לדבר אליה	3
ותלכנה שתיהם עד־באנה בית לחם	19.1
ויהי כבאנה בית לחם	2
ותהם כל־העיר עליהן	3
ותאמרנה	4
הזאת נעמי	5

20.1   ותאמר אליהן

2   אל־תקראנה לי נעמי
3   קראן לי מרא

4   כי־המר שדי לי מאד
21.1   אני מלאה הלכתי
2   וריקם השיבני יהוה

3   למה תקראנה לי נעמי
4   ויהוה ענה בי
5   ושדי הרע לי

22.1   ותשב נעמי
2a   ורות המואביה כלתה עמה השבה
b   משדי מואב
3   והמה באו בית לחם בתחלת קציר שערים
2.1.1a   ולנעמי מודע ⟨Q⟩ לאישה איש גבור חיל
b   ממשפחת אלימלך
2   ושמו בעז
2.1   ותאמר רות המואביה אל־נעמי

2   אלכה־נא השדה
3   ואלקטה בשבלים

4   אחר אשר אמצא־חן בעיניו

5   ותאמר לה

6   לכי בתי

3.1   ותלך
2   ותבוא
3   ותלקט בשדה אחרי הקצרים
4   ויקר מקרה חלקת השדה לבעז

5   אשר ממשפחת אלימלך

4.1   והנה־בעז בא מבית לחם
2   ויאמר לקוצרים

3   יהוה עמכם

4   ויאמרו לו

יברכך יהוה	5
ויאמר בעז לנערו הנצב על־הקוצרים	5.1
למי הנערה הזאת	2
ויען הנער הנצב על־הקוצרים	6.1
ויאמר	2
נערה מואביה	3
היא השבה עם־נעמי משדה מואב	4
ותאמר	5
אלקטה־נא	7.1
ואספתי בעמרים אחרי הקוצרים	2
ותבוא	3
ותעמוד מאז הבקר ועד־עתה	4
זה שבתה הבית מעט	5
ויאמר בעז אל־רות	8.1
הלוא שמעת בתי	2
אל־תלכי ללקט בשדה אחר	3
וגם לא תעבורי מזה	4
וכה תדבקין עם־נערתי	5
עיניך בשדה	9.1
אשר־יקצרון	2
והלכת אחריהן	3
הלוא צויתי את־הנערים לבלתי נגעך	4
וצמת	5
והלכת אל־הכלים	6
ושתית	7
מאשר ישאבון הנערים	8
ותפל על־פניה	10.1
ותשתחו ארצה	2
ותאמר אליו	3
מדוע מצאתי חן בעיניך להכירני	4
ואנכי נכריה	5

ויען בעז	11.1
ויאמר לה	2
הנד הגד לי	3
כל אשר־עשית את־חמותך	4 a
אחרי מות אישך	b
ותעזבי אביך ואמך וארץ	5 a
מולדתך	b
ותלכי אל־עם	6
אשר לא־ידעת תמול שלשום	7
ישלם יהוה פעלך	12.1
ותהי משכרתך שלמה מעם יהוה אלהי	2 a
ישראל	b
אשר־באת לחסות תחת־כנפיו	3
ותאמר	13.1
אמצא־חן בעיניך אדני	2
כי נחמתני	3
וכי דברת על־לב שפחתך	4
ואנכי לא אהיה כאחת שפחתיך	5
ויאמר לה בעז לעת האכל	14.1
גשי הלם	2
ואכלת מן־הלחם	3
וטבלת פתך בחמץ	4
ותשב מצד הקוצרים	5
ויצבט־לה קלי	6
ותאכל	7
ותשבע	8
ותתר	9
ותקם ללקט	15.1
ויצו בעז את־נעריו לאמר	2
גם בין העמרים תלקט	3
ולא תכלימוה	4
וגם של־תשלו לה מן־הצבתים	16.1
ועזבתם	2
ולקטה	3

ולא תנערו־בה   4

ותלקט בשדה עד־הערב   17.1
ותחבט   2

את אשר־לקטה   3

ויהי כאיפה שערים   4
ותשא   18.1
ותבוא העיר   2
ותרא חמותה   3

את אשר־לקטה   4

ותוצא   5
ותתן־לה   6

את אשר־הותרה משבעה   7

ותאמר לה חמותה   19.1

איפה לקטת היום   2
ואנה עשית   3
יהי מכירך ברוך   4

ותגד לחמותה   5

את אשר־עשתה עמו   6

ותאמר   7

שם האיש ++++++ בעז   8

+++ אשר עשיתי עמו היום +++   9

ותאמר נעמי לכלתה   20.1

ברוך הוא ליהוה   2

אשר לא־עזב חסדו את־החיים   3 a
ואת־המתים   b

ותאמר לה נעמי   4

קרוב לנו האיש   5
מגאלנו הוא   6

21.1	ותאמר רות המואביה
2	גם [...]
3	כי־אמר אלי
4	עם־הנערים +++++ תדבקין
5	+++ אשר־לי +++
6	עד אם־כלו את כל־הקציר
7	אשר־לי
22.1	ותאמר נעמי אל־רות כלתה
2	טוב בתי
3	כי תצאי עם־נערותיו
4	ולא יפנעו־בך בשדה אחר
23.1 a	ותדבק בנערות בעז ללקט עד־כלות
b	קציר־השערים וקציר החטים
2	ותשב את־חמותה
3.1.1	ותאמר לה נעמי חמותה
2	בתי הלא אבקש־לך מנוח
3	אשר ייטב־לך
2.1	ועתה הלא בעז מדעתנו
2	אשר היית את־נערותיו
3	הנה־הוא זרה את־גרן השערים הלילה
3.1	ורחצת
2	וסכת
3	ושמת שמלתיך ⟨Q⟩ עליך
4	וירדת ⟨Q⟩ הגרן
5	אל־תודעי לאיש עד כלתו לאכל ולשתות
4.1	ויהי בשכבו
2	וידעת את־המקום
3	אשר ישכב־שם

ובאת	4
וגלית מרגלתיו	5
ושכבת ⟨Q⟩	6
והוא יגיד לך	7
את אשר תעשין	8
ותאמר אליה	5.1
כל +++++ אעשה	2
+++ אשר־תאמרי אלי ⟨Q⟩ +++	3
ותרד הגרן	6.1
ותעש	2
ככל אשר־צותה חמותה	3
ויאכל בעז	7.1
וישת	2
וייטב לבו	3
ויבא לשכב בקצה הערמה	4
ותבא בלט	5
ותגל מרגלתיו	6
ותשכב	7
ויהי בחצי הלילה	8.1
ויחרד האיש	2
וילפת	3
והנה אשה שכבת מרגלתיו	4
ויאמר	9.1
מי־את	2
ותאמר	3
אנכי רות אמתך	4
ופרשת כנפך על־אמתך	5
כי גאל אתה	6
ויאמר	10.1
ברוכה את ליהוה בתי	2
היטבת חסדך האחרון מן־הראשון	3 a
לבלתי־לכת אחרי הבחורים אם־דל	b

	c
ואם־עשיר	
ועתה בתי אל־תיראי	11.1
+++++ אעשה־לך	2
+++ כל אשר־תאמרי +++	3
כי יודע כל־שער עמי	4
כי אשת חיל את	5
ועתה [...]	12.1
כי אמנם	2
כי ⟨אם K,⟩ גאל אנכי	3
וגם יש גאל קרוב ממני	4
ליני הלילה	13.1
והיה בבקר	2
אם־יגאלך	3
טוב	4
יגאל	5
ואם־לא יחפץ לגאלך	6
וגאלתיך אנכי	7
חי־יהוה	8
שכבי עד־הבקר	9
ותשכב מרגלותיו ⟨Q⟩ עד־הבקר	14.1
ותקם	2
בטרם ⟨Q⟩ יכיר איש את־רעהו	3
ויאמר	4
אל־יודע	5
כי־באה האשה הגרן	6
ויאמר	15.1
הבי המטפחת	2
אשר־עליך	3
ואחזי־בה	4
ותאחז בה	5

6	וימד שש־שערים
7	וישת עליה
8	ויבא העיר
16.1	ותבוא אל־חמותה
2	ותאמר
3	מי־את בתי
4	ותגד־לה
5	את כל־אשר עשה־לה האיש
17.1	ותאמר
2	שש־השערים האלה נתן לי
3	כי אמר אלי ‹Q›
4	אל־תבואי ריקם אל־חמותך
18.1	ותאמר
2	שבי בתי
3	עד אשר תדעין
4	איך יפל דבר
5	כי לא ישקט האיש
6	כי־אם־כלה הדבר היום
4.1.1	ובעז עלה השער
2	וישב שם
3	והנה הגאל עבר
4	אשר דבר־בעז
5	ויאמר
6	סורה
7	שבה־פה פלני אלמני
8	ויסר
9	וישב
2.1	ויקח עשרה אנשים מזקני העיר

ויאמר	2
שבו־פה	3
וישבו	4
ויאמר לגאל	3.1
חלקת השדה +++++ מכרה נעמי השבה	2 a
משדה מואב	b
+++ אשר לאחינו לאלימלך +++	3
ואני אמרתי	4.1
אגלה אזנך לאמר	2
קנה נגד הישבים ונגד זקני עמי	3
אם־תגאל	4
גאל	5
ואם־לא יגאל	6
הגידה לי	7
ואדעה ⟨Q⟩	8
כי אין זולתך לגאול	9
ואנכי אחריך	10
ויאמר	11
אנכי אגאל	12
ויאמר	5.1
בעז ביום־קנותך השדה מיד נעמי ומאת	2 a
רות המואביה אשת־המת קניתה להקים	b
שם־ המת על־נחלתו	c
ויאמר הגאל	6.1
לא אוכל לגאל־לי ⟨Q⟩	2
פן־אשחית את־נחלתי	3
גאל־לך אתה את־גאלתי	4
כי לא־אוכל לגאל	5

7.1 a	וזאת לפנים בישראל על־הגאולה
b	ועל־התמורה לקים כל־דבר
2	שלף איש נעלו
3	ונתן לרעהו
4	וזאת התעודה בישראל
8.1	ויאמר הגאל לבעז
2	קנה־לך
3	וישלף נעלו
9.1	ויאמר בעז לזקנים וכל־העם
2	עדים אתם היום
3 a	כי קניתי ++++++ ++++++ ++++++ מיד
b	נעמי
4	+++ את־כל־אשר לאלימלך +++
5 a	+++ ואת כל־אשר לכליון
b	ומחלון +++
10.1 a	וגם את־רות המאביה אשת מחלון קניתי
b	לי לאשה להקים שם־המת על־ נחלתו
2 a	ולא־יכרת שם־המת מעם אחיו ומשער
b	מקומו עדים אתם היום
11.1	ויאמרו כל־העם ++++++ והזקנים
2	+++ אשר־בשער +++
3	עדים
4 a	יתן יהוה את־האשה הבאה אל־ביתך
b	כרחל וכלאה
5	אשר בנו שתיהם את־בית ישראל
6	ועשה־חיל באפרתה
7	וקרא־שם בבית לחם
12.1	ויהי ביתך כבית פרץ ++++++ מן־הזרע
2	+++ אשר־ילדה תמר ליהודה +++
3 a	אשר יתן יהוה לך מן־הנערה

הזאת   b

ויקח בעז את־רות	13.1
ותהי־לו לאשה	2
ויבא אליה	3
ויתן יהוה לה הריון	4
ותלד בן	5
ותאמרנה הנשים אל־נעמי	14.1

ברוך יהוה   2

אשר לא השבית לך גאל היום   3

ויקרא שמו בישראל   4
והיה לך למשיב נפש ולכלכל את־   15.1 a
שיבתך   b

כי כלתך ++++++ ילדתו   2

+++ אשר־אהבתך +++   3

אשר־היאטובה לך משבעה בנים   4

ותקח נעמי את־הילד	16.1
ותשתהו בחיקה	2
ותהי־לו לאמנת	3
ותקראנה לו השכנות שם לאמר	17.1

ילד־בן לנעמי   2

ותקראנה שמו עובד	3
הוא אבי־ישי אבי דוד	4
ואלה תולדות פרץ	18.1
פרץ הוליד את־חצרון	2
וחצרון הוליד את־רם	19.1
ורם הוליד את־עמינדב	2
ועמינדב הוליד את־נחשון	20.1
ונחשון הוליד את־שלמה	2
ושלמון הוליד את־בעז	21.1
ובעז הוליד את־עובד	2
ועבד הוליד את־ישי	22.1
וישי הוליד את־דוד	2

BIBLIOGRAPHY

Aejmelaeus, A., 'What Can we Know about the Hebrew *Vorlage* of the Septuagint?',
   ZAW 99 (1987), pp. 58-89.
Alter, R., *The Art of Biblical Narrative* (London: George Allen & Unwin, 1981).
Andersen, F.I., *The Hebrew Verbless Clause in the Pentateuch* (JBL Monograph Series,
   vol. XIV; Nashville: Abingdon, 1970).
—*The Sentence in Biblical Hebrew* (The Hague: Mouton, 1974).
Andersen, F.I., and A.D. Forbes, *A Linguistic Concordance of Ruth and Jonah: Hebrew
   Vocabulary and Idiom* (The Computer Bible, 9; Biblical Research Associates,
   1976).
Andersen, F.I., and D.N. Freedman, *Hosea* (AB, 24; Garden City, New York:
   Doubleday, 1980).
Auld, A.G., *Joshua, Judges and Ruth* (The Daily Study Bible; Edinburgh: St Andrew
   Press; Philadelphia: Westminster Press, 1984).
Bandstra, B.L., 'Word Order and Emphasis in Biblical Hebrew Narrative: Syntactic
   Observations on Genesis 22 from a Discourse Perspective [1986]', in
   W.R. Bodine (ed.), *Linguistics and Biblical Hebrew*.
Bar-Efrat, S., *Narrative Art in the Bible* (Sheffield: Almond Press, 1989).
Barr, J., *Comparative Philology and the Text of the Old Testament* (London: SCM Press,
   1983).
—*The Semantics of Biblical Language* (London: SCM Press, 1983).
Beattie, D.R.G., *Jewish Exegesis of the Book of Ruth* (JSOTSup, 2; Sheffield: JSOT
   Press, 1977).
Berlin, A., 'Lexical Cohesion and Biblical Interpretation', *Hebrew Studies* 30 (1989).
—'Point of View in Biblical Narrative', in S.A. Geller (ed.), *A Sense of Text* (1983).
Bernstein, M.J., 'Two Multivalent Readings in the Ruth Narrative', *JSOT* 50 (1991).
Bodine, W.R. (ed.), *Linguistics and Biblical Hebrew* (Winona Lake, IN: Eisenbrauns,
   1992).
—'How Linguists Study Syntax [1987]', in W.R. Bodine (ed.), *Linguistics and Biblical
   Hebrew*.
—'The Study of Linguistics and Biblical Hebrew', in W.R. Bodine (ed.), *Linguistics
   and Biblical Hebrew*.
Boling, R.G., *Judges* (AB, 6; Garden City, NY: Doubleday, 1975).
Brend, R.M. (ed.), *Kenneth L. Pike: Selected Writings* (Janua Linguarum, Series Major,
   55; The Hague: Mouton).
Brend, R.M. and K.L. Pike (eds.), *Tagmemics*. I. *Aspects of the Field* (Trends in
   Linguistics, Studies and Monographs, 1; The Hague: Mouton, 1976).
Brenner, A., 'A Triangle and a Rhombus in Narrative Structure: A Proposed Integrative
   Reading of Judges IV and V', *VT* 40.2 (1990), pp. 129-38.

Brownlee, W.H., *Ezekiel 1–19* (WBC, 28; Waco, TX: Word Books, 1986).

Burney, C.F., *The Book of Judges* (London: Rivingtons, 1918).

Buth, R.J., *Word Order in Aramaic from the Perspective of Functional Grammar and Discourse Analysis* (PhD Dissertation, UCLA: United Microfilms International, 1987).

Calloud, J., *Structural Analysis of Narrative* (trans. D. Patte; Philadelphia: Fortress Press; Missoula, MT: Scholars Press, 1976).

Campbell, E.F., *Ruth* (AB, 7; Garden City, NY: Doubleday, 2nd edn, 1975)

Cook, E.M., *Word Order in the Aramaic of Daniel* (Monographic Journals of the Near East: Afroasiatic Linguistics, 9, issue 3 [Dec. 1986]; Malibu, CA: Undena Publications).

Cotterell, P., and M. Turner, *Linguistics and Biblical Interpretation* (London: SPCK, 1989).

Dawson, D.A., 'Text Linguistics and Biblical Hebrew: An Examination of Methodologies' (PhD dissertation, University of Edinburgh, 1993).

Dearman, A. (ed.), *Studies in the Mesha' Inscription and Moab* (Archeology and Biblical Studies, 2; Atlanta: Scholars Press, 1989).

Eisenman, R., and M. Wise, *The Dead Sea Scrolls Uncovered* (Rockport, MA: Element, 1992).

Elson, B.F., and V.P. Pickett., *An Introduction to Morphology and Syntax* (Santa Ana, CA: Summer Institute of Linguistics, 2nd edn, 1964).

Eskhult, M., *Studies in Verbal Aspect and Narrative Technique in Biblical Hebrew Prose* (Uppsala: Uppsala University, 1990).

Exter Blokland, A.F. den, 'Clause Analysis in Biblical Hebrew Narrative—An Explanation and a Manual for Compilation', *Trinity Journal* 11 NS (1990), pp. 73-102.

Fewell, D.N., and D.M. Gunn, *Compromising Redemption: Relating Characters in the Book of Ruth* (Literary Currents in Biblical Interpretation; Louisville, KY: John Knox Press, 1990).

Fokkelman, J.P., *Narrative Art in Genesis: Specimens of Stylistic and Structural Analysis* (Assen: Van Gorcum, 1975).

Freedman, D.N., and K.A. Matthews, *The Paleo-Leviticus Scroll* (Cambridge, MA: American Schools of Oriental Research, 1985).

Fuchs, E., 'Marginalization, Ambiguity, Silencing: The Story of Jephthah's Daughter', *Journal of Feminist Studies in Religion* 5 (1989), pp. 35-45.

Garr, W.R., 'The Qinah: A Study of Poetic Meter, Syntax and Style', *ZAW* 95 (1983), pp. 54-75.

Geller, S.A., *A Sense of Text: The Art of Language in the Study of Biblical Literature* (JQRMS; Philadelphia: Jewish Quarterly Review, 1983).

—'Through Windows and Mirrors into the Bible. History, Literature, and Language in the Study of the Text', in S.A. Geller (ed.), *A Sense of Text* (1983).

Gerleman, G., *Ruth / Das Hohelied* (BKAT, 18; Neukirchen–Vluyn: Neukirchener Verlag, 1965).

Grant, R., 'Literary Structure in Ruth', *BibSac*, October–December, 1991, pp. 424-41.

Gray, J., *Joshua, Judges and Ruth* (The Century Bible; London: Nelson, 1967).

Greenstein, E., 'On the Prefixed Preterite in Biblical Hebrew', *Hebrew Studies* 29 (1988), pp. 7-17.

Grimes, B. (ed.), *Ethnologue* (Dallas, Texas: Summer Institute of Linguistics, 1984).

Hals, R.M., *Ezekiel* (FOTL, 19; Grand Rapids: Eerdmans, 1989).

Hoftijzer, J., *A Search for Method: A Study in the Syntactic Use of the H-Locale in Classical Hebrew* (Studies in Semitic Languages and Linguistics, 12; Leiden: Brill, 1981).

Hopper, P.J. and S.A. Thompson, 'Transitivity in Grammar and Discourse', *Language* 56 (1980), pp. 251-99.

Hospers, J.H., 'Polysemy and Homonymy', *ZAW* 6/1 (1993), pp. 114-23.

Huenergard, J., 'The Early Hebrew Prefix Conjugations', *Hebrew Studies* 29 (1988).

Hubbard, D.L., 'Ruth IV 17: A New Solution', *VT* 38 (1988), pp. 19-23.

Hurvitz, A., 'Ruth 2.7—"A Midrashic Gloss"?', *ZAW* 95 (1983), pp. 293-301.

Isaksson, B., *Studies in the Language of Qoheleth* (Acta Universitatis Upsaliensis: Studia Semitica Upsaliensia, 10; Uppsala: Uppsala University, 1987).

Jagersma, H., *Bijbels Hebreeuws: Basiscursus* (Kampen: Uitgeversmaatschappij J.H. Kok, 1991).

Jenni, E., *Lehrbuch der hebräischen Sprache des alten Testaments* (Basel: Helbing & Lichtenhahn, 2nd edn, 1981).

Johnson, B., *Hebräisches Perfekt und Imperfekt mit vorangehendem ^{we}* (ConBOT, 13; Malmö: CWK Gleerup, 1979).

Jones, L.K., 'A Synopsis of Tagmemics', *Syntax and Semantics* (Current Approaches to Syntax, 13, 1980).

Joosten, J., 'Biblical Hebrew w^eqatal and Syriac *hwa qatel* Expressing Repetition in the Past', *ZAH* 3:1 (1992).

Khan, G., *Studies in Semitic Syntax* (Oxford: Oxford University Press, 1988).

Körner, J., *Hebräische Studiengrammatik* (Leipzig: Verlag Enzyklopädie, 1988).

Lambdin, T.O., *Introduction to Biblical Hebrew* (London: Darton, Longman & Todd, 1971).

Levine, E., *The Aramaic Version of Ruth* (AnBib, 58; Rome: Biblical Institute Press, 1973).

Lilley, J.P.U., 'A Literary Approach to the Book of Judges', *TynBul* 15 (1967), pp. 94-102.

Longacre, R.E., *An Apparatus for the Identification of Paragraph Types* (Notes on Linguistics, 15; Dallas: Summer Institute of Linguistics, 1980).

—'Discourse', in R.M. Brend and K.L. Pike (eds.), *Tagmemics.*

—*Discourse, Paragraph, and Sentence Structure in Selected Philippine Languages.* I. *Discourse and Paragraph Structure* (SIL Publications in Linguistics and Related Fields, 21; Santa Ana, CA: Summer Institute of Linguistics, 1968).

—'Discourse Perspective on the Hebrew Verb: Affirmation and Restatement [1987]', in W.R. Bodine (ed.), *Linguistics and Biblical Hebrew.*

—*Grammar Discovery Procedures* (Janua Linguarum, Series Minor, 33; The Hague: Mouton, 1964).

—*The Grammar of Discourse* (Topics in Language and Linguistics; New York: Plenum Press, 1983).

—*Hierarchy and Universality of Discourse Constituents in New Guinea Languages* (2 vols.; Washington, DC: Georgetown University Press, 1972).

—*Joseph: A Story of Divine Providence: A Text Theoretical and Text-Linguistic Analysis of Genesis 37 and 39–48* (Winona Lake, IN: Eisenbrauns, 1989).

—'Tagmemics', *Word* 36.2 (1985), pp. 137-77.

—(ed.), *Theory and Application in Processing Texts in Non-Indoeuropean Languages* (Papiere zur Textlinguistik, 43; Hamburg: Helmut Buske Verlag, 1984).

Louw, J.P., 'The Function of Discourse in a Sociosemiotic Theory of Translation: Illustrated by the Translation of *zēloute* in 1 Corinthians 12.31', *The Bible Translator* 39 (1988), pp. 329-35.

MacDonald, P.J., 'Discourse Analysis and Biblical Interpretation [1986]', in W.R. Bodine (ed.), *Linguistics and Biblical Hebrew*.

MacGregor, L.J., *The Greek Text of Ezekiel: An Examination of its Homogeneity* (Septuagint and Cognate Studies, 18; Atlanta: Scholar's Press, 1985).

Magonet, J., *Form and Meaning: Studies in Literary Techniques in the Book of Jonah* (Sheffield: Almond Press, 1983).

Martin, J.D., *The Book of Judges* (CBC; Cambridge: Cambridge University Press, 1975).

McFall, L., *The Enigma of the Hebrew Verbal System* (Sheffield: Almond Press, 1982).

Meier, S.A., *Speaking of Speaking: Marking Direct Discourse in the Hebrew Bible* (VTSup, 46; Leiden: Brill, 1992).

Meyer, D.R., *Hebräische Grammatik. I. Einleitung, Schrift- und Lautlehre. II. Formenlehre, Flexionstabellen. III. Satzlehre. IV. Register, Hebräisches Textbuch* (Berlin: Walter de Gruyter, 1966).

Milne, P.J., 'The Patriarchal Stamp of Scripture: The Implications of Structuralist Analyses for Feminist Hermeneutics', *Journal of Feminist Studies in Religion* 5 (1989), pp. 17-34.

Moor, J. de, 'The Poetry of the Book of Ruth: Part I', *Or* 53 (1984), pp. 262-83; Part II, *Or* 55 (1986), pp. 16-46.

Muraoka, T., *Emphatic Words and Structures in Biblical Hebrew* (Leiden: Brill, 1985).

Murphy, R.E., and O. Carm, *Wisdom Literature: Job, Proverbs, Ruth, Canticles, Ecclesiastes, and Esther* (FOTL, 13; Grand Rapids: Eerdmans, 1981).

Myers, J.M., *The Linguistic and Literary Form of the Book of Ruth* (Leiden: Brill, 1955).

Niccacci, A., *The Syntax of the Verb in Classical Hebrew Prose* (trans. W.G.E. Watson; JSOTSup, 86; Sheffield: JSOT Press, 1990).

Noth, M., *Leviticus: A Commentary* (OTL; London: SCM Press, 1977).

Nyssönen, H., 'Steps to an Analysis of Written Discourse', in H. Nyssönen (ed.), *Issues*.

—(ed.), *Issues in Discourse Analysis, Contrastive Phonetics and Literary Communication* (Publications of the Department of English, University of Oulu, 3; Oulu, Finland: University of Oulu Press, 1983).

Nyssönen, H., *et al.* (eds.), *Bibliography of Discourse Analysis and Text Linguistics* (Publications of the Department of English, University of Oulu, 6; Oulu, Finland: University of Oulu Press, 1985).

—*Proceedings from the Second Finnish Seminar on Discourse Analysis, Oulu, September 27–28, 1988* (Publications of the Department of English, University of Oulu, 9; Oulu, Finland: University of Oulu Press, 1990).

O'Connor, M., *Hebrew Verse Structure* (Winona Lake, IN: Eisenbrauns, 1980).

Payne, D., 'Activity as the Encoding of Foreground in Narrative: A Case Study of an Asheninca Legend', in R.E. Longacre (ed.), *Theory*.

Pike, K.L., *Language in Relation to a Unified Theory of the Structure of Human Behavior* (The Hague: Mouton, 2nd edn, 1967).

—*Linguistic Concepts: An Introduction to Tagmemics* (Lincoln, NB: University of Nebraska Press, 1982).

Pike, K.L., and E.G. Pike, *Grammatical Analysis* (Dallas, TX: SIL and University of Texas at Arlington Press, 1977).

Rainey, A.F., 'Further Remarks on the Hebrew Verbal System', *Hebrew Studies* 29 (1988), pp. 35-42.

Revell, E.J., 'The System of the Verb in Standard Biblical Prose', *HUCA* 60 (1989), pp. 1-37.

Schiffrin, D., 'Tense Variation in Narrative', *Language* 57 (1981).

Schneider, W., *Übungsbuch für den Hebräische-unterricht* (Munich: Claudius Verlag, 1989).

Schoors, A., 'The Pronouns in Qoheleth', *Hebrew Studies* 30 (1989), pp. 71-90.

Schwartzschild, R., 'The Syntax of אשר in Biblical Hebrew with Special Reference to Qoheleth', *Hebrew Studies* 31 (1990), pp. 7-39.

Sihvonen-Hautecoeur, P., 'Discourse Markers and Dialogue in French', in H. Nyssönen, *et al.* (eds.), *Proceedings*, pp. 52-63.

Simpson, C.A., *Composition of the Book of Judges* (Oxford: Basil Blackwell, 1957).

Smith, M.S., 'The *Waw*-Consecutive at Qumran', *ZAW* 4 (1991), pp. 161-64.

Waard, J. de, and E.A. Nida, *A Translator's Handbook on the Book of Ruth* (New York: United Bible Societies, 1973).

Waldman, N.M., *The Recent Study of Hebrew: A Survey of the Literature with Selected Bibliography* (Bibliographica Judaica, 10; Cincinnati: Hebrew Union College Press; Winona Lake, IN: Eisenbrauns, 1989).

Waltke, B.E., and M. O'Connor, *An Introduction to Biblical Hebrew Syntax* (Winona Lake, IN: Eisenbrauns, 1990).

Waterhouse, V.G., *The History and Development of Tagmemics* (Janua Linguarum Series Critica, 16; The Hague: Mouton, 1974).

Watson, W.G.E., *Classical Hebrew Poetry: A Guide to its Techniques* (JSOTSup, 26; Sheffield: JSOT Press, 2nd edn, 1986).

Webb, B.G., *The Book of Judges: An Integrated Reading* (JSOTSup, 46; Sheffield: JSOT Press, 1987).

Wechter, P., *Ibn Barun's Arabic Works on Hebrew Grammar and Lexicography* (Philadelphia: The Dropsie College for Hebrew and Cognate Learning, 1964).

Wickes, W., *A Treatise on the Accentuation of the Twenty-One So-Called Prose Books of the Old Testament* (1887).

Wiklander, B., *Prophecy as Literature: A Text-Linguistic and Rhetorical Approach to Isaiah 2–4* (ConBOT 22; Malmö: CWK Gleerup, 1984).

Williams, J.G., 'The Structure of Judges 2.1–16.31', *JSOT* 49 (1991), pp. 77-85.

Wise, M.R., 'Language and Behavior', in R.M. Brend and K.L. Pike (eds.), *Tagmemics*.

Witzenrath, H.H., *Das Buch Rut* (SANT; Munich: Kösel-Verlag, 1975).

Wright, C.H.H. (ed.), *The Book of Ruth in Hebrew and Chaldee* (London: Williams & Norgate, 1864).

Zevit, Z., 'Talking in Biblical Henglish [sic] and Solving a Problem of the YAQTUL Past Tense' *Hebrew Studies* 29 (1988), pp. 25-33.

Zuber, B., *Das Tempussystem des biblischen Hebräisch* (Berlin: de Gruyter, 1986).

INDEX OF AUTHORS

JOURNAL FOR THE STUDY OF THE OLD TESTAMENT

Supplement Series

DATE DUE